American Cinema, 1890–1909

SCREEN
DECADES

AMERICAN CULTURE / AMERICAN CINEMA

Each volume in the Screen Decades: American Culture/American Cinema series presents a group of original essays analyzing the impact of cultural issues on the cinema and the impact of the cinema in American society. Because every chapter explores a spectrum of particularly significant motion pictures and the broad range of historical events in one year, readers will gain a continuing sense of the decade as it came to be depicted on movie screens across the continent. The integration of historical and cultural events with the sprawling progression of American cinema illuminates the pervasive themes and the essential movies that define an era. Our series represents one among many possible ways of confronting the past; we hope that these books will offer a better understanding of the connections between American culture and film history.

LESTER D. FRIEDMAN AND MURRAY POMERANCE
SERIES EDITORS

André Gaudreault, editor, *American Cinema, 1890–1909: Themes and Variations*

Charlie Keil and Ben Singer, editors, *American Cinema of the 1910s: Themes and Variations*

Ina Rae Hark, editor, *American Cinema of the 1930s: Themes and Variations*

Wheeler Winston Dixon, editor, *American Cinema of the 1940s: Themes and Variations*

Murray Pomerance, editor, *American Cinema of the 1950s: Themes and Variations*

Barry Keith Grant, editor, *American Cinema of the 1960s: Themes and Variations*

Lester D. Friedman, editor, *American Cinema of the 1970s: Themes and Variations*

Stephen Prince, editor, *American Cinema of the 1980s: Themes and Variations*

Chris Holmlund, editor, *American Cinema of the 1990s: Themes and Variations*

American Cinema, 1890–1909

Themes and Variations

EDITED BY

ANDRÉ GAUDREAULT

RUTGERS UNIVERSITY PRESS

NEW BRUNSWICK, NEW JERSEY, AND LONDON

LIBRARY OF CONGRESS CATALOGING-IN-PUBLICATION DATA

American cinema, 1890–1909 : themes and variations / edited by André Gaudreault.
    p. cm. — (Screen decades : American culture/American cinema)
  Includes bibliographical references and index.
  ISBN 978–0–8135–4442–7 (hardcover : alk. paper)—ISBN 978–0–8135–4443–4
(pbk. : alk. paper)
  1. Motion pictures—United States—History. I. Gaudreault, André.
  PN1993.5.U6A8573 2009
  791.430973'09034—dc22

                                      2008013962

A British Cataloging-in-Publication record for this book is available from the British
Library.

Visit our Web site: http://rutgerspress.rutgers.edu

Manufactured in the United States of America

To Eileen Bowser and David Francis,
who made Brighton 1978 possible

We are living between two twilights: the dusk of one
world, and the dawn of another. Twilight is imprecise,
and the outline of all things is indistinct. Only eyes
sharpened by a will to discover the primal and
invisible movement of things and beings can find their
way through the misty sight of the *anima mundi*. . . .
Through movement created by a marvelous
combination of photographic images and light, life is
shown in the movie theater at the height of its action
in a truly paroxysmal convulsion. Here is the sign of a
new art.

> Riciotto Canudo, "Triomphe du cinématographe" (1908)
> and "La naissance d'un sixième art" (1911)

CONTENTS

ACKNOWLEDGMENTS

This book would not have been possible without the support of a great number of people and institutions who contributed to it in one way or another and to whom I am extremely grateful. First of all, there are the nine scholars who each wrote a chapter under a tight deadline according to the series' guidelines, which some authors found just as "tight." These authors have been remarkable in every respect. I am certain that readers will find their articles interesting, even captivating. I am also certain that they will realize, as they turn each page, that these authors have advanced our knowledge of the highly important phenomenon that has come to be known as early cinema. These authors were also remarkable for the constant spirit of collaboration that animated their work and for which my assistant Lisa Pietrocatelli and I are most grateful because, in our concern to do things properly, the editing of this volume has been an enormous task. There is one concern, however, that we did not have, and that was running after our authors for their texts, answers to our questions, or additional information. Lisa and I are extremely grateful to them for this.

Among these authors, I would like to extend special thanks to Tom Gunning, who agreed to share with me the great responsibility (in my eyes at least) of writing the introduction. One of the principal tasks of this chapter was to bring to the fore some of the ideas of the other ten chapters that follow it and to make the reader want to continue to read the rest of the book. I also thank Tom for serving as my "special advisor" in editing the volume. His advice helped me make the right decisions at strategic moments and was thus a crucial contribution to the form the book has taken.

I also thank from the bottom of my heart Murray Pomerance, one of the series's two general editors, who put considerable effort into editing the texts, which he did with astonishing speed and inspired severity, always spot-on and well tuned. His constant presence at the other end of the line (electronically speaking) and his constant presence of mind made it possible for the chapters to respect a minimum of uniformity despite their relative formal diversity. Murray is an agreeable, interested, and interesting fellow who knows how to earn the respect of those he works with and who is able to generate enthusiasm for a project.

I would also like to thank Richard Abel, Donald Crafton, Germain Lacasse, and Charles Musser, who provided advice on one or another of the following chapters.

I can't express the debt I feel toward Paul Spehr and Jean-Marc Lamotte for their advice while I was researching the first part of the introduction. What good fortune it was for me to be able to count on *the* specialist, on this side of the Atlantic, on the invention of the Kinetograph, and on *the* specialist on the invention of the Cinématographe on the other.

Lisa and I also thank Jennifer Bean, Charles Musser, Patrick Loughney, Murray Pomerance, Paul Spehr, Lauren Rabinovitz, and Matthew Solomon for their advice on preparing the timeline. We are also indebted to the other general editor of the series, Lester D. Friedman, and to Leslie Mitchner, associate director/editor-in-chief at Rutgers University Press, for their steadfast collaboration and unwavering support throughout the work of editing the present volume.

I would also like to extend my warm thanks to my regular translator of the past few years, Timothy Barnard, himself a true scholar, with whom I enjoy working immensely and from whom I am always learning things (I can hear him grumbling as he translates these lines). Lisa and I are also grateful to him for his inspired revision of the texts and the regular advice he provided us.

The present volume is the fruit of research undertaken as part of the work of the Groupe de recherche sur l'avènement et la formation des institutions cinématographique et scénique (GRAFICS), which I have had the honor of leading at the Université de Montréal since 1994. GRAFICS receives generous funding from the Fonds québécois de recherche sur la société et la culture (FQRSC), without which it would not have been possible to work on this volume under decent conditions. The Social Sciences and Humanities Research Council of Canada (SSHRC), not to be outdone, agreed to fund a workshop held by GRAFICS in November 2006 (and presided over by Pierre Véronneau of the Cinémathèque québécoise and the author of these lines). This memorable workshop enabled members of GRAFICS to share ideas with the authors of the present volume in the series Screen Decades.

GRAFICS is housed and supported by the Département d'histoire de l'art et d'études cinématographiques at the Université de Montréal, to which this volume is also greatly indebted. Besides Jean-Pierre Sirois-Trahan, Tom Gunning, and myself as authors, and Lisa Pietrocatelli as editorial assistant, some members of GRAFICS have played a very close role in the creation of the present volume, especially Carolina Lucchesi-Lavoie

(Université de Montréal), Dominique Noujeim (Université de Montréal), and Louis Pelletier (Concordia University), and they have my sincere thanks.

Last but not least, as they say, I must in all truthfulness say that this book would not have appeared in its present state, or at the time it has, if it weren't for Lisa Pietrocatelli's enormous and high-quality work, day after day, as editorial assistant, publication secretary, special advisor, and, at times, deputy editor of this volume. Lisa is a reliable and responsible person like few others. She is also endowed with good judgment and is always ready with sound advice. She shares with the author of these lines a never-failing optimism and proverbial good humor (readers will excuse me for including myself in these remarks!). All in all, this means that the present volume has been prepared, in my view, by a terrific team of people (I call things the way I see them).

Lisa and I sincerely believe, given all of the above conditions, which these acknowledgments wish to express, that readers will not be bored by the present volume and, especially, that they will learn much from it. We hope you enjoy it.

André Gaudreault
Montréal
March 2008

TIMELINE
1890–1909

1890

25 JANUARY   Nellie Bly completes her tour of the world in seventy-two days in a hot-air balloon.

1 OCTOBER   Yosemite National Park is established.

29 DECEMBER   The U.S. Army attacks a Sioux camp at Wounded Knee, South Dakota, resulting in the deaths of between 150 and 370 Sioux men, women, and children.

1891

1 APRIL   The Wrigley Company is founded in Chicago, selling products such as soap and baking powder.

5 MAY   Opening of New York's Carnegie Hall, with Piotr Ilyich Tchaikovsky conducting the Symphony Society.

20 MAY   Thomas Edison demonstrates his Kinetoscope, the first peephole film device (it was not projected on a screen).

21 DECEMBER   The first basketball game is played in Springfield, Massachusetts.

1892

1 JANUARY   The Ellis Island immigration entry facility opens.

15 APRIL   General Electric is founded.

7 SEPTEMBER   James J. Corbett knocks out John L. Sullivan in the twenty-first round and becomes the new heavyweight champion of the world.

31 OCTOBER   *The Adventures of Sherlock Holmes* by Arthur Conan Doyle is published in the United Kingdom by Newnes Press.

1893

1 MAY   The World's Columbian Exposition opens in Chicago.

5 MAY   The Panic of 1893. The New York Stock Exchange collapses, causing an economic depression (1893–1897) followed by a flurry of corporate mergers.

9 MAY   Edison makes his first public demonstration of "modern motion pictures," using a peephole kinetoscope, at the Brooklyn Academy of Arts and Sciences. *Blacksmith Scene* and *Horse Shoeing* are shown.

11 JUNE   In Japan, Kokichi Mikimoto obtains the world's first cultured pearl.

16 DECEMBER   Antonin Dvořák's Symphony "From the New World" is premiered at Carnegie Hall.

1894

12 MARCH   For the first time, Coca-Cola is sold in bottles.

14 APRIL   Business associates of Thomas Edison open a kinetoscope parlor at 1155 Broadway, New York.

11 MAY   Workers living in Pullman City, whose wages had just been reduced by nearly a third, go on strike with the support of the American Railway Union.

1895

1 FEBRUARY   Birth of John Ford, American film director.

3 SEPTEMBER   The first professional football game is played, in Latrobe, Pennsylvania, between the Latrobe YMCA and the Jeannette Athletic Club. (Latrobe won the contest 12–0.)

8 NOVEMBER   In Germany, Wilhelm Röntgen discovers X-rays.

1896

1 FEBRUARY   In France, Henri Becquerel discovers radioactivity by accident.

26 MAY   The Dow Jones Industrial Average, now the world's oldest stock-exchange index, is established as part of the New York Stock Exchange.

2 JUNE   Guglielmo Marconi patents the radio.

29 JULY   Chop suey is invented in New York.

3 NOVEMBER   Republican William McKinley is elected president of the United States.

16 NOVEMBER   Electric power is transmitted between two cities for the first time.

1897

19 MAY   Oscar Wilde is released from Reading Gaol, where he had been imprisoned on sodomy charges.

26 MAY   *Dracula*, by Bram Stoker, goes on sale.

17 JULY   The Klondike Gold Rush begins.

1898

1 JANUARY   Manhattan, Brooklyn, Queens, and the Bronx are incorporated to form New York City. Staten Island is added on 25 January.

13 JANUARY   In France, Emile Zola's *J'accuse!* exposes the Alfred Dreyfus affair.

21 APRIL   Start of the Spanish American War, which lasts until 12 August. The Treaty of Paris between the United States and Spain forces Spain to relinquish Cuba, Puerto Rico, Guam, and the Philippines to the United States.

21 DECEMBER   In France, Marie and Pierre Curie discover radium.

1899

3 JANUARY   The *New York Times* uses the word "automobile" for the first time.

14 FEBRUARY   Voting machines are approved by the U.S. Congress for use in federal elections.

6 MARCH   Trademark is registered for Aspirin.

20 MARCH   At Sing-Sing prison in New York State, Martha M. Place becomes the first woman executed in an electric chair.

4 NOVEMBER   Sigmund Freud's *The Interpretation of Dreams* is published.

1900

19 SEPTEMBER   Butch Cassidy and the Sundance Kid commit robbery together for the first time.

2 DECEMBER   Gillette files a patent application for the safety razor.

12 DECEMBER   U.S. Steel is formed.

1901

17 MARCH   A showing of his canvases in Paris makes Vincent Van Gogh a sensation, more than a decade after his death.

2 SEPTEMBER   At the Minnesota State Fair, Theodore Roosevelt says, "Speak softly and carry a big stick."

6 SEPTEMBER   At the Pan American Exposition in Buffalo, the anarchist Leon Czolgosz shoots President William McKinley, who is seriously wounded. On 14 September, McKinley dies and Vice President Theodore Roosevelt, a forty-two-year-old New Yorker, becomes the twenty-sixth president of the United States.

12 DECEMBER   Marconi transmits the first transatlantic telegraph.

1902

21 FEBRUARY   Dr. Harvey Cushing, the first U.S. brain surgeon, performs his first operation.

25 FEBRUARY   Hubert Cecil Booth founds the Vacuum Cleaner Company.

9 AUGUST   Edward VII is crowned King of England; the Victorian Age is over.

1903

15 JANUARY   The teddy bear is introduced in America.

1 OCTOBER   The first game of the first World Series is played between the Boston Americans and the Pittsburgh Pirates.

17 DECEMBER   The first successful powered airplane flight is made by Orville and Wilbur Wright at Kitty Hawk, North Carolina.

1904

22 MARCH   The first color photograph is published in a daily newspaper, the *Daily Illustrated Mirror*.

30 APRIL   President Theodore Roosevelt inaugurates the Louisiana Purchase Exposition.

8 NOVEMBER   Roosevelt is elected to his first full term as president.

31 DECEMBER   The first New Year's Eve celebration takes place in Longacre (now Times) Square.

1905

14 JUNE   In Russia, sailors mutiny aboard the Battleship *Potemkin*.

5 SEPTEMBER   President Roosevelt acts as the mediator in peace talks between the Russians and the Japanese following the Russo-Japanese War, won by Japan.

28 OCTOBER   Sinn Féin is formed by Arthur Griffith.

1906

19 FEBRUARY   W. K. Kellogg and Charles Bolin found Battle Creek Toasted Corn Flake Company.

18 APRIL   The Great San Francisco Earthquake, estimated at 7.9 on the Richter scale, leaves thousands homeless and causes more than three thousand deaths.

22 SEPTEMBER   A white mob gathers on Decatur Street in Atlanta and begins destroying African American businesses on nearby Auburn Street. The mob kills five African Americans, burns hundreds of homes, and destroys vibrant sections of the city.

1907

21 MARCH   The United States invades Honduras.

31 MAY   Taxis first begin running in New York City.

4 JUNE   An automatic washer and dryer are introduced.

1908

11 JANUARY   The Grand Canyon National Monument is created.

24 JANUARY   General Baden-Powell starts the Boy Scouts.

12 MAY   The *Lusitania* crosses the Atlantic in a record four days, fifteen hours.

12 AUGUST   The first Model T Ford is built.

1909

12 FEBRUARY   The National Association for the Advancement of Colored People (NAACP) is founded.

6 APRIL   Robert Peary reaches the North Pole.

19 AUGUST   The first race at the Indianapolis Motor Speedway is held.

American Cinema, 1890–1909

Thomas A. Edison and his assistant William Kennedy Laurie Dickson designed a system for taking moving images and invented the Kinetograph, created in 1889 and patented in 1891.

INTRODUCTION

American Cinema Emerges (1890–1909)

ANDRÉ GAUDREAULT AND TOM GUNNING

The So-Called Invention of So-Called Cinema

Peter Bogdanovich: Was it true that one director told you not to call them "movies" but "motion pictures"?

Orson Welles: . . . Nowadays, I'm afraid the word is rather chic. It's a good English word, though—"movie." How pompous it is to call them "motion pictures." I don't mind "films," though, do you?

Peter Bogdanovich: No, but I don't like "cinema."

Orson Welles: I know what you mean.   (Bogdanovich and Welles 23)

This book deals with a very special topic: the beginnings. The beginnings of *cinema*, some would say. The beginnings of *moving pictures*, others would say. Or, to use less familiar terms—but terms that would have been familiar in the period covered by this book—the beginnings of *animated views* or *animated pictures*. The choice of words in the question we intend to formulate here is important, because each could give rise to a different answer. The answer to the question "Who invented the movies?" is not necessarily the same as the answer to the question "Who invented cinema?" or "Who invented moving pictures?" Generally speaking, these terms all refer today to the same phenomenon, but each of them involves a series of specific meanings, especially if we delve into the history of the invention of the various processes that gave rise to what we now call "cinema." The problem of the invention of what we today call "cinema" is certainly complex, but we are obliged to address it here before setting out, if only because it will enable us to put into perspective some of the conditions in which the new technology emerged. We must first of all determine who invented what, and when.

The present volume could very well have begun with the year 1895. That would have been the result of a different editorial choice than the one we have made here. Doing so would not have been completely foolish or mistaken, because, as we will see below, this truly was the year in which the projection of photographic moving pictures on two continents (Europe and the Americas) began, in the form of a variety of devices and processes. But is the projection of photographic moving pictures essential if we are to speak of "cinema"? Immediately, the question we formulated above returns: what do we mean by "motion pictures," by "cinema," by "moving pictures"? Are we necessarily talking about a projected image? Is the simple viewing of photographic moving images in itself, without projection, sufficient for cinema to exist? What really is "cinema"? Or, more precisely: *When* is there cinema?

These are entirely relevant questions, because the invention of cinema is a topic on which there is far from unanimous agreement. This was true at the time of its invention and it is even truer more than a century later. These questions about origins, it must be said, also carry with them a certain degree of subjectivity (and emotions and nationalist sentiment sometimes enter into the matter as well). In fact, one's position about the invention of cinema rests on one's choice of a supposed "inaugural moment." In the historical continuum, what is the most important thing to enable us to claim that, before the intervention of some event or another, there was no cinema? And that after this event there was cinema? What exactly was this great "inaugural moment" that determined the "birth" of cinema? Was it when such-and-such a device was invented, making possible the dissemination of animated pictures? Or was it, rather, such-and-such a demonstration, in the course of which animated views encountered an audience for the first time? These are seemingly simple questions, but they open up a true Pandora's Box, because the debates they give rise to call into question a great number of "certainties" about the invention of cinema and invariably ruffle various nationalist sentiments. And these are not the only questions that come to mind when we try to determine who invented cinema, a question that is simple only in appearance, because it opens onto numerous avenues and has given rise, for more than a hundred years, to many sharp words and passionate debates.

Thus one scholar will see Eadweard J. Muybridge's first projections using his Zoopraxiscope (the name it is known by today; Muybridge called it the Zoöpraxiscope) in May 1880 in the United States as the inaugural moment. Another will see the pioneer of chronophotography, Étienne-Jules Marey in France, as the "real founding father of cinematographic technique" (Mannoni), because even though he did not project images he was able to demonstrate, at the Académie des Sciences in Paris in October 1888, a sequence of photographs on paper taken at a rate of twenty images per second. Some other scholar will see this moment as when Louis Aimé Augustin Le Prince, in 1888 in Great Britain, obtained a patent for a moving picture camera, while yet another will prefer the German Ottomar Anschütz's demonstrations of his Electrical Schnellseher at the International Electrotechnical Exhibition in Frankfurt in May 1891; or the projections in July 1891 by the Frenchman Georges Demenÿ of his Phonoscope before, like Marey, the Académie des Sciences in Paris. All this is not to mention Émile Reynaud's projections of his Pantomimes lumineuses in 1892 in France with his Théâtre optique, or the projection on 22 January 1889, by William Friese Greene and Mortimer Evans, of images taken by a camera at the rate of four or five pictures per second. Nor is it to mention many other devices that would fill pages of this book merely to list.

Of course, every one of the premises underlying these claims of "paternity" is refuted by detractors. And so it is said that there isn't any evidence that Le Prince's device was sufficiently realistic. Or that Anschütz's Schnellseher and Demenÿ's Phonoscope have too few sequential images, most often no more than a dozen, for their inventions to earn the title "inaugural moment." But this is not a criticism one could level at Reynaud's Théâtre optique that, with its hundreds of images on a spool, created shows lasting some twenty minutes. On the other hand, it is said that these images—like those of Muybridge's Zoopraxiscope—were not *photographic* (though Muybridge's were drawn from photographs). Even so, it is clear that the Zoopraxiscope and the Théâtre optique inaugurated something: while the images that these devices show are not *photographic* moving pictures, they are, just the same, at least in a literal sense, "moving pictures."

In the French historical tradition, the Lumière brothers, despite a few squawks here and there, are generally credited with the invention of cinema. Indeed, the device that Louis and Auguste Lumière invented and developed, the Cinématographe, patented on 13 February 1895, shines brightly in the firmament of French film history. What is more, the name of their device caught on around the world, with many derivatives in existence today in many languages, most of all in French but also in English (cinema, cinematographic, cinematographer, and so on).[1] Certainly the Cinématographe was a finished device whose principles served for many years as the basis of film projection: a single strip of perforated film; intermittent movement, with the film being pulled before an aperture and stopped again and again, over and over and over; photographs taken at regular intervals. Generally speaking, historians have not chosen the date the invention was patented (February 1895) when granting the Lumière brothers a special place in the invention of cinema, but have rather pinned their attention on the fetish date of 28 December 1895. It was on that day that the Lumière brothers began commercial use of their device with what historians have long seen as the very first public projection before a paying audience (in the Salon Indien, a room annexed to the Grand Café on Boulevard des Capucines in Paris). By choosing this date, and by granting it the role of inaugural moment, historians are emphasizing, consciously or not, that what should be considered the turning point, the historical moment, is not the invention of the device but the coming together of the entire "apparatus" (projection plus public plus paying) that presides over the act of "going to the movies": buying a ticket, taking a seat in an auditorium alongside other spectators, and watching animated views unfold on a screen. Unfortunately for them, the Lumières' priorities, which for a long time dominated historical debate in the cinema, have come increasingly under attack, at least if we take the screening on 28 December 1895 as our starting point. For if we adopt as our criteria the fact that this screening was "public" and also that it was "paying," we must acknowledge not only that the supposed primacy of the Lumières has been contested by many, but also that it is entirely contestable. There is now no doubt that, as far as "public and paying projections" are concerned, the Lumière Cinématographe was beaten to the punch on several occasions, as we will see in a moment.

There is, however, one "first" to which the Lumières' device can lay claim in a much less debatable manner: a screening on 22 March 1895, when Louis spoke to the members of the Société d'Encouragement pour l'Industrie Nationale in Paris. In fact his talk was to introduce the very first public screening of a "cinematographic" film (literally speaking, given that the device was called the Cinématographe). On the program was a single film, lasting a little less than a minute: *Sortie d'usine* (the first version of the view known today in French as *La sortie des usines Lumière* and in English as *Workers Leaving the Lumière Factory*). The topic of Louis's talk was the role of the Lumière firm in the photography industry. For at the time of their invention, the Lumière brothers were, with their father, Antoine, large industrialists in the photography business and had become rich from the sale of the popular photographic plates produced in their factory. Screening the film *Sortie d'usine* thus served to illustrate Louis Lumière's talk: "Look," it seemed to say, "at all the workers who, because of our success, are leaving our factory in great numbers; moreover, watch them in *moving* images, thanks to my new invention, produced in that very same factory!" As a publicity stunt, it would be hard to find anything better.

The event was described as follows in an 1895 article:

On March 22, Mr. Louis Lumière gave a most interesting talk on the photo-graphic industry and particularly on the workshops and industrial products of the Société anonyme des plaques Lumière, based in Lyon. . . . Mr. Louis Lumière, to make his discussion clearer and more attractive, projected [fixed] views of the interior of his workshops. . . . Using a kinetoscope of his own invention, he projected a most curious scene: the employees leaving the workshop at lunchtime. This animated view, showing all these people in full movement as they hurriedly head for the street, had the most gripping effect, so much so that the entire audience, so enchanted were they, asked that the view be screened again. This scene, which took only a minute or so to unfold, contains no fewer than eight hundred successive views. It has everything: a dog coming and going, people on bicycles, horses, a fast-moving carriage, etc.

("Conférence" 125–26)

The audience for this screening was selected and limited in number (it was made up of scientists who had come to hear what Louis Lumière had to say, not to see what he had to show) and viewers did not pay. For these reasons, film history has paid little attention to this date of 22 March 1895, preferring the date of 28 December 1895, the day of the supposedly first pro-jection to a paying public. Nevertheless, fairly recent and well-documented research—with evidence to back it up—shows that there were predeces-sors to this so-called "first" on 28 December 1895 (see in this volume "1890–1895: Movies and the Kinetoscope" by Paul Spehr). Here we men-tion the three most important examples: those of the Lathams' Panoptikon in the United States; Armat and Jenkins's Phantoscope, also in the United States; and the Skladanowsky brothers' Bioskop in Germany.

1. On 20 May 1895, using their Panoptikon (sometimes written Pantop-tikon or Panopticon, aka the Eidoloscope), the Latham family (father Woodville with sons Otway and Grey) projected a film of a boxing match (between "Young Griffo" and Charles Barnett) before a paying audience on Broadway in New York City. This paying exhibition of moving images in New York went on for several months. In addition to New York, the Lathams showed their film on an irregular basis in sev-eral U.S. locations.

2. In late September 1895, C. Francis Jenkins and Thomas Armat showed films with their Phantoscope to a paying audience at the Cotton States Exhibition in Atlanta, Georgia. As Charles Musser demonstrates in this volume, the rights to this same Phantoscope, after undergoing a few modifications, were granted by Armat to Thomas A. Edison, who pre-sented it to the public under a different name—Vitascope—and under his own signature.

3. On 1 November 1895, the brothers Emil and Max Skladanowsky (the invention of cinema was most assuredly a brotherly affair!) presented a program of eight films to a paying audience at the Wintergarten variety theater in Berlin, using their Bioskop (sometimes written Bioskope, Bioscope, or Bioscop).

Each of the devices used for these paying public projections had peculiarities that distinguished them from the others and from the Lumière Cinématographe (besides the fact that none of them was as well designed as the Lumière machine).

1. The Latham family's Panoptikon had no mechanism to advance the film intermittently through the device, or any other system to compensate for the absence of an intermittent mechanism. Each image had to remain on the screen for as short a time as possible in order to avoid blurring. Hence their use, given the need for brighter images, of a larger film format (two inches wide). In fact, the Panoptikon did not perform as well as had been hoped, if we are to judge from the report of a journalist present at one of their demonstrations: "There is considerable room for improvement and many drawbacks have yet to be overcome" (qtd. by Herbert).
2. Jenkins and Armat's Phantoscope, for its part, had an intermittent mechanism and, by all accounts, gave much better results than the Latham Panoptikon. This is why it enjoyed such great success the following year under a new name (Vitascope), when it was used for the very first public screenings organized by Edison in April 1896.
3. The Skladanowsky brothers' Bioskop, finally, was based on a very complex system of projection that did not catch on. Everything in this German-designed device was found in twos. It required two light sources, two mechanisms for feeding the film, two strips of film (two copies of the same film, in fact), and two lenses. The biggest concern was to make sure that the two strips of film were perfectly synchronized, because they were masked in turn by a central shutter. The device projected image 1 of film strip A, then image 2 of film strip B, image 3 of film strip A, and so on. The alternation between two film strips was a kind of imitation of intermittent movement, with which the Bioskop was not equipped. Because its extreme complexity brought about no improvement to systems already in use, which employed the intermittent advancement of a single strip of film, this device was not used for very long and had no real future.

In this entire story of establishing various priorities for determining what constitutes the invention of the cinema apparatus, historians have to ask themselves what should matter most. In the end, it's a question of whether to make public projection the decisive criterion, and whether or not it is important that viewers paid to see what was projected. Whatever the case, if we decide that it is legitimate to make projection alone, to a restricted and selected audience, the decisive criterion, we could give strong preference to the Lumière brothers (with their screening on 22 March 1895, two months before the Lathams' screening). Indeed, from our perspective, 22 March 1895 (even if it was not a for-pay projection, even if it was not open to the general public), seems more significant than the 28 December date, which appears more frequently in the histories of cinema.

Nevertheless, anyone who privileges the work of the Lumière brothers in the history of these inventions (whether because of the primacy of the 22 March screening or by virtue of the viability of their device, which established projection standards for animated views) must ask whether their invention of the Cinématographe signaled the invention of "cinema" itself. There are at least two reasons why this question must be posed. First: when the Lumières entered the race in late 1894, photographic animated images had already been in existence for several years and had been exhibited commercially for months. In fact, five long years before the invention of the Lumière Cinématographe, Thomas Edison and his assistant William Kennedy Laurie Dickson designed a system for taking moving images and invented the Kinetograph, created in 1889 and patented in 1891. To show their Kinetograph views, Edison and Dickson designed a separate viewing device, the Kinetoscope, a rectangular cabinet about four feet high and equipped with a peephole that enabled a single viewer to watch the images unfolding inside. This is the device that set the initial standards for seeing animated views, and it was precisely this device to which the above-quoted French journalist referred in his report on the 22 March 1895 Lumière screening ("using a kinetoscope of his own invention, [Louis Lumière] projected a most curious scene"). Edison's technology for taking moving pictures was based on the principle of intermittence, but the Kinetoscope for viewing those pictures had no such capacity and viewings took the form of an uninterrupted series of images. Views taken with the Kinetograph were shown to an invited public as early as 1891, but as we see in the 1890–1895 chapter, their commercial use began only in April 1894 (still some twenty months before commercial use of the Lumière Cinématographe began in

To show their Kinetograph views, Edison and Dickson designed a separate viewing device, the Kinetoscope, a rectangular cabinet about four feet high and equipped with a peephole that enabled a single viewer to watch the images unfolding inside.

December 1895). Moreover, the discovery by the Lumières' father, Antoine, of the existence of these kinetoscopic views, when they began to be shown commercially in France in late 1894, was the Lumière brothers' prime motivation. Their goal was clear: to find a way to project views on a screen large enough for people seated together in the same hall. The essential condition for achieving this was to apply the principle of the intermittent advancement of the film strip. Because the projected image was to be much larger than the one seen in the Kinetoscope, any blurring or shaking movement through this enlargement would be irritating to the eye of the spectator. Thus it was crucial that each frame pause briefly while being shown on the screen and before being yanked away in order to be replaced with its successor, image after image.

The Lumière brothers, therefore, did not invent animated views. What they invented, rather, was a device for recording moving pictures that was designed in such a way as to project them onto a screen. Does this mean that the Lumières invented "cinema"? One might ask, as suggested above, whether the phenomenon we have in mind when we speak of "cinema" can be defined only by the *projection* of *animated views* on a screen for a *paying audience*. This question is all the more relevant today, given that a large proportion of films are consumed on DVD or downloaded from the Internet in a private space. In any event, there is a second reason for qualifying the role of the Lumières in the invention of "cinema." Isn't it perfectly legitimate to ask ourselves whether it is even possible to answer the question "Who invented cinema?" with a single name, or the names of two people working together? Common sense tells us that a new technology is not invented from one day to the next: it is created through the accumulation of many inventions, as minor as they may be, which form a cluster of like objects based on a number of principles shared by a number of researchers working more or less at the same time. Every small discovery made by one inventor or another is thus the fruit of inspiration derived from a number of discoveries made by other inventors before them. Thus, for example, we owe the principle of the synthesis of movement (ca. 1830) to Joseph Plateau (his Phénakistiscope made it possible to synthesize movement using a rotating disc bearing a series of drawings and with slots cut into it through which to view them), and we owe photographic analysis of movement (ca. 1880) to Muybridge and Marey (their respective "chronophotographic" experiences enabled them to dissect movement using multiple images on a silver gelatin base). We also owe the principle of the perforated film strip (ca. 1888) to Émile Reynaud (with a system of cog-wheels, the perforations in the strips of images he showed in his Théâtre optique made possible even and stable projection) and perhaps, most likely without any reciprocal influence, to Edison and Dickson, who had used it initially to advance the strip of paper in their stock ticker machine (using sprockets and perforations). We owe the principle of celluloid film (ca. 1889) to Edison and Dickson (they applied the idea of perforations to a strip of 35 mm film, establishing the film industry's standard to this day). Every one of these principles was essential in order one day to project animated photographic images on a screen. We might thus say that the technological advance represented by the invention of cinema was the result of a group effort to which many people contributed.

Thinking about the question in a little more depth, we can see that there is another fundamental reason—a third reason—for saying that it is pointless to try to answer the question "Who invented cinema?" with a single name. The cinema cannot be reduced at its base to the mere "picture-taking machine," to the technological apparatus alone. Isn't it true that cinema is not simply the projection on a screen of photographic images that give the illusion of movement? Above all, cinema is a complex sociocultural phenomenon rather than something one "invents" (since it cannot be patented). The cinema is a phenomenon that is gradually and collectively institutionalized. The invention of animated views (by Edison and Dickson) and the invention of the Cinématographe and the processes it competed with (the Panoptikon, the Phantoscope, and the Bioskop) may very well have occurred in the final years of the nineteenth century, but the institutionalization of cinema is a process that occurred in the early twentieth century, several years after the invention of the devices behind it. In fact, the cinema did not come into the world in the nineteenth century at all, despite the fact that Edison's Kinetograph was developed in 1890 and the Lumière Cinématographe in 1895. Cinema emerged in the first decade of the twentieth century. And it is precisely this phenomenon—the gradual emergence, the advent over time, of this new "cultural formation"—that the chapters in this book discuss: this twenty-year period, and the process it gave rise to, by which cinema developed and was legitimized.

Between 1890 and 1909 lies a period during which there reigned what we once described as a "cinema of attractions,"[2] whose tenets and products have little in common with those of the later, dominant forms of cinema, apart from the fact that both paradigms are based on the use of moving images. Indeed, we believe that the specificity of the "animated views" of so-called early cinema must be recognized with respect to the films that the institution "cinema" produced after 1910, and that it is impossible to compare the conditions under which trivial little views were produced at the turn of the twentieth century with those that prevailed when feature films were first produced, roughly at the time of the Great War. We must come to terms with the fact that so-called early cinema was, in a sense, not yet . . . cinema (at least as Hollywood would later define it).

The First Two Decades

The two decades we cover in this volume move the United States from the end of the nineteenth century to the beginning of the twentieth. They involve such enormous transformations socially and politically that to attempt to briefly summarize them can only lead to a superficial view of a complex history. This is an era in which America joined the rush for imperial spheres of control, when recent immigration (from Europe as well as the Great Migration of southern African Americans to northern cities) seemed to change the nature and appearance of American society, and when the industrial might of the United States established the nation's position as the upcoming if not dominant economic power in the world. But the history of film always reveals the intensely social nature of cinema, directly dependent on technology, industrialization, and changes in audience demographics, and subject to intense sociological scrutiny and attempts at control. Therefore, our account of cinema immerses us in the social and cultural history of the United States. Cinema was both affected by and influenced major changes in this period, such as the nature of leisure time, how gender roles were understood, and the way race and ethnicity were represented and encountered. Each of our chapters spends some time relating cinema to the larger horizon of social and cultural history. But a few aspects of a historical overview are essential to keep in mind.

From 1890 to 1909 the modernization of America begun after the Civil War continued and accelerated: the growth of major industry and the creation of major incorporations, the urbanization of large parts of the American population, and the heightening of tensions between labor and capital. With the Spanish-American War in 1898, the United States challenged the weakest of the European colonial powers in the Western Hemisphere and then took control of their former colonies, thus becoming an imperial power itself, suppressing native independence movements in Cuba and the Philippines. Labor during this period transformed, due partly to the new regularization of labor time and processes known as Taylorization, in which workers were forced to regularize their work process with an eye toward efficiency and speed. At the same time, working-class activism and unionization gained some elevation in the standard of living, yielding slightly more expendable income and an increase in leisure time—just enough to fuel the growth in cheap film theaters known as nickelodeons. The first audiences for film primarily attended the predominately middle-class vaudeville theaters in which films often premiered during the 1890s. Although films continued to be shown in vaudeville theaters throughout our period, except for the few films that became hits on the vaudeville circuit (often those portraying current events, such as the Spanish-American War), from 1905 on cinema became associated primarily with a new working-class audience. Especially in urban areas, this audience could be very diverse. This was also an era of massive immigration and, particularly in urban areas, an increase in foreign-born inhabitants. Many accounts of urban nickelodeons emphasize the fascination film had for those who did not speak English well. Likewise, the mass movement of African Americans from the rural South to northern urban areas began toward the end of the era covered by this book and exerted an influence on the development of film audiences, as shown in Jackie Stewart's pioneering work *Migrating to the Movies*. Although middle-class women had been courted by vaudeville during the previous decades, movies provided a new pastime for working-class women and children, and many early accounts of the nickelodeon describe women and children crowding the theaters.

All these transformations intertwine with the history of film, dependent as it is on technical development in photography, chemistry, and precision engineering, and on the growth especially in urban areas of a working-class audience, one particularly receptive to a visual mode of representation. Electrification, accomplished a few decades before in urban areas and still being extended to smaller towns, allowed film exhibition to expand, while the film industry itself especially toward the end of this period used the economic strategies that other industries had used to control profits and minimize competition—for example, Edison's use of patent law to intimidate and ultimately dominate his rivals. Cinema stands as an emblem of modernizing America, a form of entertainment possible only because of the confluence of transformations already mentioned, but it is also the most modern form of representation, founded on technological innovation, presented as a new mass phenomenon: for the first time audiences across the nation could see the exact same performance more or less at the same time in a variety of locales. Its revolutionary nature cannot be overstated.

The trajectory of the history, specifically of film form and of the film industry, also involves a revolution. Cinema emerged at the end of the nineteenth century as a new technological wonder with the ability to produce extended sequences of perceived motion. The technology that allowed this was fairly simple. Motion pictures depended primarily on two separate innovations that emerged at the end of the nineteenth century. First, recent transformations in film stock allowed brief exposures that could register stable images of an instant of motion. Second, a flexible base for the photographic image, which eventually became primarily celluloid film, allowed the long continuous strip of images necessary for films lasting more than an instant. Over the two decades covered by this book, the basic technology of cinema changed only slightly. But enormous transformations occurred in film's role in society and in the way films were produced and shown. The American motion picture companies formed at the end of the nineteenth century were primarily engaged in manufacturing apparatuses of their own invention—motion picture cameras and projectors. As Paul Spehr puts it in his opening chapter, "Edison was fundamentally in the business of making machines, not images." The first years of American film history focused on the perfection and proliferation of an apparatus and its modes of exhibition, through the formation of new companies who produced machines and the films that they showed. Many of the first film companies bore the names of the devices they originally marketed, such as the Biograph and Mutoscope Company or the Vitagraph Company.

By 1909 a very different terrain appeared; an industry dedicated primarily to the production of films rather than machines had emerged from these pioneers. In contemporary terms we could describe this as a gradual emphasis on software (the movies) over hardware (the camera and projectors). This is not to claim that films were of limited importance in the cinema's first years, since several of them (the kinetoscope films of Edison, such as Annabelle's dances, or the view of the Lumière Cinématographe on the same subject) remain key films in film history, still shown today. But one could claim that most of these first films were primarily designed to exploit and demonstrate the cinematic apparatus, through the realistic presentation of familiar forms of images and entertainment (illustrations of current events, family scenes, travel images, comic skits, and vaudeville acts). Film was seen initially as a mode of technological reproduction, whether the realistic capturing of the movements of everyday life or a presentation of the likenesses of public figures and events or the stars and acts of the variety stage. This period could be referred to as the novelty era, during which film was displayed primarily as a new technological device and scientific curiosity. Although it is hard to specify an exact end to this period, since film remained a novelty to some audiences for years, by the beginning of the new century film's status as a novelty had essentially been exhausted in the United States.

Initially, cinema companies supplied vaudeville theaters and other venues with a complete service, which included the films made with their cameras, projectors of their own design, and operators who would project the films. Often, as in the case of Biograph's Billy Bitzer, the projectionist was the same person who had operated the camera in taking the films. But soon this originally self-contained service separated into interconnecting but independent aspects. As Charles Musser has detailed, film projectors became easier to operate and were placed on the commercial market, so that exhibitors could own and operate them separately from the manufacturers ("Emergence" 366–67). Separating the projecting of films from their production also meant the realm of exhibition was free to expand independently. A new basis for the industry appeared.

During most of the period covered by this book, films were sold directly by the companies that produced them, priced generally at so much per foot. Such a system favored traveling exhibitors who moved from town to town showing their films for a limited amount of time, vaudeville managers who had chains of theaters and could share films among their theaters, or exhibition services that were engaged to supply films for a variety of venues. Early film exhibitors played a very different role from the chains of movie theaters that dominate today's film industry. Since the films they showed were short (often barely a minute), exhibitors assembled them into programs that often displayed a degree of creativity. An exhibitor might decide to purchase and exhibit films with a common theme, such as views of the 1900 World Exposition in Paris, or scenes of the Boer War then raging in South Africa. Such thematic grouping might include projected lanternslides as well, and frequently included an oral commentary spoken or arranged by the exhibitor. Or the exhibitor might decide to follow the dominant vaudeville aesthetic and present a "variety program," emphasizing a diverse range

Famous final close-up
(*The Great Train Robbery*,
Edison, 1903). Digital frame
enlargement.

of entertainment rather than a single theme. Thus, comic gags might jostle with scenes of state funerals, or films of war might be followed by a dance or acrobatic number. Further, as Charles Musser stresses in his chapter on 1896–1897 in this volume, until nearly the end of the period covered by this book exhibitors frequently "were in charge of what would later be called 'post-production.'" In other words, they not only determined the order of films in their programs but sometimes did their own editing, cutting, or combining of different shots within films. Some production companies, especially Edison, encouraged this practice by selling different versions of a film, or by indicating that a specific shot—such as the famous close-up of the outlaw firing his pistol in *The Great Train Robbery* (1903)—could be rearranged as the exhibitor decided.

As more permanent sites of film exhibition appeared with the growth of small film theaters, a service that provided a regular supply of different films became a necessity. Film distributors, the middlemen between production and exhibition, appeared to make a steady, reliable, ongoing, and varied supply of films available to exhibitors. Thus, although film production companies continued to sell rather than lease or rent their films until 1909, this did not mean that owners of film theaters had to buy individual prints of the films they showed, since businessmen known as exchangemen stepped in to obtain prints from the producers and then rent or lease them to the individual film theaters for a shorter period. Although there has been less research on the history of the film exchange business than on the histories of film production and exhibition, which have been studied quite thoroughly in recent years, its basic outlines are clear. Film exchanges began to appear as businesses in large cities, especially in centrally located Chicago, and conducted a nationwide business that depended on the railway system to ship films across the country to exhibitors. Exhibitors now dealt with an agent that intervened between them and the production companies. Exchanges offered exhibitors at least a weekly change of films (most film theaters in rural areas changed at least once a week; many urban theaters changed twice a week, and at the height of the nickelodeon craze they offered a daily change of films in order to compete with neighboring theaters). After their exhibition the films were returned to exchanges and a new program was shipped out. The degree of choice that exhibitors had of these films varied greatly, with exchangemen often giving them what was available rather than anything they specifically requested. Further, limited information was available to exhibitors about the films they were about to show. Exchangemen claimed they selected the best films from those offered by production companies, but exhibitors often complained about what they were sent. Production companies sent out publicity bulletins describing their releases, and from 1907 onward trade journals began to appear, targeting the exhibitor and describing and often reviewing individual films as they were released. In this way exhibitors tried to gain the information that allowed them to make an informed choice.

The exchange business thus made possible the second major transformation of the film industry (after its initial invention and public presentation) in the era covered by this volume: the growth of theaters whose main business was the showing of films (as opposed to films shown in vaudeville or other theaters as part of a diverse program). Although some theaters opened showing films as their main attraction from early in the novelty era, before 1905 films were primarily shown in other venues: fairgrounds, minstrel shows, street fairs, circuses, and—primarily—vaudeville theaters. From 1905 on a number of small theaters opened, first in metropolitan areas generally in close proximity to downtown shopping districts. These small theaters, often housed in vacant storefronts, presented short programs (usually around half an hour) of a number of reels of film, accompanied almost always by "illustrated songs," songs performed by a live singer with the lyrics illustrated by projected lantern slides. Such brightly colored slides were made up specially for each song (and were carried by exchanges, or even by their own separate exchanges that had hundreds of titles). These film theaters took their name from the price most often charged for admission, a nickel—hence nickelodeons.

It would be hard to overestimate the importance of the nickelodeon revolution for American film history. Instead of remaining as merely one component of a vaudeville program, films now became the center of a program. The relatively cheap cost of running these theaters allowed a very low admission price, well within the reach of most working men and their families. The informality of the theaters and the brevity of their shows (as opposed to the full evening required when attending vaudeville, legitimate theater, or musical concerts) also fit into the schedule of laborers with a limited leisure time. A new form of entertainment found a new audience— the working class—and the nickelodeons were often called "the poor man's theater." The growth of these theaters from 1906 on (most major cities had hundreds of nickelodeons by 1908, and few small towns lacked them entirely) greatly increased the demand for films. Lauren Rabinovitz describes the arrangement of typical nickelodeons in her chapter on 1906.

The nickelodeon triggered a severe crisis, both within the film industry and in American society. The proliferation of nickel film theaters and their popularity among the working class meant that a whole class of people now possessed a form of entertainment and representation that had seemed to appear without either the blessing or the control of the better classes. From 1907 the social elite campaigned for the regulation of films and the places they were shown, with a variety of both conservative and progressive reformers demanding that this new entertainment become safe (fear of fire was rampant during the early days of film), clean (the single most remarked-upon aspect of nickel theaters next to their popularity was their smell, often augmented by attendants spraying atomizers of perfume to cover the body odor of the viewers), and moral. As Matthew Solomon details in his 1908 chapter, after newspaper and clergy led campaigns claiming film shows were vicious and obscene, various attempts were made to clean up films. Chicago and Ohio were prominent among city and state governments that, unlike the federal government, instituted censorship. In 1909 the film industry itself introduced the National Board of Censorship, which reviewed films and suggested changes, similar to self-regulating boards that would later appear during the Hollywood era. This organization, still in existence, later changed its name to the National Board of Review to emphasize that it had no power to legally ban a film.

The industrial crisis sparked by the nickelodeon revolution came largely from the fact that the production side of the industry had lost control over the exhibition and distribution sides. (Later, during the era of major Hollywood studios, distribution, exhibition, and production became vertically integrated in a small number of large film companies.) As Eileen Bowser details in her 1907 chapter, Edison kept American production under a stranglehold with his threat of patent suits. Faced with an uncertain future in 1907, only a trickle of American product was being produced. Richard Abel has demonstrated that foreign films, imported mainly from France and principally from the Pathé studio, supplied the films needed for the nickelodeon boom. Thus, from at least 1906 to 1909, French films dominated American screens.

By 1908 the production of American films was dominated by a duel between titans: Edison, who had originated motion pictures in the United States, and the American Mutoscope and Biograph Company, whose patents, largely designed by William K. L. Dickson (the guiding engineer behind Edison's motion picture devices), had circumvented aspects of Edison's design. Biograph also had the industrial capital to fight off an Edison suit. J. J. Kennedy, who had come in to liquidate Biograph when it seemed no longer a profitable business, decided instead to expand the business, regularize it, and launch a full-scale offensive against Edison. Although both sides blustered, they reached a compromise (probably brokered by exchangeman and film importer George Kleine) that involved Edison and Biograph mutually recognizing their respective patents and instituting a licensing system by which a limited number of production companies would be allowed to produce films, provided they paid a royalty fee to the holding company organized to pool the various patents. This company was known as the Motion Picture Patents Company (MPPC), but its opponents often referred to it as the Film Trust, referring to the tendency in American industry of the era to form combinations that would limit competition, a practice many considered illegal. Besides Edison and Biograph, Essanay, Kalem, Lubin, and Vitagraph were licensed to produce films, and the foreign companies Pathé and Méliès as well as Kleine were licensed to import films from Europe (and Méliès and Pathé eventually also produced films in the United States). The MPPC also instituted controls that would regulate the exchanges (setting up release dates and a policy of leasing and retiring old films) as well as exhibition (including an unpopular royalty on projectors paid to the MPPC). Instituted in 1909, the MPPC immediately encountered resistance from the exchanges, exhibitors, and a few small production companies and film importers, and the next few years would see a battle waged between the "Film Trust" or "Licensed" films, as the MPPC and its products were known, and the growing independent movement. But the MPPC certainly put the American film industry on a new basis: it allowed expansion of American production, regularized the distribution of film, and limited the number of foreign imports (Pathé lost its earlier prominence and even began setting up an American branch in recognition of the increasing importance of the vast American market). After 1909, America reconquered its own screens and began producing homegrown genres (such as the western, enormously popular by 1909) and inventing techniques (a style based on action and tempo).

The demand of the nickelodeon for a steady flow of new films forced filmmaking into a mode of systematic production, with a regularized number of one-reel films produced every week. The switch from the predominance of actuality to the predominance of fiction films took place during the dawn of the nickelodeon era (although, as Musser has shown, even granted that more actuality films were made before the rise of nickelodeons, fictional films were more popular and therefore shown more widely and frequently). Likewise, the switch to story films allowed a degree of preplanning far beyond that of actuality films, dependent as they were on current events for both topics and popularity. Fictional films could be devised ahead of time. Indeed, regular production could be systematized with stock companies of actors, studios equipped with electrical light, and a battery of props and sets.

The development of film form over these years shows a rather coherent shape. First, films became progressively longer. The first film programs featured very brief scenes (often less than a minute) of staged performances or scenes of daily life. But films could be longer when the subject demanded. Thus, early in our period longer films were made of Passion Plays and prize fights, although programs of shorter films grouped together were more frequent. Vaudeville shows tended to favor topical subjects (such as the films of the Spanish-American War described by Patrick Loughney in the 1898–1899 chapter). However, after the initial novelty period, a number of fictional genres became popular. Trick films, often in versions that featured applied color, were especially popular among the vaudeville patrons, particularly those made by French producer Georges Méliès such as *A Trip to the Moon* (1902) or *Fairyland* (1903). Comic films involving chases (led by Biograph's hit *Personal* in 1904) or daring exploits of criminals (such as Edison's *The Great Train Robbery*) emerged next as enduring genres. Trick films, gag comedies, and chase films (both dramatic and comic) were easy to understand without dialogue, dependent as they were mainly on physical action. All these genres involved some form of editing, splicing, and joining the film strip, whether as a way of refining tricks of disappearance or transformation, or the "jump cuts" that Jean-Pierre Sirois-Trahan describes in the 1900–1901 chapter as occurring even within early actuality films, or the more visible joining of shots in different locations to create an action that moved through extensive space.

The earliest film primarily displayed a "view," presenting something that filmmakers thought would grab the audience's attention. This means that the earliest films dealt less with telling stories (let alone developing characters) and concentrated more on presenting what we have called "attractions," usually brief items of visual interest. During the novelty era, the reproduction of motion served as a film's main attraction and filmmakers used film form to emphasize this (as in scenes of rapid motion, films shot from trains, movement directly toward the camera, the unpredictable movements of an urban crowd, or even the natural attractions of pounding surf, waterfalls, or billowing smoke). Trick films, facial contortions, acrobatic acts, or even simple gags also provided a form of attractions that filmmakers might control to a greater degree. Likewise, filmmakers learned that tricks, gags, or any combination of short attractions could be strung together to make longer and more varied films, as the pure novelty of motion faded. Simple story lines offered one way of stringing attractions together. But the stories themselves, with their narrative progression and even suspense, began also to play an increasing role in making films popular, yielding many films in which storytelling and the display of attractions seem to intertwine to keep the viewer's interest (one could argue that even today films with extensive special effects use a similar combination). As André Gaudreault discusses in his 1904–1905 chapter, the genre of the "chase" film (in which crowds of people pursued a character) appeared in 1904. This simple action of pursuit channeled the attraction of motion into an easily comprehensible narrative form, using editing to create an extensive space as the chase moved through various locations shot by shot.

As fiction films became dominant (this happens in terms of raw numbers in 1907, as Eileen Bowser shows, although fictional films had been the most popular for several years before), more complex narrative formulas emerged, and making films with complex action—such as Vitagraph's *The Mill Girl*, which Bowser discusses—required the filmmaker to develop more complex editing strategies. During this period the one-reel length of 1,000 feet became the standard for production, and so most films had a running time of about fifteen minutes. From 1908 on, adaptations of famous novels, poems, and plays became frequent, partly as an attempt to mollify social critics who claimed films were obscene and partly to attract more middle-class patrons to the cinemas. These and other story films also depended to a greater degree on developing characters who could convey individual personality and motivations, a tendency also aided by a new style of acting and by closer camera positions that allowed more vivid presentations of unique characters. The dramatic effect of D. W. Griffith's entrance into filmmaking at Biograph in 1908 must be seen as the result of a film industry trying to refashion itself and aspiring to cultural roles as a narrative form. While the same "uplift" and increased systematization of narration (with stronger characterization carried by actors such as John Bunny or Florence Turner) was evident at Vitagraph and other MPPC-affiliated producers, the sophistication of Griffith's editing and narrative structure is shown in a film like *A Corner in Wheat*, whose background is explored in this volume in the 1909 chapter by Jennifer Bean. This is a film that aspires to both social commentary and poetic form.

With the invention of cinema, a new apparatus appeared as a scientific novelty with possibly only a brief period of commercial interest (as was true of the Kinetoscope peepshow device first offered by Edison). By 1909, cinema was establishing itself as a major form of entertainment, one whose social and aesthetic roles began to define themselves. From the manufacture of machines and the exhibition of brief actuality films of daily life or current events, the film industry refocused on the production of a constantly renewed supply of films, primarily of a fictional nature and of a standard length of one reel. Taking in the movies had become an important pastime, especially for working-class patrons, initially in urban areas. But by the end of this period most Americans had the opportunity to see films. The industry had made its first attempt at systematic coordination of all its aspects and offered a steady supply of product, intent on establishing American films as dominant in American theaters and on gaining social respectability.

NOTES

The authors of this introduction are, of course, jointly responsible for it. However, the section "The So-Called Invention of So-Called Cinema" is mostly the work of André Gaudreault (translated by Timothy Barnard), while Tom Gunning was in charge of the section "The First Two Decades." For the first section, André Gaudreault is much indebted to Paul Spehr and to Jean-Marc Lamotte, Lumière collections manager at the Institut Lumière in Lyon, for their constructive and well-founded ideas exchanged over years of research. The editors of and contributors to this volume used as a reference source not only the Internet Movie Database (which is standard for the series) but also the silent film database on the web site of the American Film Institute.

    1. Nevertheless, we must also take into account the fact that in the early twentieth century the root *kinema* was more widespread in the United States and especially in England.

In some languages, when you say that you are going to the "cinema" you use words from an entirely different tradition. Thus in Flemish, cinema is called the *bioscoop,* and in Chinese, *dien ying* ("electric shadows").

2. At the suggestion of Tom Gunning, the present authors proposed this expression in the summer of 1985 at a film history conference in Cerisy, France. The original text from Cerisy (published initially in Japanese and then in French) has finally appeared in English. See Gaudreault and Gunning, "Early Cinema" 365–80. It should be noted that André Gaudreault has recently criticized the expression "cinema of attractions" and suggested that we use instead the expression "kine-attractography" (the English equivalent of the French term "cinématographie-attraction"). See Gaudreault, "'Primitive Cinema'" 85–104.

1890–1895

Movies and the Kinetoscope

PAUL C. SPEHR

The period between 1890 and 1895 was a rich one in terms of scientific, cultural, and social developments, but it was also a period of growing unrest. Karl Benz constructed the first automobile on four wheels and Henry Ford built his first gasoline-powered engine. Women's suffrage was adopted in Colorado. Coxey's army marched from Ohio to Washington to protest widespread unemployment. Workers at the Pullman Palace Car Company struck and Eugene Debs's American Railway Union declared a sympathy strike. Wilhelm Röntgen discovered X-rays; Guglielmo Marconi invented radio telegraphy. For the first time people heard Mahler's Second and Dvořák's "New World" Symphonies, Verdi's *Falstaff*, Sibelius's "Finlandia," Debussy's "Prélude à l'après-midi d'un faune," and Tchaikovsky's *Swan Lake*. At the theater, they saw George Bernard Shaw's *Arms and the Man* and Oscar Wilde's *A Woman of No Importance*. By their (gas, kerosene, and increasingly electric) lamplight they read Rudyard Kipling's *Jungle Book* and H. G. Wells's *The Time Machine*. A partial list of prominent persons who died and were born during these years symbolizes this era of change. Among those who died: Vincent van Gogh, Guy de Maupassant, and Louis Pasteur. Among those born were Dwight D. Eisenhower, Fritz Lang, Mary Pickford, Josef von Sternberg, Jean Renoir, John Ford (Sean Aloysius O'Feeney), and Buster Keaton (Joseph Francis Keaton). But something even more than new was on the horizon, something that would enchant and mystify viewers for ages to come.

The Kinetoscope

The opening was scheduled for Monday, the sixteenth of April, but the films and ten Kinetoscope machines arrived on Friday and the members of the Kinetoscope syndicate had them set up and ready by noon on Saturday. When Al Tate, who was Edison's personal secretary, saw a large crowd gathered outside, he turned to Tom Lombard of the Chicago Central Phonograph Company and suggested that they open early and let the crowd pay for the celebratory supper planned for that evening at Delmonico's. So the doors were opened. Tate sold tickets, Lombard monitored the crowd, and Tate's brother Bert kept the machines running. They hoped to close at six, but the press of the crowd kept them busy until one A.M. Tate said that it would have taken a squad of police to clear the hall if they had tried to close earlier. They had sold almost 500 tickets at twenty-five cents each and the take was more than enough to pay for supper. Unfortunately, they did not record the name of the first person to buy a ticket, but the opening of the Holland Brothers Kinetoscope parlor on 14 April 1894 was a promising beginning for the American motion picture industry. Tate and company happily regaled themselves with boiled lobster—but at an all-night restaurant. Delmonico's was closed.

What the crowd saw were not movies in the sense that most of us understand them today, that is, images moving on a screen in an experience shared with others gathered in a darkened space. Instead, the patrons at the Holland Brothers parlor paid their quarters to view five different films, each exhibited in one of five large wooden boxes. One by one they bent over and looked at the movie through a slot in the top. Each film lasted from twenty to thirty seconds, and after watching the first they could move to the second and so on. If a patron was pleased and could afford it, another twenty-five cents made it possible to see the films on the remaining five machines. They saw a mixture of subjects: Eugene Sandow, the European strongman, with his quizzical face and bulging muscles; the innocent-looking contortionist Bertholdi (Beatrice Mary Claxton); a Highland dance; a trapeze artist; a wrestling match; a cockfight; and two staged scenes: a blacksmith and assistants at work and men gathered in a barbershop. The films bore Thomas Edison's name, the machines were designed and built by him, and a bust of Edison was prominently displayed in the center of the parlor.

The Kinetoscope had had a long gestation. Edison, the "Wizard of Menlo Park," had promised in October 1888 to make a device to "do for the eye what the phonograph does for the ear." Attempts to record microscopic images on a cylinder proved futile and in 1889, when George Eastman announced that he was marketing strips of celluloid on rolls, Edison got one of the first samples. By 1890 a prototype camera was built that used a strip of film and took circular images three-quarters of an inch in diameter. A crude viewing machine was built and in 1891 it was demonstrated to a group of women visiting Mrs. Edison. Eastman's celluloid, introduced in 1889, made the breakthrough feasible. It was transparent and flexible and came in lengths that made it possible to take a succession of images at speeds rapid enough to create the illusion of movement. But Eastman had trouble producing a consistent product, and Edison's assistant William Kennedy Laurie Dickson spent much of 1891 and 1892 redesigning the machines and working with Eastman to improve the strength and photo-sensitivity of his celluloid. A revised version of the camera, called the Kine-tograph, was completed in 1892, using film in the modern 35 mm format, a frame one inch wide and three-quarters of an inch high with four perfo-rations on either side to advance the film by engaging with sprockets on a wheel. A prototype of the viewing machine, the Kinetoscope, was com-pleted that fall, and by the end of 1892 a studio designed for film produc-tion was being built (the famous Black Maria in West Orange, New Jersey).

Edison had promised to feature the Kinetoscope in his exhibit for the World's Columbian Exposition in Chicago. The 1893 fair came and went but the Kinetoscope was not among its wonders. This was not for lack of antic-ipation and preparation—or want of publicity. The machine was demon-strated publicly for the first time—to an invited audience in Brooklyn—and contracts to exhibit the Kinetoscope were negotiated. The potential exhibitors remained hopeful as the opening of the fair approached, but at the last minute Edison pulled the plug, delaying the debut for almost a year.

An accumulation of problems and uncertainties caused Edison to pull back. Of immediate concern was a decision by the Eastman Kodak Com-pany to discontinue manufacture of celluloid film. Up in Rochester, George Eastman had encountered serious manufacturing problems. Dickson, the photographic specialist who had done much of the work creating the Kine-toscope, had struggled with Eastman to produce a product that was sensi-tive enough to take multiple exposures, up to forty-six each second, and at the same time tough enough to stand up to the rapid start-stop movement through the camera. Without acceptable film, it was impossible to move ahead. No new subjects could be filmed and no copies produced for view-ing. Eastman's decision, coming late in 1892, forced Dickson to turn to East-man's competitor, the Blair Camera Company, the only other manufacturer of celluloid camera film. Dickson had by this point spent so much time working with Eastman's staff that he turned only reluctantly to Blair, knowing that film designed for still cameras would have to be tried, tested, and modified before production could begin.

Before Blair's film could be tested, however, and while the Black Maria was being completed, Dickson fell seriously ill. Edison called it "brain exhaustion" and was so concerned he sent Dickson to Florida to convalesce at his vacation home in Fort Myers. With Dickson away for all of February and March 1893, work on the Kinetoscope was curtailed. On 7 April, Edi-son told the officials of the Columbian Exposition that the Kinetoscope was not ready and surrendered his concession. A few days later Dickson returned, but too late to revive the concession. The exact nature of his ailment is a mystery (it was probably neurasthenia), but he returned fit for duty and there was no recurrence. So this was a temporary but very inopportune setback.

Edison, however, may not have felt that it was badly timed. In fact, he may have been relieved by the postponement. He held very conflicted views about the Kinetoscope and had serious doubts about its future. He had built a business by inventing and innovating in service to the business community, and he regarded serving business as serving mankind. Producing products for amusement and diversion fell outside his experience, and his attitude toward entertainment was almost Calvinist. Although he may not have regarded them as sinful—he was not an active churchgoer—he seemed to consider products for amusement as less than dignified. He had fashioned the phonograph as a secretarial tool for business and that was how he marketed it: as a means of recording and keeping verbal information and a method of sending messages to others (voice mail!). Others did not see it that way, but their attempts to commercialize recorded music and speech met with resistance from Edison.

The Kinetoscope was the phonograph's little brother. Edison had conceived of it as an extension of the phonograph, and although the effort to join the two had borne little success, he had not given up on the idea. He found a "serious" purpose for the phonograph, but he was having trouble staking out a similar role for the Kinetograph. He talked about businessmen being able to see the person they were talking to on the phone, but the prototypes in his lab were a far cry from that objective. He also talked about making complete operas and famous players in famous roles available for home consumption, but since the machine lacked sound and could make only an image of less than a minute's duration, that was also beyond the realm of reality. Meanwhile, the parties who had been pressing to exhibit the Kinetoscope in Chicago clearly intended to amuse, divert, and amaze the public—and for profit. Edison was not opposed to profit, but he preferred a more elevated means of achieving it.

He was also skeptical about the future of the Kinetoscope. Certainly the public would greet it as a sensation. Certainly it would enjoy early popularity. But how long would the popularity last? And then what?

He was mulling over these problems at the beginning of 1893 when the group of businessmen who had wanted to exhibit the Kinetoscope at the Chicago fair began to press for a contract. The proposal came from the Chicago Central Phonograph Company, one of the largest and most influential branches of the North American Phonograph Company, the Edison-dominated organization that controlled North American rights to Edison's Phonograph and Alexander Graham Bell's Graphophone. The Chicago company was managed by Tom Lombard, who was also the acting head of the North American Phonograph Company. He had financial backing from Erastus Benson, a wealthy banker from Omaha who was also an officer of North American Phonograph. The proposal was negotiated by Edison's personal secretary, Al Tate. Tate's duties went beyond taking dictation and handling correspondence. He was responsible for most of Edison's financial affairs, and among his duties was management of the phonograph business. He was on the board of directors of North American Phonograph and Chicago Central Phonograph.

The Chicago company had ambitious plans. They expected to have 350 phonographs and hoped to have 150 Kinetoscopes. They enticed Edison with estimates of a take of $180,000 (more than $30 million today) from that many machines. Edison balked when he learned that the fair wanted one-third of the net, so Lombard negotiated to reduce that to 15 percent. But the negotiations became more complicated when Edison received a similar proposal from H. E. Dick, the brother of A. B. Dick, who had turned Edison's electric pen, a prototype of the mimeograph, into a successful office supply business. Because Edison was negotiating with the Dicks about a place to stay in Chicago when he took his family to the fair, he could not refuse to at least consider their bid.

So, by canceling the concession, Edison eased away from a problematic situation. With the opening of the Exposition less than a month away, no machines were being built (there were one or two prototypes at the lab), there were only a few films completed, and even those had been made as tests; worse, Dickson, his key person in the project, was just returning from convalescence. Despite the setback, Lombard hoped that Edison might supply a reduced number of Kinetoscopes that could be exhibited with the phonographs at the fair or in downtown Chicago. With Tate's support, Lombard proposed twenty-five machines. Edison agreed, and at the end of June he gave James Egan, a machinist at his lab, a contract to build mechanisms for twenty-five "kinetos."

Edison's reluctance to push manufacture of the Kinetoscope was provident. Four days after the fair opened, on 5 May 1893, the stock market faltered, initiating a series of bank and corporate failures that threw the economy into a tailspin. Among the victims were several railroads, one of the backbones of America's industrial growth. It proved to be one of the worst economic slumps between the Civil War and the crash of 1929. The troubles affected everybody's business. Erastus Benson's banks in Omaha were in trouble and he was the principal backer of Lombard's proposal. George Eastman's partner and the president of Eastman Kodak, Henry Strong, lost his bank in Tacoma, Washington. With help from Eastman he reopened, but in 1894 the bank failed a second time. Closer to home, on 1 August, the *New York Herald* reported that Superintendent Ballin of the Edison Phonograph had resigned because he was unable to face laying off 400 workers. The manufacture of phonographs and recording cylinders was thus drastically reduced, as was the staff of the lab. Machinists, carpenters, pattern makers, and laborers were the first to go, but the staff of experimenters eventually declined, too. By the end of 1893, Dickson was one of the few senior experimenters left on staff and the Kinetoscope was one of the few bright spots in an otherwise gloomy picture.

The contract to make twenty-five kinetos remained in place, but Mr. Egan was not up to the task. The project dragged on through the remainder of 1893; late in the year Egan, who apparently had problems with alcohol, was dismissed. William Heise, Dickson's assistant, was assigned to finish it. And finish it he did. The mechanisms were ready early in 1894, and orders were placed for the wooden cabinets to hold them and the lenses through which eager patrons' eyes would peek. Rolls of film stock were received from Blair and serious film production had begun. By late March, most of the first ten machines had been assembled. They had to be converted from starting by coin to a manual switch located at the rear of the machine, one of the last modifications made before the machines could be commercialized. By late March, Dickson had set up facilities to print films in large quantities. With everything ready for the mid-April 1894 opening of the Holland Brothers parlor, Edison transferred the Kinetoscope project from the lab to the Edison Phonograph Works, a branch of the Edison Manufacturing Company.

Marketing Kinetoscopes

The syndicate that had contracted for twenty-five Kinetoscopes evolved. It had been initiated by the Chicago Central Phonograph Company and members of that company still dominated it, but it had now become a semi-independent body. Economic troubles apparently caused Erastus Benson to reduce his role, so to fund the project Tate and Lombard turned to a pair of newcomers, Norman Raff and Frank Gammon. Raff was the son of George W. Raff, a prominent judge and banker from Canton, Ohio, whose law office and bank were near the law office of William

McKinley, Ohio governor, congressman, and future president of the United States. Though the Raff family was prominent in the Democratic Party, McKinley, a Republican, was a director of the Raff's Central Savings Bank. In the 1880s, Raff had gone west and prospered through ventures in mining and oil. Rather than labor with pick and sluice, he set up a bank in a remote part of southern New Mexico where he provided safekeeping for those who actually struck pay dirt. Among his customers there was Charles R. Canfield, who later became a partner in the oil business with Edward L. Doheny, of Sinclair Oil and Teapot Dome infamy. After leaving New Mexico, Raff set up one of the first banks in Guthrie in the recently opened Oklahoma Territory. In Oklahoma he reaped new profits from oil prospectors. With his pockets well-lined, he retired from prospecting and with his brother-in-law, Frank Gammon, took a flyer in the phonograph business.

Raff joined the Chicago Central Phonograph Company in late 1892 or early 1893, and it was probably Erastus Benson who introduced him to the phonograph. Benson had made money in mining and probably felt a kinship with the young prospector. Speculating in the moving picture business soon followed. Sometime during 1893 Tate and Lombard added the Holland brothers to their syndicate. George and Andrew Holland had been secretaries to the Canadian parliament and were the Canadian concessionaires for the North American Phonograph Company. They had formed a close relationship with Lombard and their fellow Canadian, Tate. The Hollands apparently helped fund both the purchase of the twenty-five Kinetoscopes and the setup of the exhibition parlor at 1155 Broadway. At any rate, their name went on the door, although they do not seem to have been in New York for the opening.

The syndicate's arrangement with Edison did not extend beyond the first twenty-five machines, even though Tate presented a more specific long-term proposition. Edison was to be paid a $10,000 bonus (in two $5,000 payments) and assured a minimum business of $10,000 a year. The syndicate would pay Dickson and his assistant to complete work on the Kinetograph and Kinetophone and to make films. Dickson would also receive a commission. Kinetoscopes would be ordered in lots of fifty at a cost not to exceed $60 apiece and they would pay a royalty of fifty cents for each roll of film used. Edison was not prepared for a long-term deal, however, and continued to consider offers from others to purchase machines. Although it was not accepted, Tate's proposal contained elements of the ultimate agreements.

Edison's reluctance to jump into this lucrative offer was the consequence of a long-term crisis in the phonograph business. Even before the stock market collapsed, things had not been going well. The troubles had begun when Jessie Lippincott, the wealthy drinking glass manufacturer who set up the North American Phonograph Company, found himself overextended and unable to meet payments for his rights to Edison's patents. He also owed Edison a huge amount for phonographs the company had ordered. To settle some of the debts Edison took stock in the company and eventually gained control. In the midst of the gathering crisis, Lippincott suffered a stroke and lingered at death's door for several months, with Lombard filling in as president. In addition, the enterprise was not developing as planned. The stenographic business never performed up to expectations and was in decline. After originally leasing the machines, Edison began to sell them, but with a price of about $200 they were beyond the reach of most customers. Many who had leased them did not renew and a glut of unused phonographs resulted. From England, where machines were still being leased, came a flood of complaints that pirated machines were being sold at relatively low prices. Back in the United States, Emile Berliner, a young technician allied with the Columbia Phonograph Company in Washington, D.C., introduced an inexpensive machine that played disks and eliminated dependence on electricity by using a wind-up spring mechanism. Berliner was also working on a method of pressing recordings from a master that would open the market for home use. By the spring of 1894, Edison's manufacturing and sales were at a standstill and his European clients were threatening a lawsuit.

Soon after the Holland Brothers Kinetoscope parlor opened, Edison took drastic steps to reorganize his phonograph business. To gain control of the patents he had licensed, he forced the North American Phonograph Company into bankruptcy and did the same with the company controlling sales outside the United States. To manage and reform the business he brought in William Gilmore as his general manager. Gilmore, who had worked at General Electric in Schenectady, began with Edison on 1 April 1894, two weeks before the opening of the Holland Brothers parlor. On the first of May, Al Tate was laid off.

It was amid this disarray that the Tate-Lombard syndicate's efforts to get a contract for the Kinetoscope took place; it was late summer before they were able to get Gilmore into a serious negotiation. In the interim, several other proposals were put on the table, including one from Otway Latham to purchase ten specially built machines designed to show boxing on a longer piece of film and another from Colonel George Gouraud, Edison's principal phonograph concessionaire in England, who wanted to distribute the Kinetoscope overseas. Latham represented a syndicate that consisted of him, his brother Grey (the Latham brothers were obscure southerners of modest fortune), Enoch Rector, and members of the Tilden family (the Rectors and Tildens represented established New York City money). Rector had been a classmate of the Lathams at the University of West Virginia, where Woodville Latham, the father, had been on the faculty. Otway Latham worked for the Tilden Drug Company. The syndicate proposed to show boxing films and asked that the Kinetoscope be enlarged to show one-minute rounds. Latham paid a deposit and asked for delivery by 2 July. After determining that it could be done, Edison accepted their offer.

Colonel Gouraud was an American who had lived in England for several years. He had represented a number of Edison's interests and fancied himself to be Edison's special emissary. He was a flamboyant showman and his sometimes ambitious projects often made Edison—and Tate—nervous. He was in the United States to confer on the fate of the phonograph, and a visit to the Kinetoscope parlor caused him to make a spur-of-the-moment proposal that 200 machines be purchased at a price of $200 each. He promised to deposit $20,000 in a bank of Edison's choice to begin the deal. Despite his reservations about Gouraud's style, Edison knew him as a business associate who could handle a large-scale operation, so he accepted the offer.

It took a while to get the Phonograph Works tooled for Kinetoscopes and the staff trained, but by July work was under way to fill these orders. By August, Edison and Gilmore had decided to pattern the market for the Kinetoscope after that of the phonograph, but with modifications. Unlike the contract with North American Phonograph, Edison did not include rights to his patents. Instead, they offered two contracts, one for distribution rights for North America, the other for territories outside North America. The contract for North America was signed by Raff & Gammon in August. They agreed to buy one hundred machines at $200 each within a two-month period. It was a short-term contract, but it was renewable. They paid $10,000 down and formed the Kinetoscope Company to handle their business. The special agreement with the Latham syndicate remained in force as well, but restricted to boxing films. The Latham group set up a company with the similar name of the Kinetoscope Exhibiting Company. (To avoid confusion, historians have stuck to "Raff & Gammon" and "the Lathams" in hopes of keeping matters clear.)

The negotiations for an agreement for distribution outside the United States went through a period of disorder. Gouraud ran into financial problems and several parties, among them Raff & Gammon, vied for his rights. In early September 1894, agreement was reached with Frank Z. Maguire, a long-time distributor of mimeographs and phonographs for Edison, and

Joseph D. Baucus, a Wall Street lawyer, to purchase the Kinetoscopes that Gouraud had ordered. Maguire and Baucus set up the Continental Commerce Co. to handle affairs outside North America. Each of these companies marketed their Kinetoscopes to the public through sub-contracts with regional distributors. Although their agreements were short-term, they remained in place for the next two years.

Film Production

Edison was fundamentally in the business of making machines, not images. He expected profit to come from the manufacture and sale of his Kinetoscopes. Although he understood that it was images rather than the machine that attracted paying customers, he looked upon the making of films as a secondary aspect, albeit a necessary one.

Arrangements for producing a specific film were often made by the concessionaires, but film production was the responsibility of Dickson. Dickson, an enthusiastic amateur photographer, was uniquely suited for making films. He came from a family of artists and musicians and was educated in the Renaissance tradition that stressed the classics, music, art, and literature as well as science. He possessed a strong sense of pictorial composition and had learned photography in the era when enthusiasts had to combine artistry with knowledge and skill in the use of chemistry and

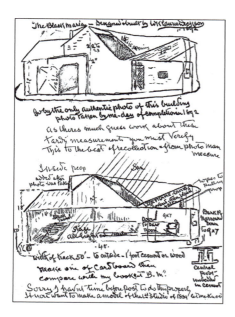

Dickson drawing of Black Maria, for Earl Thiesen, 5 July 1933.

optics. He is one of the few filmmakers who designed all the tools used for the trade: film, camera, studio, laboratory, and viewer.

In the course of the Kinetoscope experiments, Dickson designed three photo studios, the last of which was the Black Maria, purposefully built for Kinetoscope production. It was an awkward, humpbacked structure built upon a rail and designed to swivel 360 degrees on a central pivot. The off-center hump covered the stage area and its roof section opened to expose the shooting stage to direct sunlight. There was a blackened recess behind the stage, darkened to provide maximum contrast by absorbing ambient light. The camera was mounted on a table that could move backward and forward on rails. The rails led into a dark room where the film was loaded and unloaded.

The design of the Black Maria reflected exposure problems that plagued Dickson throughout the camera's long gestation. Although emulsions improved and exposure time was reduced to a fraction of a second, Dickson stretched it to the limit. In order to present a steady image and eliminate annoying flicker he felt it necessary to expose between thirty and forty frames per second (fps). (The films first shown by the Holland brothers were taken at about forty fps. Today, this compares with thirty frames for TV, twenty-four frames for sound motion pictures, and sixteen to twenty frames for most silent films.) To compensate for the film's relative slowness in responding chemically to light, filming took place during midday when the subject was typically bathed in sunlight against the light-absorbing black background.

The camera was cumbersome. It was driven by an electric motor, and to keep vibration at a minimum the mechanism was mounted on cast iron. It was large and heavy, but the design of the studio made it flexible. In addition to moving backward and forward, the camera could be raised and lowered. It had a through-the-lens viewfinder and the aperture speed was regulated by a rheostat. Each take could thus be carefully planned and whenever possible the action rehearsed and timed and the camera carefully positioned. The camera was not designed for use outside the studio and the three or four pictures taken in open air were made adjacent to the studio, with the camera positioned in the building and pointing out the open side door or the rear of the building.

The film stock was custom-made to Dickson's specifications. In addition to being coated with a sensitive emulsion, it had to be tough enough to withstand the rapid start-stop movement through the camera's mechanism. It was supplied without perforations and ordered a bit wider than was necessary to fit the camera. A perforator-trimmer was designed to prepare each reel for camera use. This device was propelled by a sewing-machine treadle and operated in a dark room by Dickson's assistant. This was but one element of a complete system that had to be designed and built before production could begin. There were separate dark rooms for developing negatives and prints, reels for drying film, and a printer to make positives from negatives (by contact).

Moving pictures were produced by a team. Although the various jobs had not yet gelled, Dickson worked as the director and sometimes as producer. His assistant, William Heise, acted as camera operator and did many of the tasks now handled by a production crew. Dickson oversaw the work, planned and rehearsed the shot, and evaluated the results. Heise prepared the film and loaded and set up the camera per instructions. After the "take" he removed the film, developed it, operated the contact printer, and so on. Almost a hundred films were produced during this period; because they established precedents for subsequent productions we will examine the particulars of several of them.

Sandow

Regular film production began in early March 1894. On 6 March, the European strongman Eugene Sandow came to Edison's lab to be filmed. Billed as the Modern Hercules, his display of strength, muscle, and flesh made Sandow one of the top draws on the theater scene. He had opened at the Casino the previous June and was on the bill at Koster & Bial's Music Hall at the time of the filming. Accompanied by John Koster of Koster & Bial's, Koster's business manager C. B. Kline, and Richard T. Haines of the North American Phonograph Company, he arrived at about

Souvenir strip of the Edison Kinetoscope
(*Sandow*, Edison, 1894).
Digital frame enlargements.

noon in order to be filmed at midday. The group was welcomed by Dickson, who apologized for Edison, who was napping after an all-night session and planned to join them for lunch after the filming. Sandow stripped for action and three short films were taken.

Dickson framed the shots in medium-close-up, displaying Sandow's torso from just above the knees. Dressed in the briefest of briefs, Sandow performed muscle flexes and demonstrated his chest expansion. It was an intimate view, and there was no attempt to show the sensational tricks that wowed New York audiences. (The stage of the Maria was too small to show him bent backward supporting a platform bearing a pianist, a grand piano, and a Hungarian band on his chest.) But Dickson's staging gave glimpses of the strongman that only a few front-row spectators could have seen, an intimate view of the play of Sandow's muscles. The films' intensely erotic overtones have caused modern viewers to speculate about what they say about late Victorian taste.

These films, and many other early productions, owe a debt to the chronophotographic images that Eadweard Muybridge, Ottomar Anschütz, and Étienne-Jules Marey had already published—and sometimes projected. Chronophotography is the analysis of movement by use of rapidly photographed images. It was pioneered by Eadweard Muybridge and perfected by Étienne-Jules Marey.

Marey also photographed Sandow and had used photography to study muscle movement and breathing. We don't know if Dickson had seen these pictures, but he was familiar with the genre. He used it as a model but was trying to achieve something extra. Though the picture itself was short by modern standards, the action was much longer than the twelve to twenty-four frames typically used to study motion, and was not cyclical as were most of the public exhibitions that Muybridge and Anschütz presented at the Chicago Exposition and elsewhere. There was no attempt to analyze the movements. Instead, the films were produced and staged to display action.

Dickson made filmmaking an event. After the Sandow filming, Edison joined the group for lunch at Davis's, the best local restaurant. Sandow was so pleased by Edison's presence that he waived his usual $250 fee. The next day Sandow returned and Dickson took him for a tour of Glenmont, Edison's nearby mansion; to another lunch at Davis's; and for a drive and a visit to Dickson's home, where his sister Antonia entertained on the piano. That evening Sandow was the guest of honor at the dinner meeting of the Orange Camera Club.

The films of Sandow provided diversion and entertainment for the public, but that was not their sole purpose. John Koster's presence shows he appreciated the valuable publicity the filming provided—as did Mr. Edison. It promoted both Sandow's performance *and* the Kinetoscope. The press was given advance notice and articles appeared in the *New York World* and in papers in Orange and Newark. Dickson took still photographs, provided strips of film frames for the articles, and prepared a card with frames from the film as a souvenir item. When the Holland Brothers parlor opened on 14 April 1894, the films of Sandow were a prominent feature and Dickson's souvenir card was probably available as a remembrance. This interaction between exhibition and publicity is characteristic of film's early years. Edison, Dickson, and a number of others saw filmmaking as a form of advertising, promotion, and public information. It was a practical use for his invention that made popular entertainment more palatable for Edison.

Sandow was the first of a string of featured variety performers who took the ferry from Manhattan to New Jersey to appear in the Kinetoscope, many of them headliners from Koster & Bial's. Sandow was followed by Carmencita, a sensational Spanish dancer whom some have credited with making vaudeville fashionable; Bertholdi, a popular British-born contortionist; Mlle Armand'Ary, a stylish chanteuse known for her humorous delivery; Caicedo, King of the Wire Walkers; and others. There were also animal acts—some, such as dancing dogs, innocuous. But trained bears, boxing cats and monkeys, fighting cocks, and dogs that fought or killed rats and weasels challenge modern sensibilities.

Annabelle the Dancer

The serpentine dance is one of the favorite images from early cinema. It was filmed dozens of times, and surviving versions are often chosen as prime examples of the era. While dance historians credit Loïe Fuller with popularizing it, the widely seen filmed versions probably made it familiar to the public. Though Fuller was filmed, the first performance for camera was by Annabelle Whitford (later Annabelle Moore). She came to Orange in the summer of 1894 and performed three dances: a butterfly dance, a sun dance, and the serpentine, each with a different costume and choreography. The serpentine was performed with a billowing, diaphanous full-length gown. The sleeves were extended by hand-held sticks that were maneuvered to create graceful patterns of sheer billowing cloth. In the theater, the billows were illuminated through changing colored gels, an effect that was sometimes emulated on film by hand coloring each frame.

Annabelle, known popularly as Annabelle the Dancer, established her reputation at the Chicago Exposition and for several years was a featured performer in New York theater. Her filmed dances were so popular that she returned to New Jersey twice to make replacements for negatives that had worn out.

While it may seem odd to watch a dance without music, this seems not to have bothered early viewers, as dance performances were a staple. The range of selections was quite broad, sometimes featuring solo dancers like Annabelle, Carmencita, and Ruth Denis (later Ruth St. Denis) and some-time groups like the Gaiety Girls, the latter constituting one of several scenes from theatrical productions filmed during the fall of 1894. Beyond dance, Kinetoscope patrons enjoyed a generous sampling of popular enter-tainment. Among the theatrical presentations filmed in the fall of 1894 were scenes from the *Passing Show*, *Milk White Flag*, *1492*, *Little Christopher Columbus*, *The South before the War*, and *Rob Roy*.

Corbett and Courtney before the Kinetograph

Not surprisingly, the first large investment in motion picture production by outsiders came from the sporting world. Also not surpris-ingly, it involved boxing. Boxing was popular and interest was keen after James J. Corbett won the heavyweight championship from John L. Sullivan in a legendary match on 7 September 1892. This had been the first bout fought under the Marquess of Queensberry rules (which mandated padded gloves, the twenty-four-foot ring, and three-minute rounds, and excluded seconds from the ring), and both fighters were colorful crowd pleasers. The sporting public's appetite was quickened because it was difficult for many to experience the action first-hand. Boxing was illegal in most states, par-ticularly in the populous East and Midwest, so matches were held sub-rosa or in seemingly remote locations like New Orleans (where the Corbett-Sullivan bout was held). Theatrical exhibitions were permitted, however, and both Sullivan and Corbett performed in stage productions with boxing as a theme. The possibility of staging a match for the camera was raised soon after the Kinetoscope appeared.

James J. Corbett and Peter Courtney from the *Police Gazette*.

In early August 1894, Otway Latham wrote William Brady, the theatrical producer who was Corbett's manager, proposing a match with Peter Jackson, a prominent contender. Latham proposed a purse of $15,000 for a fight to be filmed in the Black Maria. Brady sent Latham's letter and his response to the *New York Journal*. He did not turn the proposition down, but asked that Latham match an offer of $25,000 he had received from the Olympic Club of New Orleans. He commented that "Mr. Corbett would be delighted to have his motions and actions in the ring preserved for future generations." Nothing came of this proposal, but at the end of the month Corbett agreed to fight Peter Courtney, an obscure challenger styled as the heavyweight champion of New Jersey. The Lathams hoped that by "staging" the bout as a demonstration of skill and technique, they could circumvent the proscription. It was a theory that Edison was happy to accept. The bout took place on 7 September 1894. It lasted six rounds, and a knockout conveniently close to the end of round six left Corbett in possession of his crown and a purse of $4,750. Courtney took home $250.

This was the second match filmed for the Lathams. A bout between welterweights Michael Leonard and Jack Cushing had been filmed the previous June. It was staged in the Black Maria with ropes strung across the front and back to emulate a ring. The twelve-foot-wide area used then proved to be too confining, so the stage was widened to fourteen feet for Corbett and Courtney. But this "ring" was still much smaller than required by the Queensberry rules. To protect the fighters, the walls were padded and the floor smoothed and covered with resin. For Corbett, the rounds were stretched to last a bit longer than one minute but were still much shorter than the officially required three minutes. (The temporal extension was apparently achieved by running the camera a bit slower than usual.) Even though enlarged, the stage of the Black Maria did not please Corbett. The *New York Sun* reported that upon entering the stage Corbett commented: "My, but this is small. There's no chance to bring any foot movement into play here, that's sure. A fellow has got to stand right up and fight for his life."

The principals came to Orange on 6 September, but the match had to be postponed because of poor weather. At noon the next day, all was ready and the six rounds were filmed. There was a break of about three minutes between rounds so the camera could be reloaded. Following the fight, Corbett took the 2:00 P.M. train to the ferry, accompanied by an entourage of assistants, reporters, and fans. It was a special occasion though with less festivity than there had been for Sandow, probably because of nervousness that the authorities might intervene. Corbett made it back to Manhattan, but a few days after the bout a grand jury in Newark was asked to investigate Edison for a possible violation of the law. Edison and Dickson were called to testify in the case but were not charged. The court accepted the claim that this was a staged bout, so the door was opened for boxing to become one of the most popular film genres. Indeed, as long as real matches were difficult to see, boxing films were especially popular, attracting large investments and spawning a number of significant technical improvements.

Sioux Ghost Dance

Although the Kinetograph camera remained in the Black Maria and never roamed the world, exotic subjects came to Orange to be filmed. A few weeks after Dickson filmed Corbett, Buffalo Bill brought members of his Wild West company to Orange. Among the performers was a group of Native Americans, members of the Brule and Oglala Sioux tribes. After Buffalo Bill was filmed, the Indians performed the Ghost Dance, staged a "War Council," and finished with the Buffalo Dance.

The recording of the Sioux Ghost Dance has particular significance. The cult of the Ghost Dance was an attempt to rehabilitate Native American culture. It involved a ritual dance in which many participants fell into trances where they received songs or were healed by ghosts they believed they encountered. It was influenced by Christian teachings, but the rapid spread of the Ghost Dance cult alarmed many white settlers. Indeed, it was misguided concern about the cult that led to the massacre at Wounded Knee at the end of 1890. The dance fell out of favor and for many years it was rarely performed, so this filmed record is a unique document, all the more so since one member of the troupe, Johnny-No-Neck Burke, was a survivor of Wounded Knee.

Although this example is dramatic, it was only one of a number of native groups that were filmed in the Black Maria. Interest in ethnic groups was high at the time, stimulated by recent international expositions that brought musicians, dancers, artisans, and other cultural representatives from distant lands. Edison had met Buffalo Bill when he visited the Paris Exposition of 1889, where international cultures were an important feature. In addition to the Native Americans, Buffalo Bill brought performers from Mexico and the Middle East to Orange to be filmed. A few months later, when Barnum and Bailey's Circus was in the area, dancers from Samoa, Fiji, India, Ceylon, and Egypt were filmed. This was recognition that moving images could open new vistas and provide a unique record of unfamiliar cultures. For such cultures, these efforts, when they survive, are all the more valuable since advancing globalization already threatened their survival.

Peep Shows and Screen Machines

Edison's skepticism about the future of the Kinetoscope was well founded. As predicted, it was received enthusiastically by the public and the press, and during the first months Edison and his licensees made good money. In fact, in 1894 the profits from the Kinetoscope saw Edison though an otherwise financially disastrous year. Phonograph, cylinder, and battery profits plunged to a paltry $3,752, while sales of Kinetoscopes and films yielded $155,585 with a resulting profit of $73,455. But the novelty lapsed, and by early 1895 profits began to wither. Edison hoped that combining the Kinetoscope with the phonograph would revive business, but efforts to synchronize them came to naught. In April 1895 the Kineto-phonograph was introduced, but it only accompanied films with unsynchronized recordings and never caught on. Only forty-five of these were marketed. Raff & Gammon pressed Edison to produce a projector, but Edison was not convinced it was worthwhile.

Although a "screen machine" was tested during the experimental period, Edison opted for the peep show. He was sure that only a few projectors would be needed and his factory would make many more Kinetoscopes. He felt that a device that could be placed in various locations, make money twenty-four hours a day, and not require an on-site worker was a desirable commercial venture. Others did not agree. Almost as soon as the Kinetoscope appeared, work began on devices to project images. In 1895 several notable examples became available.

Soon after opening their New York Kinetoscope parlor, the Latham brothers asked their father if movies couldn't be projected. He said they could and so the Lathams approached Dickson with a proposal to make a projector. Initially the project was offered to Edison but he wasn't interested. Dickson was, and thus began a controversial relationship with the Lathams. After recommending his close friend Eugene Lauste as their principal machinist, he visited their New York workshop frequently. By the end of December 1894, a prototype projector was built. It could run Edison film but the camera that followed used a wider film than Edison's. It was tested near the end of February and a projector, dubbed the Eidoloscope, followed. On 20 May 1895, a film of a boxing match between "Young Griffo" and Charles Barnett was presented to the public at 156 Broadway in New York City.

The Lathams went on to film Niagara Falls, street scenes in New York City, and a bullfight in Mexico City. While continuing to exhibit in New York, during 1895 they sent projectors and films to several other locations. The Eidoloscope lacked an intermittent movement (which would grasp the film and pull it, frame by frame, past the aperture) and the resulting flicker has led it to be regarded as inferior, but the Lathams have the distinction of being the first to publicly project moving pictures as they are understood today. Their enterprise was also short lived. Despite their apparent success, they were overextended and accumulating debt. Dickson became disillusioned and curtailed his involvement with them, but his activities led to a confrontation with Edison on 1 April 1895, which resulted in his resignation. Although he was more experienced and knowledgeable than any of the Lathams, the extent of his contribution to the design of the Eidoloscope is a matter of speculation.

New Competitors

C. Francis Jenkins, a secretarial clerk at the U.S. Life Saving Service (later the U.S. Coast Guard), built a version of the Kinetoscope. In November 1894, he exhibited it at the annual "Pure Food Exposition" in Washington, D.C. Jenkins was a peripatetic dabbler who worked on a myriad of projects during his lifetime. His interest in the phonograph led to an association with the Columbia Phonograph Company of Washington (the parent of CBS), which had the concession for the Kinetoscope in the D.C. area. Since Raff & Gammon could not supply as many machines as Columbia wanted, it supported Jenkins's version of the Kinetoscope and continued to encourage his interest in making a projector. While working on it and taking a course in electricity at the Bliss School, he met Thomas Armat, who was also interested in projection. Armat came from a prosperous Virginia family and had relatives in Washington real estate. They joined forces and together developed a projector they dubbed the "Phantoscope." Using Edison films, it was presented to the public at the Cotton States Exhibition, which opened in Atlanta on 18 September 1895.

The Phantoscope was the most successful of the first U.S. projection designs, but its introduction was a disaster for Armat and Jenkins. The partners found themselves competing with the Kinetoscope and Eidoloscope, both of which were on offer elsewhere in Atlanta. The public proved reluctant to enter their darkened tent-like exhibit booth. After a fire at an adjacent exhibit damaged their exhibit and destroyed one of their projectors, the two men quarreled, parted ways, and never spoke to each other again.

They had been ill matched. Jenkins was an impatient, impulsive gadabout experimenter and an extroverted self-promoter. Armat was patient, conservative, and methodical. They squabbled in court and in print about who contributed most to the Phantoscope, Jenkins claiming that Armat simply financed the work and Armat charging that he made the critical improvements and that Jenkins did not understand that the film had to be stopped in the gate behind the aperture in order that enough light would be thrown on the screen. At the end of 1895, Jenkins took his version of the projector to the Columbia Phonograph Company, which made plans to manufacture and market it. In December, Armat bought Frank Gammon a railway ticket to come to Washington to see his version of the Phantoscope. Gammon liked what he saw and recommended it as a replacement for the Kinetoscope.

Not everyone focused on projection. A former Edison associate, Charles Chinnock, designed and marketed his version of the Kinetoscope. He built a camera and made several films, but he was never a serious economic threat to Edison. More serious competition came from Dickson and several of his associates. After seeing the Kinetoscope, Dickson's friend and former co-worker Harry Marvin approached him, asking if it could be improved. Dickson sketched a flip-card device—something like a thumbbook. Marvin took it to another friend, Herman Casler, who converted Dickson's sketch into a hand-cranked peep-show device they dubbed the Mutoscope. Like the Lathams, they offered their design to Edison. He rejected the offer, so they began work on a camera and in June 1895 they tested it by filming a mock boxing match between the six-foot-plus Marvin and the very diminutive Casler. Both devices used ordinary Kodak still camera film. The image produced was almost three inches wide and two inches high, larger than any competitor's. In the fall, with New York businessman Elias B. Koopman joining them, they formed the KMCD syndicate (from their initials Koopman, Marvin, Casler, and Dickson). Marvin and Koopman began exploring formal commercial opportunities and at the very end of 1895 they launched a well-funded rival to Edison, the American Mutoscope Company. At the outset they intended to market the Mutoscope as a rival peep-show machine, but future events would cause them to revise their plans.

By the end of 1895, with public interest in the Kinetoscope fading, Raff & Gammon were looking to projection as a way to rescue their business. Although Edison was still resisting the "Screen Machine," he had given them a sop by hiring a former machinist, Charles Kayser, to work on converting a Kinetoscope into a projector. His efforts came to naught. Gammon was impressed with the Phantoscope and told Armat he hoped it would not be made available to anyone else. As 1895 ended, change was in the air.

Conclusion

In the history of film, the years before 1896 are generally regarded as a prelude to the main event, the coming of projected film. There have been disputes about who should be credited with invention; Edison and his Kinetoscope, the Lathams, and Armat and Jenkins have been either ignored or considered merely a preview to more important events. For most film devotees, cinema begins in 1896, launched by the exhibition of the Lumière Cinématographe at the very end of 1895. This has been particularly true in Europe, but many American scholars have followed suit, ignoring the hundred or more motion pictures Edison's company produced before the Cinématographe's debut. Edison's images seemed inconsequential. They were small, viewed awkwardly in a wooden box, and only one person at a time could see them—quite different from the shared experience of watching dramas and comedies on a screen in a darkened room. Edison became better known for his unsavory role in patent suits. But, though his resistance to a "screen machine" doomed him to a subordinate place, Edison's contribution to cinema was significant— even decisive. The American motion picture industry began with Edison in 1894 and, for better or for worse, he dominated it during its formative years.

And yet there were valid reasons for dating the beginning of "cinema" with the Lumière brothers. Theirs was a contrasting system and the difference between it and the Kinetoscope was and is striking. The Cinématographe was a clever device that could be used as either camera or projector. It was compact, versatile, portable, and capable of bringing exciting images to a worldwide audience. It roved the world, reached a larger audience than the Kinetoscope, and presented exciting views of people, places, and things both familiar and novel. Edison's Kinetoscope was awkward, heavy, and expensive, and it showed tiny studio-produced images that were ultimately seen by relatively few people. It was a novelty that was soon replaced by "screen machines."

On the surface, Edison's system seems stodgy; the product of limited imagination. But was it? The short-lived Kinetoscope was part of a system, and the system that Edison introduced proved very durable. Edison introduced the 35 mm format; produced films in a purpose-built studio; shot on negative film; and developed his negative in a laboratory where it was copied to positive film on a contact printer and then shown to the public on a separate machine. These methods of production and exhibition have been used—and are still used today—by the industry in the United States and elsewhere in the world. Of particular importance, the "Edison standard" format, today's 35 mm film, was adopted by filmmaker after filmmaker and became *the* universal standard that, more than any other factor, facilitated the rapid spread of cinema about the globe. Then and now, movies made in 35 mm with four perforations on each side of the frame could and can still be seen from Hollywood to Hanoi by audiences large and small. This is true despite changes in the aspect ratio of the frame and modifications to the shape of the perforations. Remarkably, a film made in 1893 is essentially the same as today's and can still be viewed. To understand the value of this consistency, one only has to recall the fate of 78 rpm and LP records, Beta-max and the now-threatened half-inch videotapes.

The films made during these early years also suffer from disregard and misunderstanding. They were and sometimes are characterized as "primitive." This implies that they were the inferior product of learners groping their way toward some golden future that emerged after years of trial and error, which is a misleading view. The first films were short and lacked the complexity that would develop later, but many were capably produced by skilled craftsmen with a strong artistic bent. From the beginning the most successful producers used experienced photographers who were capable of producing striking images that could and did engage viewers intellectually and emotionally. Dickson set the standard, and Edison's chief rivals responded by engaging similarly skilled artists. In England, Birt Acres, a photographer with a substantial reputation, worked for Robert Paul; the Lumières were leading photographic entrepreneurs who trained their camera operators to produce quality images. The limitations these first film producers faced were technical rather than artistic. Film stock came in short lengths, emulsions were relatively slow, and the available celluloid had technical flaws that required knowledge and experience to overcome.

Edison's pioneering work fell short of the quality set by theatrical cinema, but recent scholarship has broadened our perspective and provided a fresh outlook on the beginning years. This comes as new technologies and changing popular tastes are altering the way moving images are used and viewed. Digital projection threatens to replace Edison's 35 mm celluloid film in theaters, and older films are now transferred from film to tape or disk and watched at home on a television screen. Digital technology is replacing analog. Ironically, even as the system that Edison introduced in 1894 is threatened, his emphasis on viewing by individuals has become more valid. And with hand-held, multi-format devices becoming commonplace, the tiny images that seemed so inadequate in 1895 are becoming acceptable in the twenty-first century. Perhaps the Wizard was more perceptive than supposed.

1896–1897

Movies and the Beginnings of Cinema

CHARLES MUSSER

The "cinema," defined here as projected motion pictures in a theatrical setting, was one of the major technological and cultural innovations of 1896–1897. But it shared this distinction with the X-ray, discovered by Wilhelm Röntgen in late 1895, which gained public attention during the same period. While the cinema captured and re-presented images of life in motion, by early 1896 the X-ray was used to produce photographs of what could not be seen (the invisible). In March 1896 Thomas A. Edison used X-rays to develop the fluoroscope, which had medical applications. As cinema and the X-ray entered the public realm, they were in some sense complementary and did much to change the ways people experienced and imagined the visible world. Perhaps it was fitting, then, that Soviet filmmaker Dziga Vertov was born in 1896, the same year that saw the birth of Howard Hawks, F. Scott Fitzgerald, John Dos Passos, and Ethel Waters. In February, Giacomo Puccini's opera *La Bohème* was first performed in Turin, Italy, and Oscar Wilde's play *Salomé*, though published in 1893, was first performed onstage in Paris. At the time Wilde was locked up in a British prison for his homosexuality and not released until May 1897. The month following his release, Queen Victoria celebrated her Diamond Jubilee, marking the sixtieth anniversary of her reign. The first modern Olympic Games were held in Athens, Greece, during April 1896—with the United States winning the equivalent of eleven gold medals, more than any other country. The Klondike Gold Rush in Alaska began little more than a year later.

The cinema made its first commercially successful appearance in the United States on 23 April 1896, with the premiere of Edison's Vitascope at Koster & Bial's Music Hall, located on Herald Square in New York City. Within a few weeks, local premieres were beginning to occur all over the country; by the end of 1897, traveling showmen had screened films in even the nation's smallest towns. As this broad diffusion proceeded, projected moving pictures began to transform many aspects of American life and culture—and to have an impact on photographic practices, screen practices (the illustrated lecture, the magic lantern, and so forth), theatrical culture, the newspaper, politics, art, religion, sports, and the nature of representation itself. Film companies and exhibitors also presented views of the world with different aesthetic and ideological perspectives.

Until 1896, the combination of technological accomplishment, commercial skill, and good fortune necessary for the successful diffusion of cinema was absent. C. Francis Jenkins and Thomas Armat's motion picture projector, which they called the Phantoscope, had an intermittent mechanism—which held the film frame momentarily stationary in front of the light source—but its first use, late the previous year, was ended by fire. Nonetheless, an agent for Norman C. Raff and Frank R. Gammon (heads of the Kinetoscope Company, which had a contract with Edison to distribute his machines) saw the impressive results and met with Armat. This resulted in a contract on 15 January 1896, whereby Armat assigned the Raff & Gammon partnership sole rights to exploit the projector. As Raff & Gammon were agents for Edison's peephole Kinetoscope, this provided an unexpected opportunity to revive Edison's flagging motion picture business. This commercial arrangement relied on the good-faith efforts and coordination of three groups—Armat, Raff & Gammon, and the Edison Manufacturing Company—this latter, solely owned by Thomas A. Edison, would not only build the needed projectors but also supply the films.

For commercial purposes, the Phantoscope was soon renamed Edison's Vitascope (emphasizing "showing life" rather than "showing phantoms"). The renowned inventor's name was used to promote the invention while his associate Armat—occasionally mentioned as a promising young inventor from Washington, D.C.—was kept in the background. An exhibition was staged for the press, with Edison in attendance, on 9 April at the Edison Laboratory in West Orange, New Jersey. By this time, Raff & Gammon were facing an array of challenges. First, they learned that their contractee Armat had a co-inventor, Jenkins, who was threatening to undermine the exclusive nature of this arrangement. They wanted Armat to pay him off (something that did not materialize). Second, they learned of rival screen machines overseas: the Lumière Cinématographe and Robert Paul's Theatrograph were showing in London during February and were certain to reach American shores soon. Raff & Gammon, who had set up the Vitascope Company to handle this new business, moved ahead rapidly. The Vitascope's New York premiere was followed by debuts at Keith's New Theater in Boston on 18 May; Hartford on 21 May; Keith's Theater in Philadelphia on 25 May; New Haven on 28 May; Providence on 4 June; Buffalo and San Francisco on 8 June; Nashville on 13 June; Baltimore on 15 June; Brooklyn, Scranton, and Portland, Maine, on 22 June; and New Orleans on 28 June. Meanwhile, Woodville Latham and his sons Grey and Otway added an intermittent mechanism to their Eidoloscope and became credible competitors, opening at the Olympia Theater in New York on 11 May. On 29 June, the Lumière Cinématographe opened at Keith's Union Square Theater. The Jenkins-affiliated Phantoscope, sometimes under different names, also began to appear in theaters by late June.

Initially, companies tried to sell exhibition rights for their machines on an exclusive, states' rights basis. This was as true for the Lumières as it was for Raff & Gammon and the Lathams (though the Lumières often divided up the globe by countries rather than dividing nations by states). Vaudeville impresario B. F. Keith apparently acquired exclusive rights to the Cinématographe in the United States for the first few months. Raff & Gammon sold states' rights to entrepreneurs, then leased them projectors and sold them films—with an exchange policy. (Only Manhattan screenings were under their direct auspices.) Raff & Gammon's business strategy was to use these initial cash payments to bind rights holders to their Vitascope enterprise, for they would do whatever they could to protect their investments. This worked for a time, but as the number of rival machines proliferated, the value of these rights became worthless. Armat and Jenkins had applied for patents to their invention but the patents took time to be issued and they were either challenged by rivals or disregarded.

By the fall, numerous skilled machinists were manufacturing their own motion picture projectors. Some of these machines were for the exclusive use of one or more showmen (e.g., Lyman Howe's Animatoscope), while others were for sale on the open market—the International Film Company's Projectograph, Edward Amet's Maginscope, the Cinographoscope, the Wonderful Panoramographe, Lubin's Cineograph, and so forth. By fall, the Edison Company broke with Raff & Gammon and was selling films directly to all takers, not just those licensed by the Vitascope Company, and was building its own projector for sale on the open market. Such moves were dictated by commercial realities on the ground. The Vitascope Company all but disappeared by the end of 1896. The Lumières began to sell projectors and films to independent exhibitors in April 1897.

The most successful motion picture company in the United States by the end of cinema's first twenty months was clearly the American Mutoscope Company (later the American Mutoscope & Biograph Company, often called simply Biograph). The company used a larger film format (68 mm/70 mm) and showed more frames per second than its 35 mm rivals. As a result, the quality of its projected image was far superior. Biograph did not sell states' rights to entrepreneurs but dealt directly with top theaters. In this respect, it is worth noting that the Lumière Cinématographe, which often replaced the Vitascope in vaudeville houses during the late summer and fall of 1896, was displaced in turn by the Biograph system late in 1896 and into 1897. This shift was evident in Keith's theaters along the East Coast as well as the Orpheum circuit on the West Coast, and with other smaller vaudeville entrepreneurs as well. By February, one of Biograph's principal owners reported that the company was showing films in twenty-five different locations. Biograph was also expanding internationally, starting sister companies overseas, notably the British Mutoscope & Biograph Company. Biograph's London premiere came on 18 March 1897, and its first filming in the United Kingdom was of Queen Victoria's Diamond Jubilee celebrations on 22 June.

Biograph was at the high end of cinema culture while a miscellaneous group of small-time exhibitors, who bought projectors and films from dealers or manufacturers, were at the low end. In between these two extremes, there were a few ambitious 35 mm film companies that combined the manufacture of films and projectors with exhibition. These included Sigmund Lubin in Philadelphia, the International Film Company and the Eden Musee in New York, and Edward Amet (working with George Spoor) and William Selig in Chicago. Their exhibition services offered a selection of films that often included their own exclusive productions, a trained projectionist, and a projector. Once their original productions had been shown on their own circuits as exclusives, they offered them for sale. This reliance on exhibition services would continue for years to be one of the principal means of distribution.

Film companies proliferated rapidly over the course of 1896–1897, generating a commercial free-for-all that rapidly reduced prices and allowed for experimentation. This was evident in the appearance of *The Phonoscope*, a popular monthly trade journal for the phonograph and film industries, which had its first issue in December 1896. There was a brash openness to such endeavors, which quickly came to an end when Edison sued his rivals for patent violations, beginning with Charles H. Webster and Edmund Kuhn's International Film Company and Maguire & Baucus, Ltd. on 7 December 1897. Many of these defendants were terrified to confront the mythic Edison, and either quickly became his licensees or withdrew from the motion picture business. Although a few would persist, these suits quickly changed the mood of the American film world. People in the film business had to be more secretive and act defensively. They not only faced the commercial risks of any fledgling enterprise but added legal risks (fines, bankruptcy, and jail). Edison could lure away an employee and then use him as a key witness in a patent suit. No one felt safe.

By the end of 1897, the American film firmament was dominated by two bold constellations, orbiting around the Edison Manufacturing Company on one hand and the American Mutoscope and Biograph Company on the other. Edison did not yet sue Biograph, because its financial resources and motion picture patents made such a challenge especially difficult. The intermediate-sized companies, which were active in multiple aspects of the business and used Edison 35 mm film formats, were particularly vulnerable to Edison's legal actions. Finally, there were a large number of small-time exhibitors, many of whom were traveling showmen, whose fortunes were affected by the resulting disruptions but were rarely the direct target of patent suits. They suffered collateral damage.

Cinema and Current Events

Important local, national, and world events occurring over the course of 1896–1897 often influenced activities within the motion picture field. American filmmakers responded to such events through their choice of film subjects and more generally in the ways that cinema functioned within the cultural realm. Within a few months of commercial projection, filmmakers were filming important news events. Edison camera operators filmed the *Suburban Handicap* at Sheepshead Bay Race Track, Coney Island, N.Y. They filmed *Baby Parade at Asbury Park* on 15 August, *The Arrival of Li Huang Chang* (Li Huang Chang being the former Chinese viceroy) on 23 August, and various scenes of the Pro-McKinley Sound Money Parade in New York City (that is, *The Great McKinley Parade*) on 31 October—less than a week before the presidential election. William McKinley's presidential inauguration in Washington, D.C., on 4 March 1897 and Grant's Day celebration in New York on 27 April generated numerous pictures. Grover Cleveland was filmed on the way to McKinley's inauguration, making him the first U.S. president to be filmed in office.

The cinema increasingly functioned as a visual newspaper, with a mix of news films, short cartoon-like comedies, and human-interest stories forming part of an evening's program in many vaudeville houses. One of Lubin's first films was *Unveiling of the Washington Monument*, taken in Philadelphia on 15 May 1897. Biograph filmed similar events, including Li Huang Chang at Grant's Tomb, taken on 30 August 1896, and the Harvard-

Yale-Cornell Boat Races in Poughkeepsie, New York, on 25 June 1897. All were extensively covered by the press. Press coverage assured interest in these events among potential theatergoers, who could then see them reproduced in "life-like," "life-sized" motion picture form. Of course, outside a few major cities such as New York, Philadelphia, Boston, and Chicago, film programs more likely resembled a monthly magazine, but it was the dynamics in these few cities that drove the choice of subject matter. Cinema was quintessentially urban in its orientation.

Correspondingly, the filming of performers or staged events was considered newsworthy and was extensively covered by local newspapers. Fire runs were particularly popular: Biograph's filming of Hartford's horseless fire engine made the front page of the *Hartford Times* on two separate occasions ("Biographing Jumbo"; "Fine Day"). Newspapers and cinema were sometimes used for cross-promotion. In mid-April 1896, the *New York World* brought performers John C. Rice and May Irwin to Edison's Black Maria studio so that Edison camera operator William Heise could shoot the couple's kissing scene from the musical comedy *The Widow Jones*. These images appeared in the *Sunday World*, accompanied by an article on the actors' studio visit. The Edison Company filmed *The New York "World" Sick Baby Fund* in early August, and *New York World* graphic artist J. Stuart Blackton made several lightning sketches for the camera, including one of Edison. The following year Biograph visited a summer camp designed to teach the children of immigrants American political values; it was run by William Randolph Hearst's rival *New York Journal*. The American Mutoscope Company also developed a close relationship with the *New York Mail & Express*, which published extensive articles on the company's activities, with stills and frame enlargements from the company's films.

Many early films functioned in the political realm and began to subtly change the nature of the political season. Grover Cleveland was president of the United States as commercial cinema began, but Republican William McKinley ran on a "Sound Money" platform against William Jennings Bryan, the Populist and Democrat, who was running on a "Free Silver" platform. It was thought that Free Silver would ease credit and help farmers and others burdened with debts. Others feared it would create dangerous inflation. In mid-September, W.K.L. Dickson filmed Republican political demonstrations in Canton, Ohio, and the Republican presidential candidate himself (*McKinley at Home, Canton, O*). Like virtually all the films from this period, *McKinley at Home* is a single shot, and it shows the presidential candidate in front of his house receiving a telegram, reading it, and then walking toward the camera. When the latter film was shown in Hammerstein's

From *McKinley at Home, Canton, O*
(Biograph, September 1896), an early
political campaign film. Frame enlargement.

Olympia Theater in New York, "pandemonium broke loose for five minutes. Men stood up in their seats and yelled with might and main, and flags were waved by dainty hands that would fain cast a vote on November 3, for the good cause. To satisfy the audience the Major [i.e., McKinley] was brought forth again with like result" (*Mail and Express* 4).

McKinley was famously waging his campaign from his back porch in Canton, but his virtual self effectively moved about the country galvanizing pro-Republican demonstrations. At a subsequent screening at the Olympia, a lonely Democrat dared to hiss McKinley's screen image and was chased from the theater. McKinley's brother Abner was one of the investors in the American Mutoscope Company. Exhibitors showing 35 mm films hoped to use pictures of New York's Sound Money parade to provoke similar demonstrations; but given the date of this political demonstration, their window of opportunity could only be measured in days. Although the Edison Company did take a film of McKinley's Democratic rival William Jennings Bryan, it was not widely seen: many backing his pro-silver candidacy complained of this imbalance. As film historian Terry Ramsaye would later note, "the screen was Republican from the beginning."

Other shifts in subject matter and treatment can be linked to political events, but less directly. On 18 May 1896, in *Plessy v. Ferguson*, the U.S. Supreme Court affirmed the doctrine of "separate but equal," effectively legalizing racial segregation in the United States. This affirmation of state-sponsored racism coincided with a significant shift in representations of people of color, particularly African Americans. During the two years before commercial projection, the Edison Company offered a limited series of pictures showing African Americans. These involved professional performers who danced before the camera, displaying a variety of their best moves. Blacks were shown executing characteristic dances, but then performers from a wide variety of backgrounds were also filmed doing their own ethnically distinct dances, from a Scottish Highland Dance to Annabelle Whitford's Butterfly Dance and a Sioux Indian Buffalo Dance. With the onset of projection, this changed. African Americans are soon shown enacting a range of stereotypes drawn from American visual culture: eating watermelon, stealing chickens, and washing their dusky children in the naive hope they might get "clean" (i.e., white). Many of these subjects were first made by the American Mutoscope Company, but they were quickly remade by its rivals.

████████████ Cinema, Nationalism, and the Imperial Imaginary

The shift in racial imagery was part of a larger shift in the ideological orientation of motion pictures, which again can be tied to political events, though explanations for this shift have more proximate causes. This was epitomized by a film shown on the Vitascope's opening night: *The Monroe Doctrine*, also known as *The Venezuela Case*, which responded to a crisis in foreign affairs. A longstanding border dispute between British Guiana and Venezuela had heated up after gold miners rushed into the disputed area. When Great Britain threatened to use force to assert its claims, the United States intervened by evoking the Monroe Doctrine, "the favorite dogma of the American people" (Perkins 136). The Monroe Doctrine hardly had the stature of international law, and its new and expanded application in this context could be seen to signal the true beginning of "the American century." The Edison film, which was doubtlessly inspired by a political cartoon on the subject, "showed John Bull bombarding a South American shore, supposedly to represent Venezuela. John is seemingly getting the better of the argument when the tall lanky figure of Uncle Sam emerges from the back of the picture. He grasped John Bull by the neck, forced him to his knees and made him take off his hat to Venezuela" (*Boston Herald* 32). A burlesque, this editorial cartoon on film showed "Uncle Sam teaching John Bull a lesson" (*Catalogue* 31). England was only the specific object of a doctrine that the United States sought to apply to all European powers. Another way to analyze this film, however, is in terms of allegorical self-interest: might not this interference of Europeans in American affairs be expanded to include the Lumières' threatened expansion into the American market—at least in national sentiment if not in action by the state?

The imminent threat of an invasion of foreign machines, which reports from abroad suggested likely outclassed anything Edison could offer, was motivating the Edison group to reconceptualize what it would make, select, and show (and in what way). Largely abandoning their cosmopolitan subject matter, they now appealed to American audiences based on a patriotic nationalism, which was already being mobilized due to events in Venezuela and elsewhere. This point of view was articulated in the Vitascope's opening night program. The order of the films was (1) *Umbrella Dance*, (2) *The*

Wave a k a *Rough Sea at Dover*, (3) *Walton & Slavin*, (4) *Band Drill*, (5) *The Monroe Doctrine*, and (6) a serpentine or skirt dance (see Musser, *Emergence* 116). The program thus started off with a film showing two female dancers (the Leigh Sisters), asserting continuity between stage and screen. According to one critic, "It seemed as though they were actually on the stage, so natural was the dance, with its many and graceful motions" ("Wonderful is the Vitascope" 11).

And yet the dancers were not on the stage, and their bodily absence, this displaced view, was liberating: the spectator's position in relation to the dancers on the screen was not the same as the camera's position in relation to the dancers. The dancers did not dance for the theatergoers as they would have with a "normal," live performance. The spectators watched them as they danced for the camera. This triangulation opened up a wide range of responses as the looped film was shown again and again.

The proscenium arch established by this first film on the program was then broken by *The Wave*. It was crucial that spectators know that this wave was British—at least if the narrative that I discern in this sequence of images is to be intelligible. Reviews consistently indicate this to be the case. This cut from dancers to the wave was a crucial moment in early cinema: it was nothing less, I would suggest, than the first example of early cinema's distinctive form of spectatorial identification. Given who was participating in this exhibition—Edwin Porter would claim to be assisting with the projection, James White was there, and one suspects that the Lathams, W.K.L. Dickson, and others were also in attendance—its effect would likely have been broadly felt and noted. The British wave metaphorically washed away the stage and the Leigh Sisters, even as it assaulted Koster & Bial's patrons, causing initial consternation and excitement (a shock that gradually receded as the film continued to loop through the projector). The spectators found themselves in the same position as the dancers from the previous shot. They became bound together and this shared identity was nothing less than a nationalistic one. Dancers and spectators, women and men (the audience was overwhelming male), were brought together as they were collectively attacked by this *British* wave.

If the wave's assault initially pushed the spectators out of the picture, *Walton & Slavin* provided the audiences with a new surrogate. On behalf of the newly constructed community of Americans (patrons and performers), Uncle Sam responded. That is, this wave was followed by a familiar subject: the burlesque boxing bout between "the long and the short of it," featuring lanky Charles Walton and the short, stout John Slavin. According to some sources, Walton also appeared in *The Monroe Doctrine*: he played Uncle Sam

From *The John C. Rice–May Irwin Kiss* (Edison, 1896), extracted from the musical comedy *The Widow Jones* (1895). Frame enlargement.

while Slavin's replacement, John Mayon, was John Bull. In any case, Walton and Slavin visually evoked Uncle Sam and John Bull engaging in a fistic encounter. It is worth noting that in this looped film, "the little fellow was knocked down several times" (*New York Daily News*).

Uncle Sam was beating up John Bull for his presumptuous wave. That is, the relationship between the second and third film was one of cause and effect. The fourth film, *Band Drill*, showed a marching band in uniform: suggesting a mobilization of the American military, it "elicited loud cries of 'Bravo!'" from the audience ("Wonderful is the Vitascope" 11). Uncle Sam and John Bull of *Walton & Slavin* had been only symbolic figures of the nation. This next scene was less symbolic in that it showed a group of soldiers marching as if to war, as if in response to the British assault. *Band Drill* thus prepared the way for *The Monroe Doctrine*, which "twinned" *Rough Sea at Dover* even as it returned to and reworked the fistic exchange in *Walton & Slavin*. The British bombarded the shoreline of another American nation (Venezuela)—with guns instead of cinematic waves. Uncle Sam (Walton) forced John Bull (Mayon) to stop. According to one report, "This delighted the audience, and applause and cheers rang through the house, while someone cried, 'Hurrah for Edison'" ("Wonderful is the Vitascope" 11).

After this imaginary but much wished for American victory, there was a return to the status quo as patrons once again viewed a dance film that was similar in style and subject matter to the opening selection. The program ended as it began, with a film of a woman that indulged male voyeuristic pleasures but also remobilized the possibility of identification. Might this dancer not evoke Columbia or Liberty (as in the Statue of Liberty in New York harbor)? A masculinist-nationalist (English American) confrontation thus forced these pleasures aside until an American triumph was achieved (on the screen) and audiences were able to return to their sensual pleasures.

Future Vitascope programs generally favored American material. *Picture of a Kiss*—which soon became known by such titles as *The John C. Rice–May Irwin Kiss*, *The Widow Jones Kiss*, and eventually *The May Irwin Kiss* or just *The Kiss*—featured a kiss extracted from the musical comedy *The Widow Jones*.

Filmed in a "close view," it showed a middle-aged couple (Billy Bilke played by John C. Rice and Beatrice Byke played by May Irwin) in a long, drawn-out kiss. Their kiss, which sealed their agreement to be married, was celebrated as a good old American kiss and also seen as a burlesque on the Nethersole kiss from a dramatic version of *Carmen*. Olga Nethersole, a British actress with Mediterranean blood (hence her passionate performances), starred in *Camille* and *Carmen* and in other plays about scandalous, amoral women. In *Carmen* she had kissed three different men (at great length) and married none of them. Here again a short, simple film of a kiss promoted a self-congratulatory American agenda. In Boston, it was shown with *The Village Blacksmith Shop*. This was an earlier Edison film, either *Blacksmithing Scene* (1893) or *New Blacksmithing Scene* (1895), which in itself evoked little sense of national identity. By changing its title, showmen linked it to the famed poem by Henry Wadsworth Longfellow (1807–1882), "The Village Blacksmith" (1839). According to the *Boston Herald*, "'The Village Blacksmith Shop' will recall to many young men and women who have resided in the city for long periods familiar scenes of their early childhood; it is a work of art" ("Keith's New Theater"). The memories of childhood that the film was said in the press announcement to evoke were, in fact, those described in the poem's fourth stanza:

> And children coming home from school
> Look in at the open door;
> They love to see the flaming forge,
> And hear the bellows roar,
> And catch the burning sparks that fly
> Like chaff from a threshing-floor.

Firemen were quintessential nineteenth-century American heroes, and *Fire Rescue Scene* (1894) was also shown on early Vitascope programs. In November, Edison produced a new series of fire films, including *A Morning Alarm*, *Going to the Fire*, and *Fighting the Fire*. The cinema's rapid embrace of racial stereotypes in many of these early film programs—particularly of African Americans eating watermelon and stealing chickens—became a not-so-subtle celebration of good old fashioned American racism and the racial hierarchies on which its socioeconomic and cultural system operated.

The cosmopolitan, internationalist position, which was once occupied by Edison's Kinetoscope, was quickly filled by the Lumière Cinématographe. Its scenes of foreign lands often corresponded to the national identities of Edison's earliest motion picture performers. This was likewise a shift for the Lumières, who had occupied the nationalist position in

France (celebrating family, nation, and state) in the face of the Kineto-scope's internationalism. In the United States, however, the Ciné-matographe's internationalism had quite distinct qualities. The Lumière programs contained numerous military subjects. In Philadelphia, the city of brotherly love, audiences cheered *Charge of Seventh Cavalry*, which was retained on the program for many weeks. According to the *Philadelphia Record*:

> The possibility of instantaneous photography in fixing life motion on a mov-ing film and of the cinematographe to reproduce the life motion with absolute fidelity are superbly illustrated in the cinematographe exhibition, which is the telling feature at the Bijou. Those representing scenes from mil-itary life are realistic to a wonderful degree, and they are made marvelously effective by the splendidly worked effects appropriate to each scene. This is especially true of the charge of the Seventh Cavalry and the sham battle, which always arouses the greatest enthusiasm. These two dashing scenes will be retained for this week's exhibition and another will be added. It is called the march of the Ninety-sixth Regiment of the French Infantry.
>
> ("Theatrical World")

The playing of "La Marseillaise" and the introduction of noise and battle din "also added to the wonderful realism of the scene" and "stirred the audi-ence to a pitch of enthusiasm that has rarely been equaled by any form of entertainment" ("Bijou").

Not all military scenes were of French forces. The Spanish, Italian, Russian, English, and German military were also represented. Audiences could compare the armies of different nations and perhaps fantasize about the outcome of future wars as suggested by the "sham battles" on the screen. Although the Lumière camera operator Alexandre Promio came to the United States in September 1896 to take films in New York, Chicago, and elsewhere, these were not used to cater to (or challenge) the Ameri-canist position of Edison, Biograph, and others. Although the Ciné-matographe was a combination camera, printer, and projector, Promio's films were sent back to Lyon, France, for development and dispersion around the world. This happened again when the Lumières covered the inauguration of President McKinley. Rather than quickly develop the films in the United States and project these images on American screens in a timely, competitive fashion, they sent these films back to France to ensure maximum quality and worldwide distribution.

The American Mutoscope Company, as its very name suggests, began its career by aggressively wrapping itself in the flag of patriotism. When it was shown in the nation's capital, according to one review,

American invention is bound to lead the world when it gets the opportunity, and it is the popular verdict that the biograph, a purely American invention and manufacture, leads all the moving picture machines yet seen here. . . . Not only Americans, but foreigners as well admit this fact. Last evening a large delegation from the Chinese Legation attended the exhibition, and afterward expressed themselves through an interpreter as highly pleased and surprised. Among the most popular pictures shown are the flight of the famous Empire express train, Old Glory flaunting the breeze, Niagara Falls and rapids, Rip Van Winkle in his toast scene, President-elect McKinley and a political parade; Union Square, New York; the kissing scene from "Trilby," a darkey baby taking a bath, and the turn out of a fire department—all characteristic American scenes. ("Biograph Better")

Biograph possessed a repertoire of quintessentially American scenes, including famed American actor Joseph Jefferson in excerpts from his classic performance of *Rip Van Winkle*, majestic scenes of America's natural beauty such as Niagara Falls, and pictures of the American flag itself. Scenes of the Empire State Express, a famed train that was breaking speed records on the New York Central Railroad, were shot in a far more dynamic fashion than earlier Lumière scenes of a train entering a station. The express train is moving rapidly from the distant background toward the camera at full speed, though it veers offscreen left as the film nears its conclusion—purposefully designed to disconcert spectators as they experience the train's power and speed. The Biograph was to the Cinématographe as the onrushing Empire State Express was to the quaint French train chugging into La Ciotat. The company quite successfully outflanked the Edison groups' own jingoism. The Edison Company responded by offering *The Black Diamond Express* as an equivalent to *The Empire State Express*. Edison and American Mutoscope personnel also began to take films of the American military over the course of 1896–1897. Commercial rivalry heated up, a surrogate for the real thing. These strategies would be given more immediate and intense application early the following year, in the run-up to the Spanish-American War.

Biograph and Edison entered the era of cinema by wrapping themselves in the flag of patriotism, but as their production capabilities expanded and as they dispatched their European competitors (the Lumière company was not a serious rival by the second half of 1897), their ideological framework became more nuanced. The Biograph group developed a long-term strategy that melded patriotic nationalism with cosmopolitan internationalism. The launching of the British Mutoscope & Biograph Company as well as W.K.L. Dickson's filming trips throughout Europe (and later South Africa) made the world a part of America's purview. The head of Edison's Kinetograph Department, James White, and his British collaborator, the camera operator Fred Blechyden, also embarked on a filmmaking tour of the world in the latter part of 1897, first traveling to the West Coast and then, by November, into Mexico. The following year they would visit Japan and China. Perhaps more than mere coincidence, putting the world on American screens was preparatory to the United States actually acquiring an overseas empire of its own—just like its European rivals.

Breaking Down Prohibitions and Dynamizing American Culture

Cinema's onset dynamized American culture in other areas besides its imperial ambitions. Illegal or semi-legal forms of entertainment were purified through the absence of bodily presence and the cleansing purity of light. This happened most strikingly in the realm of boxing and religion. As the new era of cinema began, prize fighting remained illegal in every state of the nation. Fight films were popular but their status was ambiguous for they could easily serve as evidence of illegal activity. To film a championship bout between James J. Corbett and Robert Fitzsimmons, promoters managed to bribe and otherwise convince the Nevada legislature to legalize the sport. The event—indeed the sport itself—was now legal, at least in Nevada. The Veriscope Company filmed the championship bout on 17 March 1897 with special wide-gauge film, well-suited for photographing the whole ring. Fitzsimmons won the match in the fourteenth round, perfect for repackaging as an evening-length entertainment. In the face of considerable controversy, many states, cities, and towns sought to ban fight films in general and *The Corbett-Fitzsimmons Fight* in particular. Their efforts generally proved unsuccessful, and the subsequent premiere at the Academy of Music in New York City on 22 May was a huge success. A controversy over the fight was nurtured. Corbett's corner suggested that Fitzsimmons's decisive blow was a late hit and thus a foul: if the referee had seen it, Corbett would still have been the champion. Fitzsimmons rejected these accusations. People went to see the Veriscope ("truth viewer") to decide the real winner for themselves, though the telling moment on the screen passed too quickly for anyone to see clearly what had happened.

As *The Corbett-Fitzsimmons Fight* played cities, towns, and eventually villages—often with return engagements—over the next few years, boxing became a familiar form of entertainment to many Americans, albeit in virtual form. Corbett, Fitzsimmons, and various promoters enjoyed an

From *The Corbett-Fitzsimmons Fight* (Veriscope, March 1897), showing Fitzsimmons stand-ing over the fallen Corbett—incapacitated by a blow to the heart. Cropped frame enlargement.

unprecedented large and extended payday. Prior to the arrival of motion pictures, fighters made money off wagers and by using their resulting noto-riety to appear on the stage. Now the fight itself could generate a large income through pictures. As a result of the successful exhibition of these films, boxing was legalized in many states, including New York. Soon prize-fights were large, well-publicized events that were often organized around their filming. Less than a year after the premiere of Edison's Vitascope, cin-ema had totally transformed the boxing world, which was at this time a crucial slice of the sporting world.

A similar transformation occurred at the other end of the spectrum. Efforts to perform the Passion Play had been prohibited in most parts of the United States, particularly New York, for decades. A staging in a Little Italy puppet theater was shut down. Likewise, a pageant by children mounted at a Catholic church in Long Island was prohibited. For anyone to imperson-ate the role of Christ was deemed a blasphemous sacrilege. Perhaps the most notable exceptions were lantern shows of the Passion. John Stod-dard's illustrated lecture of the Passion Play of Oberammergau proved unexpectedly popular with clergy as well as cultural elites. Because the images of the play were still photographs, they were not "performances." Moreover, because they were photographs, the actors were not literally present. What was seen was their shadow, their image purified by the light of the educational lantern. In the summer of 1897, theatrical impresarios Marc Klaw and Abraham Erlanger sent Walter W. Freeman and camera operator Charles Webster to film a similar Passion Play performed by the people of Horitz, Bohemia. They returned with a large number of films and a selection of photographs (which would serve as lantern slides). These were assembled into an evening-length illustrated lecture, entitled *The Horitz Passion Play*. The leading performers—Jordan Willochko as Christ, Anna Wenzieger as Mary, and Joseph Frephies as Caiaphas—were introduced with lantern-slide portraits ("Passion Play in Pictures"). Some of the play's opening tableaux, such as Adam and Eve being expelled from the Garden of Eden, were also presented as lantern slides (*New York Herald*). The Horitz rendition moved quickly through the Old Testament and Christ's early years before focusing on the traditional events leading up to the crucifixion. The full program of thirty negatives totals 2,400 feet of film. (Unfortunately, neither prints nor frame enlargements would survive to tell us any more about this ambitious project.) The resulting premiere occurred on 22 November 1897 at Philadelphia's Academy of Music and received a favorable response. Local clergy made up a substantial portion of the appreciative audience.

The principle was established: films of the Passion Play (like films of boxing matches) would be allowed even if their embodied performances were forbidden. The use of projected images somehow cleansed and purified, transforming the ways that Christianity's most sacred story could be told, at least in the United States. *The Horitz Passion Play* thus opened the way for the production and exhibition of similar kinds of programs, most notably *The Passion Play of Oberammergau*, which was being filmed at the end of 1897 by Richard Hollaman of the Eden Musee. Here again, once virtual performances were allowed, the banning of embodied performances seemed foolishly out of date. By the turn of the century, the Passion Play would even be performed on Broadway.

The impact of cinema extended into other areas of religion as well. For a number of Protestant groups, notably Methodists and Baptists, attendance in the theater was strictly forbidden. The theater was a den of iniquity, the devil's entertainment. And yet, these churches were losing ground to an increasingly dynamic and vibrant popular culture. As traveling showmen such as Lyman Howe began to tour the nation's smaller cities and towns, their exhibitions were often sponsored by Baptist and Methodist churches as a way to raise money but also to attract the wavering faithful and perhaps even gain converts. In some cases these films were shown in their churches. Among the films shown were excerpts of plays such as *The John C.*

Rice–May Irwin Kiss from *The Widow Jones*. Again, in quite fundamental ways, the cinema immediately challenged and subtly rearranged the cultural agenda of many religious groups, transforming their modus operandi.

In many areas of American life, the well-defined boundaries between the sexes were being blurred as women showed growing independence in work, dress, and mobility. When *The Corbett-Fitzsimmons Fight* was shown in theaters, women often went to see it, particularly during matinees. In Boston, "women formed a considerable portion of the audience" ("Does Its Work Well" 7). In some instances the trend was absolutely extraordinary. According to at least one source, women constituted fully 60 percent of Chicago's patronage (*Phonoscope* 11). For many, this fact was at once shocking and puzzling. Why would women, the gentler sex, ever want to see such violence? Was the absence of noise and the physical absence of brutalized bodies at least a partial explanation? Or perhaps, many of them attended "with the expectation of being shocked and horrified" ("Does Its Work Well" 7). In fact, at least some of these women were fans of James Corbett, who had established himself as something of a matinee idol in the previous few years as he acted on the stage. Moreover, it was perhaps a gesture of group rebellion and independence, as women went to see the perfectly trained, semi-naked male bodies perform their brutal rituals. They would at least take a peek at this traditionally all-male domain. Seventy-five years later their counterparts would be those women who lined up at the World Theater in New York to see *Deep Throat* (1972). However, not unlike their latter-day counterparts, these women would rarely return to the theaters when similar offerings (boxing films) came along.

Production, Exhibition, Spectatorship

The motion picture system that Thomas A. Edison had introduced in 1893–1894 went through a fundamental transformation with the introduction of projection. Another way to express this would be to say that the adaptation of motion pictures to the magic lantern transformed screen practice—the projected image and its sound accompaniment. This coincided with significant changes in the methods of film production. Cameras were becoming much more portable (though they were still often bulky and heavy), and American camera crews often left the confines of the studio area. It was in this period that the motion picture camera had its first sustained encounter with the world. Edison's camera crew made films around New York City on 11 May 1896, including *Herald Square*. The proliferation of camera technology also resulted in a variety of different and incompatible systems and formats. The elaborate process of print production was little changed except for the shift from a translucent base (well suited for the peephole Kinetoscope) to a transparent stock more suitable for projection. Although Edison had used Blair stock for making prints, the Blair Company had difficulty making a transparent stock that retained the emulsion. As a result the Edison Manufacturing Company, perhaps following the lead of some of its competitors, became a customer of Eastman Kodak in the middle of 1896.

Projection profoundly changed the mode of exhibition and also reception. Projection technology was highly variable. Although the use of an intermittent mechanism was the basis for all commercially viable projection, other aspects of the technology were not so readily agreed on. As an example, some projectors had a shutter blade that covered the projected light while one film frame replaced the next. Others did not, since many preferred the blurring of the image to the flickering of the light. The Vitascope and other Edison-influenced exhibitors (using Edison-based projection technology) showed films as loops. This worked particularly well for certain kinds of subjects: waves crashing on the beach, Serpentine dances, water falls, kissing scenes, and so forth. Because the projection speed was relatively high (around thirty frames per second) and most of the films were only forty-two feet long (or even somewhat shorter), this meant a film lasted only about twenty seconds on the screen if it was not repeated. Since it took about ninety seconds to replace a film on a projector, exhibitors sometimes had two Vitascopes and alternate projectors to keep up a more or less continuous show. This means each film was repeated at least five or six times. Even if "long films," which were closer to 150 feet, were shown, they would need to be repeated twice, though such films were often less well suited for looping. The popularity of film loops faded over the course of late 1896–1897. The number of frames per second when taking or projecting films also began to decline within the Edison sphere of influence during this same period.

Although Lumière pictures used roughly the same amount of film footage, a single showing lasted longer on the screen because they were projected at fewer frames per second (fps). Lumière films were not looped when they were projected, though they could be fished out of a pick-up bin and shown again—or shown in reverse motion. Biograph films, with their large format and high speed for taking and projecting, were less versatile, though the last film in a film program could be—and sometimes was—repeated. Also, a separate projector was sometimes used to project title slides, though the titles of films were also sometimes identified by a lecturer, by the printed program, or through announcement cards arranged by the side of the stage.

Virtually every lantern show and film program involved the sequencing of images in some form. (Very occasionally, when cinema was first being introduced, an exhibitor showed a single film between successive acts of a vaudeville program.) By the time cinema appeared, lantern exhibitors had developed a full repertoire of ways to structure images, sometimes using two (or more) slides to move from day to night or to create other contrasts and comparisons. They often sequenced numerous slides to tell elaborate narratives, typically with the showman's accompanying live commentary. Some exhibitors presented unified evening-length illustrated lectures, particularly on travel topics. Others showed a miscellaneous selection of images, each a self-contained attraction. These projected images often employed different methods for creating movement: slip slides, mechanical slides, and dissolving views. This continued interest in the discrete spectacular image continued and was revitalized in the era of cinema with what Tom Gunning and André Gaudreault have called "the cinema of attractions." At the same time, as analyzed above, the very first Vitascope program presented an imaginative if distended narrative. Likewise, by December 1896, Lyman H. Howe was already sequencing three to five fire scenes into a short narrative of a fire rescue. By March 1897, Henry Evans Northrop was giving a full-length illustrated lecture at the Brooklyn Institute of Arts and Science: periodically interspersed among his colored lantern slides was a film projected on the Lumière machine (at the ratio of four to five slides for every motion picture). The program, which was repeated several times, was alternately called *An Evening with the Cinematograph* and *A Bicycle Trip Through Europe*.

Exhibitors were in charge of what would later be called "postproduction." They chose the one-shot images, provided an order, determined the way they would be projected, and chose the sound accompaniment. The functions of what would later be called "editing" and "programming" were not yet clearly differentiated. Projection technology also influenced the form of reception. Again the American Mutoscope Company, with its brief, spectacular images, strongly favored a variety of images that surprised and even shocked audiences. When *The Empire State Express* was first shown, spectators sometimes screamed and a woman at an early screening was reported to have fainted. In contrast, the use of loops and the much more extended projection time that was common for showing a film on Edison's Vitascope generated images that spectators could contemplate in the manner of a painting. Indeed, Vitascope films were often shown inside an elaborate, gilded picture frame, underscoring the affinities between paintings and films (and indeed, some of the early films were actually "painted" or hand-tinted). Many films evoked subjects that had been or still were popular with painters—for instance, Niagara Falls and other scenes of nature. Exhibitors might offer their patrons a cinema of astonishment, of contemplation, or some version of narrative absorption.

Finally, we might consider the ways that the arrival of cinema began to change the nature of representation itself. Projected motion pictures meant the introduction of virtual performances into cultural life. While films shown in the peephole Kinetoscope provided significant antecedents, cinema was a decisive break as it placed these virtual performances in a theatrical setting. Indeed, we can say that cinema in this respect began to disrupt and change the world of theatrical entertainment. These virtual performances were also now life-sized; and there were, in theory at least, few practical limits as to the length of such performances. *The John C. Rice–May Irwin Kiss* was particularly illuminating. The stage musical *The Widow Jones* had a successful run in New York's Bijou Theater until 18 May 1896. The film counterpart, taken in mid-April at the behest of the *New York World*, was not shown on the screen until Monday, 11 May. For one week, then, New York theatergoers had a choice between seeing Rice and Irwin kiss live and onstage at the Bijou or seeing their virtual kiss performed repeatedly and in medium close-up at Koster & Bial's. For the first time, the same action by the same actors was being performed in two different places, in two different modes and, potentially at least, at the same time. The film continued to be screened at Koster & Bial's Music Hall long after the stage show closed and Irwin went to Europe for the summer.

Now another Vitascope opened at Keith's Boston theater, also with the Rice-Irwin kiss. The performers were now performing their kiss—virtually of course—in two different theaters in two different cities at the same time. And when the Vitascope opened in Philadelphia and elsewhere, the number of kissing performances grew rapidly, for everywhere it was on the bill.

Before *Picture of a Kiss* was shown, however, Irwin's management announced that Rice was to be replaced as Irwin's romantic lead onstage by a more youthful and debonair actor—Charles Dickson. Undeterred, Rice went into rehearsals for Richard Sheridan's comedy *The Rivals*, playing the role of Captain Absolute—the youthful heartthrob. Rice and his troupe then made a lightning tour of the East Coast. In every city he played, *The Rice–Irwin Kiss* was being shown in another theater. Audiences could go see Billy Byke (i.e., Rice) seduce the Widow with a long, drawn-out kiss in one theater—or see the actor successfully seduce a much younger woman in the

Sheridan play in another. This was one of the first times that an actor performed two different roles in two different theaters at the same time—and of course in two different modes. This made Rice a kissing star, and he was soon playing the role of acting teacher in a vaudeville skit that topped the bill in the leading venues along the East Coast. Naturally, he instructed his attractive pupil how to kiss for the movies.

As the fall theatrical season approached and the film continued to play to enthusiastic crowds, Irwin and her management resumed their tour with *The Widow Jones*. People flocked to *The Widow Jones*, eager to see the famous kiss performed live by its real-life star(s). Instead, to the audience's distress, they were greeted by Irwin and an interloper—Charles Dickson, who proved to be an inept kisser. Despite their individual successes, Rice and Irwin had one problem in common: Rice may have been happily kissing his wife (Sally Cohen) onstage in the vaudeville skit for which she played the willing pupil, and May Irwin may have been awkwardly kissing Dickson, but neither was kissing the person they kissed in the film—which continued to be a popular hit. Their short film kiss created an overwhelming demand for a reunion of Rice and Irwin in *The Widow Jones*. Indeed, Irwin's management made a number of concessions to lure Rice back; a month into the theatrical season Irwin dumped Dickson and rehired her old co-star. Together again, they hammed up their kissing scene for all it was worth—delighting audiences in the process. Here we see the way that virtual performances took over the theatrical realm, indeed the very lives of its actors. Irwin—the star of her show—was upstaged by a man she had fired. And even when they no longer appeared onstage together, their performance went on and on. Certainly this was an early and powerful experience of cinema as a force for modernity. In the world of theater, cinema demonstrated its power to disrupt and enhance the theatrical careers of several stars, hinting at what it would be capable of doing in the future.

1898–1899

Movies and Entrepreneurs

PATRICK LOUGHNEY

Movies were invented to make money, and although they would later come to be recognized as a medium capable of great artistic achievement, the North American motion picture industry of the last two years of the 1800s was not primarily concerned with art. In 1898 inventor C. Francis Jenkins published *Animated Pictures*, a historical survey of the technological development of motion pictures. In a section titled "A Multinomial Machine," Jenkins provided a "selected" list of names for over one hundred motion picture machines, relating only to cameras and projectors incorporating the Latin and Greek root words "graph" and "scope," that had appeared in the marketplace up to that time. One device on that list, "Getthemoneygraph," included as a satiric commentary, humorously yet accurately captured the chaotic entrepreneurial spirit of the movie world of the period. Jenkins was in a position to know, for he was one of the rapidly growing number of inventors, producers, showmen, and investors in an array of business enterprises then emerging as the aggregation of a new and substantial area of industrial activity by the close of 1899.

The progress of the motion picture business during the last two years of the nineteenth century occurred during a time of growing prosperity in North America. The principal nations—Canada, Mexico, and the United States—were all in the midst of a strong recovery period of economic expansion, following the depression years of the early 1890s. Under the leadership of José de la Cruz Porfirio Díaz (1876–1911), Mexico was reaching the height of a sustained period of "order and progress" unprecedented in the country's history. Canada was likewise beginning to record nationwide increases in investments and exports at historic levels. And the United States, which had been the engine of largely unregulated economic growth for the entire continent since the 1860s, entered a new phase of aggressive international expansion in 1898 that would dramatically upset the centuries-old order of European world dominance in military, economic, and social affairs.

The emergence of the United States as a world military power in the final years of the nineteenth century was only one aspect in a complex and often paradoxical array of achievements in the arts, literature, and culture that defined America as truly distinct from any nation in history. Examples appeared in every field of endeavor. In architecture, construction of Louis Sullivan's Schlesinger & Mayer department store in Chicago (1898–1899) revolutionized the design of modern-era office buildings. In contrast to the unbridled American pursuit and accumulation of wealth of the time, Frank Norris's *McTeague* (1899) analyzed the corrosive influence of money on personal relationships, while political economist Thorsten Veblen introduced the concept of "conspicuous consumption" in his examination of newly rich entrepreneurs, *The Theory of the Leisure Class* (1899). At a time when New York's "tin pan alley" mass-produced songs with countless rhyme variations on "June, moon, spoon, swoon, and croon," Scott Joplin published "Maple Leaf Rag" (1899), establishing ragtime and an African American composer as major influences on the course of popular music. Philosopher and educator John Dewey published *The School and Society* (1899), summarizing his research into pedagogical method, which had a lasting influence on national educational reform. And, with the founding of the American Anti-Imperialist League (1898), leading artists, poets, writers, dramatists, politicians, and social critics of the day publicly demonstrated their strong disagreement with the nation's decision to initiate war with Spain. Members of the League included writer Mark Twain, politician George S. Boutwell, poet Edgar Lee Masters, humorist Finley Peter Dunne, philosopher John Dewey, former president Grover Cleveland, writer William Dean Howells, psychologist-philosopher William James, social reformer Jane Addams, journalist Ambrose Bierce, industrialist Andrew Carnegie, labor leader Samuel Gompers, progressive reformers Moorfield Storey and Josephine Shaw Lowell, influential editor-journalist Oswald Garrison Villard, and industrialist Charles Francis Adams Jr. In spite of the League's strenuous efforts, Cuba, Hawaii, Samoa, Guam, the Philippines, and Puerto Rico were annexed to the United States during 1898–1899.

■ The Motion Picture Patent and Copyright War

In the midst of this general turmoil of creative expression, social reform, economic growth, and international ambition, the disjointed elements of the motion picture business in North America collectively faced the challenge of advancing beyond the limiting factors of the "novelty" era, which had ended in 1897 (Musser, *Emergence* 109ff).[1] Motion pictures as a new kind of entertainment phenomenon had proven their staying power with the public during that introductory phase, and their potential as an important area for capital investment and income was recognized. And, although the general history of motion pictures in 1898–1899 is a tale of aesthetic experimentation, technological development, and economic success, it was, upon closer inspection, also a period beset by mini-cycles of boom and bust, copyright piracy and patent infringement, aggressive litigation, competing film and equipment formats, and wide variation in the quality of projected image entertainments.

Eighteen ninety-eight dawned on a movie industry mired in its first sustained period of stagnation, with producers, exhibitors, and showmen alike searching for better exhibition ideas and new film subjects that might revive attendance. In the midst of these troubles came the most widespread, serious, and sustained blow to occur in the industry during 1898–1899: the decision by the Edison Company, under the direction of business manager William Gilmore, to initiate a barrage of lawsuits against virtually all major competitors operating in America. Gilmore's intention was to seize control of the films and technology of the entire North American movie industry. The first steps were taken in December 1897, but the full force began to fall on 10 January 1898 with suits filed in Pennsylvania against film producer Sigmund Lubin of Philadelphia and in Illinois against Edward H. Amet, a producer of films and related equipment. The pressure continued in February with additional suits against the Eden Musee and its president, Richard Hollaman, and many others filed in various jurisdictions through the end of December (Ramsaye 379–85). During this two-year period, Edison's lawyers aggressively enjoined every prominent exhibitor, film producer, and equipment manufacturer in the business, including the vaudeville impresario B. F. Keith, because many of his theaters were licensing films and projectors made by rival companies (Ramsaye 379–85).

The response by most of Edison's competitors was to bow to the legal pressure and sign a licensing or royalty compensation agreement. Some went out of business or moved their operations to Europe. Lubin did both by temporarily ceasing production and going to Europe until the situation cooled down, but he also eventually took actions to oppose Edison and stayed in business. J. Stuart Blackton and Albert Smith of the Vitagraph Company also stopped producing for a time during 1898 and surrendered their film negatives to Edison. When Vitagraph began production again in the fall of 1898, its film prints were sold under an Edison license. And, although Edison's actions were ruinous to some companies, the new licensing arrangement did allow for profitable growth. Vitagraph earned net profits of $4,750 in 1898, increasing by over 60 percent in 1899 to $7,975 (Smith 250). The one company strong enough to withstand Edison's challenge and remain fully engaged in the business was the American Mutoscope Company (AM&B).[2] The main reason was that the designs of the basic technologies of the AM&B company, the Mustocope peephole machine and Biograph motion picture camera, differed sufficiently from those covered by the Edison patents that they could be defended as unique. Another reason was that AM&B was sufficiently capitalized to bear the costs of continuous litigation and still remain in business. Writing in 1926, the historian Terry Ramsaye characterized the struggle between the Edison and AM&B companies that began in 1898 as "one of the longest and most desperate patent fights in the history of American industry" (Ramsaye 379).

In spite of the intensity of Gilmore's legal onslaught, the economic base of the film industry was sufficiently broad in 1898 that the Edison Company was never finally able to achieve its goal of controlling the American movie business. Another important contributing factor was the inherent weakness of Edison's patent claims. The theft of mechanical ideas (and films) within the film industry reached epidemic proportions in 1898, and Edison's staff took their share. In addition, so many people made original inventive contributions to the overall improvement of cameras and projectors since the Kinetoscope and Kinetograph had been introduced that the important lawsuits of 1898 took many years to resolve. Indeed, some of the claims of original invention in this period continue to be studied by historians to this day. Furthermore, although the New York area was the dominant center of the industry in this period, there were enough strong entrepreneurs dispersed throughout other important cities that the film business was able to function profitably, in spite of the legal distractions.

The Industry Moves Forward

The majority of motion picture–related activities in North America were concentrated in the United States, particularly in the vicinity of New York City, which continued during 1898–1899 as the major center for production, distribution, exhibition, and investment. And, because of its relative size and wealth compared to Canada and Mexico, the United States was also established by this time as the major consumer market in the Western Hemisphere for domestic and foreign film production. However, in spite of its dominant position, the United States was not the only place where filmmakers were thriving and developing their own new paths of production. In Mexico, Salvador Toscano Barragan (1872–1947) produced

Mexico's first fictional narrative film, *Don Juan Tenorio* (de los Reyes). Eighteen ninety-eight was also a historic year of first production in Canada. With support from the Canadian Pacific Railway, James S. Freer produced the more ambitious narrative film *Ten Years in Manitoba*, based on his own experiences, and took the film on tour to England in April 1898, where he successfully screened the film in many venues with an accompanying lecture (Morris).

In addition to the New York and Northern New Jersey region, there were also important motion picture–related activities concentrated in and around Chicago and Philadelphia. By 1898 those areas had also emerged as important centers for production, equipment manufacturing, sales, and, particularly in Chicago, catalogue distribution of a full range of films, equipment, and supplies to showmen throughout North America. William Selig, George Spoor, Edward Amet, and George Kleine were all major figures in the Chicago area film industry of 1898–1899. Selig is typical of the energetic film entrepreneur of the period. Starting as an exhibitor in 1896, he began the regular production of actuality films in 1898. In the same year, using designs copied from a Lumière Cinématographe, Selig developed his own camera and Polyscope projector and began supplying films and equipment to Sears, Roebuck, and Company for catalogue sales until he was sued by Edison (Herbert and McKernan). Sears, Roebuck had offered magic lanterns, slides, and equipment prior to the age of motion pictures. However, under the leadership of Alvah C. Roebuck, the company also actively entered the film business on its own in 1898 with the introduction of the Optigraph, a projection attachment developed by Roebuck to augment the company's "Double Dissolving" magic lantern package. The new combination projector for lantern slides and movies, which could be augmented with "talking machines," lighting systems, advertising materials, ticket rolls, and all the equipment necessary for a professional show, provided a relatively inexpensive way for small-time showmen far from major urban centers to try their fortunes in the new field of motion picture entertainment. The most popular films advertised in the Sears, Roebuck catalogue in 1898 were those from a variety of producers depicting scenes of Alaska and the Klondike gold fields, and the remarkably wide variety of reportorial films relating to the Spanish-American War, the great international incident that dominated world news during the final years of the nineteenth century.

In addition to Amet and Spoor, who sold equipment and produced films on subjects related to the Spanish-American War, another important Chicagoan was Kleine. With the founding of the Kleine Optical Company in 1893, he began selling magic lanterns, slides, and optical equipment as a competitor to Sears, Roebuck. In addition to being one of the first businessmen to recognize the market potential connected with the sale and distribution of film prints and equipment, Kleine made an exclusive agreement in 1899 to distribute Edison Company films and projectors. In doing so he avoided being caught up in the tangle of Edison's lawsuits, which by then were seriously limiting the business activities of Kleine's Chicago-area competitors.

New York's lead was also challenged from Philadelphia by Lubin who, until he was forced to temporarily shut down by Edison, likewise produced films and equipment and began making gains among New York venues with his films (Musser, *Emergence* 284). Historian Charles Musser speculates that Lubin may even have rivaled Edison as a producer, not only in the number of films produced during this period but also in the range of comedies and dramas, led by his well-received creative reenactments of Spanish-American War battle scenes.

However, unique in this period for their importance as exponents of a personal presentation mode of traveling film exhibition were Burton Holmes and Lyman Howe. By 1898 Holmes and Howe were well established as traveling film exhibitors in North America and, although they had many competitors, none surpassed them. Both flourished at a time when even in major cities there were few fixed venues where motion pictures were regularly scheduled for more than a few weeks or months at a time. When ticket sales started declining because a slate of motion pictures had run its course of popularity, house managers in urban venues routinely eliminated movies from their programs and replaced them with live acts or anything else that filled seats. Traveling film exhibitors competed successfully with film programs offered in vaudeville and variety theaters because they owned their own projectors and film prints. Thus, because of their itinerant status, many were able to avoid paying fees to Edison and the owners of other "multinomial" machines that were booked on a license basis in fixed venues.

The success of Holmes, Howe, and other traveling showmen depended on their ability to brand themselves as learned interpreters for middle- and upper-middle-class audiences of the still and moving image programs that they presented on a seasonal or regular basis. Whereas the advertising for the majority of film programs in fixed venues of the period emphasized the wonders and perfection of featured projection equipment, such as the Vitascope, the Biograph, and the Cinématographe, Holmes and Howe hit on the idea of marketing themselves instead of their projection equipment as the basis for attracting audiences. By presenting movies as a form of edifying entertainment more akin to an educational activity, they operated outside the standard entertainment model of exhibition at the close of the nineteenth century.

Film programs accompanied by lecturers were a major mode of presentation in this period. According to Musser and Nelson, there were at least thirteen film lecturing companies traveling America in 1898–1899, bringing their programs to three major audience segments: church-oriented Protestant groups, secular audiences primarily interested in popular culture events of the day, and refined audiences oriented to elite programs (Musser and Nelson 69, 76). While others were successfully presenting films of championship boxing matches, cock fights, and other secular actuality films of the day, Howe and Holmes created more specialized presentations for audiences who generally avoided the type of venues where standard film exhibitions were presented.

During the 1898–1899 season Howe used his Animotoscope to present his "high class moving pictures," most often to groups with religious affiliations. In the novelty era, he gave his presentations in churches, community halls, and other venues not normally associated with commercial film exhibition in those years. However, in reaction to his growing popularity, in 1898 he began accommodating larger audiences in a wider range of venues, including opera houses and large commercial theaters in major cities. By the end of his second season in the same year, Howe had established a popular schedule of performances in cities and towns of the northeast United States, through which he presented a sophisticated mixed program of films supplemented by both sound recordings and recorded sound effects. Like other non-film-producing exhibitors of the period, Howe's fortunes were tied to the popularity of the films he was able to acquire. In the first half of 1898 his performances and those of his competitors were on the decline; the reverse of that trend, in 1898 and early 1899, was due to the timely outbreak of the Spanish-American War and the resulting films that became available to independent exhibitors (Musser and Nelson 289). By the fall of 1899, Howe was so successful that he began staying at his home base in Wilkes-Barre, Pennsylvania, and put his program under the control of a tour manager. According to Musser and Nelson, at this time Howe's traveling lecturers achieved a level of popularity that put him on par with the leading exhibitors in major urban areas (96).

Burton Holmes stood apart from Howe and his other competitors not only because he had a unique ability to attract the most elite audiences but also because he produced his own films.[3] Mentored as a young man by John L. Stoddard, the most famous American travel lecturer of the nineteenth century, Holmes was recognized as the leading presenter of illus-trated lectures of the day. The Sears, Roebuck catalogue from fall 1898 headlined its section on "Special Lecture Outfits" with the question, "Do You Want to Make Big Money with Little Effort?" referring to Holmes as "lecturing to the very best and most intelligent audiences" and calculating his average income at "several hundred dollars per night" (107, 206). Although his audiences were upper class, Holmes built a loyal fan base in established venues for annual or semi-annual appearances by artfully mix-ing humor and topical information, illustrated by a constantly updated pro-gram of lantern slides and films on an extraordinarily wide range of subjects, ranging from exotic scenery to sports events. A typical Holmes program is described in a contemporary review:

> E. Burton Holmes delivered the first of his series of Lenten lectures at Daly's Theatre yesterday before a large and appreciative audience. His subject was "The Wonders of Thessaly, from the Vale of Tempo to the Monasteries of the Air."
>
> He took his audiences through the Thessalian plain, describing quaint cus-toms of the inhabitants and the wonders of the scenery, and in addition por-trayed the leading incidents of the Graeco-Turkish war. After leaving the Thessalian scenes he gave a humorous description of the lofty residences of the monks of the Meteora and the unaccessibility of the monastery.
>
> At the conclusion of the lecture a number of motion pictures were shown on the following subjects: A street scene in Naples, the departure of the Kaiser Wilhelm, the dancing of the Tarantella, review of the United States troops at Fort Sheridan, the brink of the upper falls of the Yellowstone, an alarm of fire, and Whigham, MacDonald, Tyng, and other golfing celebrities, playing off the finals in the amateur golf tournament of 1897.   ("Astoria Concerts")

Eastman Kodak and Motion Picture Film Stock

So far, this chapter has focused on film producers, exhibit-ors, lecturers, and distributors, but brief mention must be made of a basic component of the industry that is little regarded in traditional histories: raw film stock. Once the basic mechanical principles of motion picture cameras and projectors were understood, virtually any talented engineer or machin-ist of this era could manufacture reasonably competent movie equipment, thereby making it possible for producers and exhibitors who wished to avoid purchasing patented or licensed machines, such as the Edison Vita-graph projector, to do so. However, the two products essential to the entire industry that could not be produced in great quantity at reasonable cost, with high standards of precision and quality control, were negative and positive motion picture film stock. George Eastman was the first industrialist to understand that the manufacture of the large and growing amount of film stock needed by the industry required the construction of a large, complex, and centralized chemical plant operation with hundreds of highly trained employees. Thus, while the Edison Company ultimately was not able to monopolize the film industry by controlling all relevant technology patents, the Eastman Kodak Company succeeded in achieving a virtual monopoly control of film stock production with essentially the same combined strategy of buying out competitors and aggressive litigation. This is important to our understanding of the movie history of this period because it was in 1898 that George Eastman purchased his principal competitor, the Blair Camera Company of Boston, leaving Eastman Kodak in a commanding position as the major supplier of raw film stock to the American industry.

In 1899 the Eastman Kodak company also transformed the production method for making film stock from one based on cooling and drying the celluloid base material on long glass tables to one involving a large continuously revolving polished steel wheel. This manufacturing breakthrough greatly increased the rate of production and the cost efficiencies of producing both negative and positive film stock, and also permitted the production of virtually endless film rolls without splices—a development that could now make possible longer shots and longer films.

Popular Film Genres of 1898–1899

The motion picture industry relied on the regular publication of descriptive sale catalogues as the primary mode of advertising films to exhibitors and showmen of the period. The single most important influence on the first generation of film producers in Europe and North America, in terms of the types or genres of films produced, was the commercial photography industry. Major companies, such as the Keystone View, Underwood & Underwood, and the Detroit Publishing companies, produced and mass-marketed photographs on an industrial and international scale while motion pictures were just beginning to emerge. One of the primary marketing methods employed by the photography industry for advertising was the sales catalogue, cross-indexed under specific headings for genre, subject, topic, geographic location, and so on. Taking their cue from this successful model of production and marketing, film producers not only adapted proven photographic subjects to movies but also began publishing their own descriptive sales catalogues, in which actuality film subjects were organized under headings derived from those developed by the commercial photography companies, for example, Fire-Rescue, Disasters, Industrial, Military, Parades, Personalities, Scenic & Travel, Sports Events, and Novelty films (Loughney 123). U.S. copyright records from the period show that over 80 percent of the motion pictures copyrighted during 1898–1899 were actuality films that can be classified in these general topical categories. In effect, both the producers and exhibitors of the time came to recognize that the types or genres of "still" images that were commercially successful would also attract audiences to the same subjects presented "in motion." Of all the actuality films produced during 1898–1899, the most popular and frequently produced were those of military and war-related events, famous persons, and scenic and travel subjects (Loughney 158).

The doldrums in which film exhibitors and producers found themselves drifting at the beginning of 1898 was soon broken by the appearance of a sequence of topically unrelated films that best characterize the variety of films that were most popular during the last years of the century. They include films in four general categories representing three major areas of actuality production: famous persons, sporting events, and military sub-jects, and a fourth category embracing Passion Play films, an anomalous combination of quasi-actuality, proto-narrative production that proved to be enormously popular and a predictor of things to come.

Passion Play Films

Passion Plays had a complex history in America because they dealt with the life of Jesus Christ, the most often repeated yet carefully guarded narrative tale in the history of Western culture. Based on the bib-lical account of events surrounding the last days of Jesus Christ, the first authentic dramatic narrative Passion Play film produced in the United States premiered with three performances at the Eden Musee on 30 January 1898. It was filmed on a stage atop the roof of the Grand Central Palace building in New York City as something of a fraudulent effort by Richard Hollaman, president of the Eden Musee, with support from Albert Eaves, owner of a major theatrical costume company. The Hollaman-Eaves production, known as *The Passion Play of Oberammergau*, was made in relative secrecy for two main reasons. First, it was being produced without licenses either from the Edison Company or from Klaw and Erlanger, who believed they owned exclusive rights to all Passion Play films because they had purchased con-tractual rights from the villagers of Horitz in Bohemia, where internation-ally known live performances had long been produced as a religiously

The Passion Play of Oberammergau premiered at Richard Hollaman's Eden Musee in New York City on 30 January 1898. Though advertised as an authentic moving image record of the original live performance staged every decade in Oberammergau, Germany, the film was actually shot in a rooftop studio atop the Grand Central Palace building in New York.

motivated devotional expression (and where a mixed-media presentation had been produced by theatrical impresarios Klaw and Erlanger a year before). Second, it was Hollaman's intention to brazenly present his film as an authentic filmed record of the Bavarian version of the Passion Play staged in Oberammergau. In essence, the Hollaman-Eaves Passion Play film was a narrative production passed off to an unsuspecting public as an actuality film. The ruse didn't last long. On 1 February, the *New York Herald* revealed that the Eden Musee *Passion Play of Oberammergau* had been locally produced. However, the unexpected publicity didn't hurt the film's box office because it was an aesthetically superior production to the shorter, less narratively fluid Klaw & Erlanger Horitz version. The negative for the Hollaman *Passion Play of Oberammergau* measured over 2,000 feet and, depending on the speed of projection, ran about twenty minutes.

Prints of the film were sold by Hollaman for $580 and many were soon purchased by independent lecturers and other showmen (Ramsaye 370–74). Though longer and more coherent than the Horitz version, *The*

Passion Play of Oberammergau was presented in varied forms, usually padded in length with an accompanying lecture and lantern slides on related subjects, such as contemporary images of historic sites in the Holy Land. Hollaman soon organized touring companies that presented elaborate two-hour entertainments centered around the Passion Play theme (Musser, *Emergence* 217–18)—that is, until he was enjoined and forced to surrender the original negative to the Edison Company, which took over the sale and distribution of film prints under its own name. However, the Eden Musee continued operating successfully as an Edison licensee and screened the film twice a day to sold-out audiences, estimated at 30,000 people during the first three months (Musser, *Nickelodeon* 122).

Musser has shown that there was virtually no standardization in the way in which movies were presented in this period. Long-form, multi-scene actuality films, such as those of Pope Leo XIII, and the proto-narrative Passion Play films were offered for sale as component parts, that is, under separately titled scenes that, according to the needs or constraints of individual showmen, could be assembled or edited into programs of their own arrangement. Since there was no established tradition for exhibiting movies, individual lecturers and house managers were free to develop their own presentation styles. Audiences attending the unidentified "Passion Play pictures" (probably the Klaw & Erlanger *Horitz* version) at the Grand Opera House in Washington, D.C., in November 1898 saw a program that began with lantern slide images of the "humble" peasant cast involved in the routine activities of daily life, accompanied by a lecture and background music. When the films began, the lecture continued with more commentary, interspersed with vocal music, producing an effect in which "one forgets that he is listening to a lecture or witnessing moving pictures" ("Passion Play" 23). The venue of the Grand Opera House is noteworthy as well because matinees at the special time of 4:15 P.M. were presented "so as to give the children plenty of time to get home and to the Grand Opera House after school" (ibid.).

Newspaper reviews of Passion Play film exhibitions in American cities around the country commonly describe specific variations on the above style of presentation, including the screening of films on secular subjects that sometimes suggested a casual indifference to mixing the sacred and profane. For example, when *The Passion Play of Oberammergau* was presented to an audience of nearly four hundred in December 1899 by the Sawyer Dry Goods Company at Sawyer's Café in Hartford, Connecticut, it was preceded by "several excellent moving scenes from the Dewey Parade in New York . . . and a representation of a Spanish bull fight, from the arrival of the crowd outside the arena, through the rushes of the mad bull to his final slaughter. The Passion Play was added to greatly by appropriate singing by Mrs. Warwick" ("Passion Play" 9). The reporter did not note if Mrs. Warwick performed while the bull was killed.

However, in spite of such lapses of taste, the movies of Pope Leo in combination with the Passion Play films represented a clear breakthrough on the part of producers and exhibitors to an audience segment that had previously either condemned or ignored motion pictures as too worldly. These productions demonstrated that films of religious subjects could be successfully made and marketed to family and middle-class audiences of conservative religious beliefs.

Pope Leo XIII

Films of famous people constituted one of the leading actuality genres of the 1898–1899 period, and along with monarchs and political leaders Pope Leo XIII (born 1810) was one of the public figures most sought after by film companies. He may be the oldest documented person

A series of twelve films featuring Pope Leo XIII was produced during April–May 1898, showing him in various Vatican settings. The first public screening of the films in the United States took place in Carnegie Hall on 14 December 1898. (*Pope Leo XIII in Vatican Garden*, American Mutoscope & Biograph Company, 1898.)

ever recorded on film. Previous requests made to the Vatican to film the pope had been routinely refused. However, W.K.L. Dickson, representing the American Mutoscope and Biograph Company, arrived in Rome in early 1898 with numerous references and, after a four-month effort, finally persuaded the pope to sit for a series of films. Dickson won the pope's consent when he explained that, via the movie medium, he would be able to extend his blessing to the many Catholics in America (Musser, *Emergence* 219). During April and May of that year Dickson produced a series of twelve films, including separate scenes of the pope walking in his garden, riding in a carriage, and delivering a blessing to the motion picture audience ("Pope in Moving Pictures").

The first reaction on the part of America's Catholic leaders was to consider the appropriateness of permitting the commercial exhibition of movies of the pope. The *Washington Post* reported that the "pictures will be exhibited under the absolute control of the Catholic Church of America, and will not be shown in halls or playhouses" ("Pictures of the Pope"). It was not until Cardinal Gibbons of Baltimore, the leading American prelate, gave his imprimatur on 30 November that the films of Pope Leo XIII began to be regularly presented ("Pope in Moving Pictures"). The first general public screening in America was held in Carnegie Hall on 14 December 1898 for an audience composed mainly of clergy (Musser, *Emergence* 220). Throughout 1898–1899 the presentations that followed were generally accompanied by special lectures delivered by Catholic clergymen, who rounded out the short program of films with theological and historical information about the achievements of the venerable pontiff, who was now eighty-eight years old. Headlines reporting recurring bouts of Pope Leo's ill health over a period of many months during late 1898 and early 1899 helped sustain audience interest in the films through the end of the century.

However, the approval of Catholic Church authorities was not the only barrier that American Mutoscope and Biograph had to clear before it could bring the Pope Leo series into general exhibition. As with every other profitable production of these years, AM&B was enjoined by a lawsuit from the Edison Company, claiming license infringement. According to a report in the *Washington Post*, "It is possible that the conflicting claims of companies owning patents on movie picture apparatus and the company in possession of the films showing the Pope, will delay the public exhibition of the moving pictures. Suits will be filed in the New York courts to-day by one company seeking to enjoin the Mutoscope Company from exhibiting the photographs of the Pope unless a royalty allowance is granted the complaining company" ("Pictures of the Pope").

Eighteen separate copyrights were registered for both the peepshow Mutoscope and projected Biograph film versions of the Pope Leo series, indicating a continuing market for at least one of the major single-viewer, peephole modes of exhibition in these years (the other being the Edison Kinetoscope). The image quality and composition of the films were exceptionally good, primarily because of the large 68 mm format of the Biograph film negative and Dickson's skill as a director. The informality of the animated scenes from the Pope's daily life represented an obvious and important aesthetic breakthrough beyond the static engravings and photographs by which general audiences had previously formed their impressions of the pope. Because of these movies, one of the most cloistered religious figures in history could suddenly be seen engaged in such mundane activities as walking in his garden, riding in a carriage, talking with aides, and, with a serene smile on his face, looking directly at the audience and delivering a blessing. The enduring significance of the Pope Leo XIII series to film history is the way the films humanized the pope for both Catholics and general audiences alike. Thereafter, important political and public figures in all walks of life began to recognize the significant power of moving images in shaping their popular image.

The films of Pope Leo also had a more prosaic influence on the history of film exhibition by creating an opportunity to expand the exhibition of film programs to seven days a week in cities where that was not the norm. In Boston, B. F. Keith followed a self-imposed tradition of keeping his theater closed. However, due to the popularity of the Pope Leo series, Keith began running the films on Sundays. Reporting on this action, the *Boston Daily Globe* piously observed, "If it had been possible to exhibit these pictures of the pope in the ordinary course of his every-day biograph exhibit, Mr. Keith would never have broken through his rule not to open his theater on Sunday, but he feels assured that in doing so he will be affording an opportunity for many persons to see the pictures of the sovereign pontiff who would find it impossible to attend at any other time" ("Striking Pictures of the Pope").

The Spanish-American War

The American statesman Henry Cabot Lodge observed, "The war of the United States with Spain was very brief. Its results were many, startling, and of world-wide meaning." No less so for the North American movie industry, for the extraordinary collective sequence of international events that occurred in connection with the outbreak, conduct, and aftermath of the Spanish-American War became the single most important factor in its recovery and expansion through the end of the century.

The basic events that frame filmmaking activities relating to the Spanish-American War began with news of the mysterious explosion and sinking of the battleship U.S.S. *Maine* on 15 February 1898 in Havana harbor, and ended with a series of Edison films of ceremonies honoring Admiral George Dewey in New York City, Washington, D.C., and Boston, produced in late September and October 1899. War was declared by the United States in April 1898 and, though hostilities ceased in August, the war officially ended with the signing of the Treaty of Paris in December, by which Spain ceded control of the Philippines for a payment of $20 million. During that limited period there occurred two short but devastating naval engagements, one in Manila Bay and the other near Santiago de Cuba, and a limited series of land actions in Cuba. Taken generally as a group of thematically related films, no other series in the early history of world cinema equals either in number, scope, or importance the movies of the Spanish-American War.

For both producers and exhibitors, the Spanish-American War was a godsend. Events unfolded through the course of nearly two years that created naval and military heroes, emotional burial scenes, reports on unsanitary conditions for soldiers and refugees, many public parades, presidential reviews, and even the public airing of a jealous dispute between American admirals. Thus, the war offered an array of opportunities for filmmaking previously unknown and, once the leading American newspapers began vilifying the Spanish and creating a relentless and jingoistic drumbeat for war, audiences everywhere were primed for movies on any related subject. Producers and exhibitors, mainly Edison and AM&B but also including those suffering the effects of Edison's lawsuits, made renewed efforts to cash in on the sudden wave of war fever. The first four Edison films produced were literally "flag wavers" made for the purpose of arousing audience emotions: *Old Glory and the Cuban Flag, in Colors, American Flag* [no. 1], *Old Glory and the Cuban Flag*, and *American Flag* [no. 2] (Musser, *Edison* 408–9). Produced during 15–17 March, these films were usually exhibited at the opening and closing of virtually all Spanish-American War film programs, especially in conjunction with the emotional *Burial of the "Maine" Victims*.

Naval ships in harbor, soldiers marching, and other subjects close at hand were also filmed while producers made travel plans to Havana harbor and other faraway places prominent in headlines. AM&B filmed the battleship U.S.S. *Massachusetts*, sister ship to the *Maine*, and it was advertised to audiences within a week as footage of the *Maine* prior to her sinking. This report of the film's first exhibition in Chicago in February typifies the audience expressions of patriotic fervor that greeted the first Spanish-American War films:

> Chicago, Feb. 26—A patriotic outburst occurred here to-night when the audience of a local theater, inspired by a realistic picture of the ill-fated battle-ship Maine, and the presence of a local body of naval reserves, were aroused to the highest pitch. . . . At the picture of the Maine thrown on the canvas, showing a fine perspective in full detail, there was a terrific outburst of applause, which continued for several minutes, and a number of women in the audience were overcome by the excitement and had to be removed to the reception room of the theater.   ("Crowd Cheered")

By the end of March, AM&B films taken on location showed the wreck of the *Maine*, with her superstructure above the waterline of Havana harbor and divers engaged in recovering bodies and investigating the cause of the explosion, which the Hearst newspapers were already claiming as a Spanish sneak attack (Musser, *Nickelodeon* 126–27). Edison licensees clamored for films they could show without having to pay exorbitant fees to AM&B to obtain. To make up for lost time, Edison's agent F. Z. Maguire made an agreement with the Hearst newspaper syndicate for William Paley, an independent cameraman, to travel to Havana harbor and Key West, Florida, where part of the U.S. fleet was stationed. There Paley made one of the most popular films of the entire Spanish-American War series, *The Burial of the "Maine" Victims*. That film, recorded in a single long take lasting approximately two minutes, showed the procession of horse-drawn hearses bearing the remains of some of the 266 sailors lost in the *Maine* disaster. Marching with the bodies in solemn procession were sailors, officers, and other dignitaries.

Those producers who couldn't afford to send cameramen to Cuba either looked to military installations in their vicinity for appropriate actuality subjects or turned to restaging battle scenes with as much realism as possible. For example, Chicago-based producers William Selig and Edward Amet both separately produced a series of actuality films on military activities. Selig's films included several taken at Camp Tanner in Springfield, Illinois, for example, *Soldiers at Play*, *Wash Day in Camp*, and *First Regiment Marching*. Amet also produced actualities but showed more creativity by filming patriotic narratives and re-creations of specific naval battles, using scale models of battleships in water tanks, set against painted backdrops. The final note of realism in these films was provided by heavy smoke pouring from the ship's stacks as they maneuvered, with their guns firing blanks and filling the scenes with the fog of war. Amet's films included *Bombardment of Matanzas*, which he claimed was filmed through a special "telescopic lens" that enabled the action to be safely filmed from a great distance. In keeping with the hucksterism of the era, Amet advertised his table-top films as authentic (Musser, *Emergence* 255–58).[4]

In Philadelphia, Lubin began producing battle re-creation films based on newspaper accounts and, later in the year, Blackton and Smith of the Vitagraph company also produced small-scale re-creations of naval scenes, such as the *Battle of Manila Bay*, a re-creation of Admiral Dewey's naval victory filmed in May on a table-top set with miniature battleships. In January 1899 they repeated that cost-saving effort, this time under the Edison banner, with *Raising Old Glory over Morro Castle*. Against a background of a miniature of Morro Castle, a small Spanish flag attached to a staff is pulled down and replaced by the U.S. flag. Films such as this generated wild applause, especially from American audiences.

When Spanish-American War movies began to appear regularly in exhibition venues around the country, the response was overwhelming. Film labs worked overtime to meet the surge in demand for prints. When prints became available, extra daily programs were scheduled by exhibitors to meet the extraordinary public demand. The wider exposure of audiences to such scenes undoubtedly added to the public furor over the loss of the *Maine* and added to the pressure on a reluctant President William McKinley to declare war. AM&B sent a film crew to Washington to record any government activity that might suggest preparation for war. The U.S Copyright Office in the Library of Congress soon began receiving a steady flow of new motion picture applications (*Motion Pictures 1894–1912*).

Before and after the declaration of war, most of the films dealt with subjects relating to the logistics of preparing and moving ships and soldiers to war. Filmmakers soon found that they were not just covering heroic military actions but, with films such as *Cuban Refugees Waiting for Rations* and *Cuban Volunteers Marching for Rations* (both Edison, 20 May 1898), were also unexpectedly providing an early form of motion picture news coverage of the unheroic consequences of war. When newspaper reports focused on delays in the build-up of crucial supplies for the army in Tampa, Florida, in preparation for landing in Cuba, audiences began seeing such films as *Military Camp at Tampa, Taken from Train* (Edison, 20 May 1898). These films also provided crucial scenic information that helped orient audiences at home to the geographical locations where international actions were taking place.

The sustained level of public reception for Spanish-American War films was unprecedented. In Washington, D.C., Metzerott Hall, a venue that normally accommodated lectures by the Theosophical Society and other religious and intellectual groups, was taken over by the proprietors of the Columbia Theater next door and converted for the duration into a new venue advertised as the "Wargraph." Opening on 26 September 1898, the "Wargraph" ran nothing but continuous films about the Spanish-American War. Nearly two weeks later the *Washington Post* reported:

> The old, old, but ever new strains of martial music, the stir and thrill of marching soldiers, the story of national glory and victory, are daily reproduced with startling fidelity by the War-graph moving pictures at the Metzerott Hall, next to the Columbia Theater. The management of this popular exhibition are sparing no pains to make it the most perfect and interesting pictorial review of the war to be witnessed. New and elaborate effects are being added continuously. The new pictures, *Gen. Shafter and Staff Leaving Baiquiri* [sic] *for Santiago*, *Sports in Camp*, and *Loading Pack Mules in Cuba with Ammunition for the Front*, are especially interesting. *The Execution of Cuban Prisoners by Spanish Soldiers*, *The Arrival of the Oregon at New York*, and *The Grand Naval Parade and Firing of Salutes at the Tomb of Grant on the Hudson,* are all of thrilling interest.   ("Stirring Scenes")

In cities across North America, but particularly in the United States, similar programs were regularly offered until the cycle of Spanish-American War films closed in October 1899 with the production of the last films showing *Presentation of Nation's Sword to Admiral Dewey* (Edison, 3 October) and *Admiral Dewey at State House, Boston, Mass.* (Edison, 14 October).

Over one hundred motion pictures recording a wide variety of events surrounding the Spanish-American War were copyrighted in 1898–1899, primarily by the Edison Company. However, the copyright records alone do not accurately reflect the true number of Spanish-American War films produced. For example, the majority of AM&B and Lubin films of this period were not copyrighted, nor were all the Edison films. And the majority of other producers of this period, for example Selig, Amet, and Spoor, chose not to seek formal copyright protection. A count of the Edison productions for 1898–1899, including those made for Edison by Vitagraph, shows that 73 films on Spanish-American War–Philippine Revolution subjects were produced in 1898 and 56 in 1899, for a two-year total of 129 films. Therefore, a remarkable 42 percent of the 306 Edison Company productions of the 1898–1899 period were devoted to the constellation of events relating to the Spanish-American War (Musser, *Edison* 379ff.).[5] The actual number of all the films produced relating to the Spanish-American War may never be known because of the loss of so many films of the period and the fairly rampant practice of pirating and re-releasing previously produced films under new titles. However, it is probable the total number was well over two hundred separately produced titles.

Covering the Spanish-American War presented a great challenge to the film business of 1898–1899, which it collectively met with such overall success that the industry reached new heights of public acceptance and maturity that it would never lose. In spite of the litigious atmosphere and the lack of standardization among film projectors and formats, the constant public thirst for new films propelled the industry forward.

Boxing Films and the Jeffries-Sharkey Fight

In the fall of 1899, the American Sportagraph Company was formed to produce a film of the bantamweight fight between the British champion "Pedlar" Palmer and the American champion Terry McGovern.

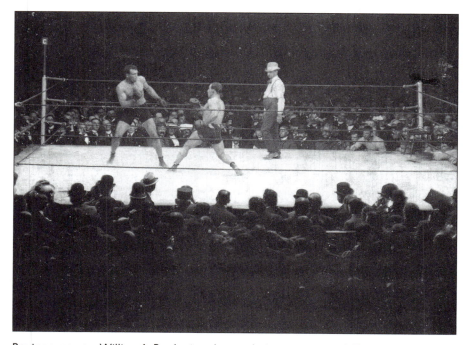

Boxing promoter William A. Brady signed an exclusive contract with Biograph to produce a full-length film record of the heavyweight contest between champion Jim Jeffries and challenger Tom Sharkey. The fight lasted twenty-five rounds and the Biograph camera negative measured over 40,000 feet, resulting in a running time of over two hours. (*The Jeffries-Sharkey Fight*, American Mutoscope & Biograph Company, 1899.)

Since film piracy was such a severe problem, especially for companies formed to invest heavily in one major film, the strategy devised by the Veriscope company, of building cameras and projectors using a unique size film stock, became the model for the owners of American Sportagraph. The expectation of this strategy was that it would be too expensive for would-be pirates to build special size printers for copying a nonstandard film gauge to 35 mm or any other competing film print format. For a variety of reasons, the Palmer-McGovern fight films generated little public interest and the American Sportagraph Company faded from history.

The wait for the next important gamble in boxing film production ended soon after with the contest between James Jeffries and Robert Fitzsimmons on 9 June 1899 at Coney Island. Lasting eleven rounds, the match was filmed by Vitagraph and released through the Edison Company in two lengths: the six-round version at 750 feet ($150), containing the highlights, and the full eleven rounds at 1,350 feet ($270) (Musser, *Edison* 508). However, during the bout the lighting system required for proper film exposure failed, making it impossible to record the conclusive rounds of the contest. Although Edison and Lubin both restaged the lost rounds with the original fighters, the completed film lacked the intensity and therefore the realism of the actual fight. Jeffries became the new champion and went on to dominate the sport for many years. He also soon appeared with Tom Sharkey in the last great boxing film of the nineteenth century, which took place on 3 November 1899.

The promoter for the Jeffries-Sharkey match was William A. Brady, who eventually went on to a long career as a producer of plays and theatrical films. Brady signed an exclusive contract with the Biograph company to produce an entire film record of the contest, regardless of length. Careful plans were made for reliable lighting and a special platform was constructed for four cameras, plenty of raw film stock, and twelve operators and staff. On the night of the fight, over ten thousand spectators filled the Coney Island arena to witness a fight that went the full twenty-five rounds, won by Jeffries in a decision. By rotating cameras, AM&B operators were able to film the entire bout without missing any of the action. The result was a motion picture of historic proportions: over 40,000 feet of film exposed under artificial light, producing a 68 mm negative seven and one-quarter miles long and a show, including fight preliminaries, advertised at two and one-quarter hours in length. Thus ended the notion that movies were inherently brief forms of public entertainment. And, if that is all that was historically important about this film, it would still rate a prominent mention in any history of cinema.

However, other events relating to this film come into play that made it the one film of the 1898–1899 period that best typifies the virtually lawless and cut-throat competition of the day. The culprits included Albert Smith of Vitagraph, the Edison Company, and Sigmund Lubin. Unbeknownst to Brady and the AM&B crew, Albert Smith smuggled his lightweight 35 mm camera into the crowd on the night of the fight and made an unauthorized film recording. Discovered before the fight concluded, Smith managed to escape pursuit and process the negative in the Vitagraph plant overnight. In the morning he discovered that someone had stolen the freshly processed film and carried it off to the Edison studio, where the staff there immediately began making 35 mm copies. Because Vitagraph was still under injunction from Edison, Smith could do nothing but negotiate for one print to be exhibited under the Vitagraph name, while the Edison Company distributed the film widely under its own name (Ramsaye 410–12). Edison, in the person of James H. White, also managed to copyright the film before Biograph could, further clouding any claims of primacy.[6] Adding to the contention that erupted between AM&B and Edison was the confusing appearance of Sigmund Lubin's *Reproduction of the Jeffries and Sharkey Fight* in the last week of November. Thus, within a matter of weeks, Brady, Jeffries, and Sharkey, who were partners in the film deal with AM&B, all found their dreams of fortune greatly diminished because of the piracy of Vitagraph and Edison, and the clever chicanery of Lubin.

Sigmund Lubin was a special case in the world of boxing films. He discovered with the Jeffries-Fitzsimmons fight (June 1899) that he could use the blow-by-blow, eyewitness accounts of the type commonly reported in newspapers to script the re-creation of championship boxing contests, featuring look-alike actors. By carefully labeling his films as "reproductions," he brazenly claimed them as "copyrighted" and authentic and, with complicit exhibitors, lured unwitting audiences into venues where they believed they were going to see films of the actual fight. The Lubin contemporary ad for the *Reproduction of the Jeffries and Sharkey Fight* in the *New York Clipper* boldly offered *$10,000 to Anybody That Can Prove that Lubin's Reproduction of the Jeffries-Sharkey Fight is Not Copyrighted* (Musser, *Emergence* 207). Part of the problem was that the public's understanding of the concept of copyright protection was no clearer in 1899 than it is today. Lubin's filmed restaging of the Jeffries-Sharkey fight was original and not pirated— unlike the Vitagraph-Edison version—and therefore could be copyrighted. Though not an authentic filmed recording of the actual fight, it was clearly promoted in a manner intended to dupe audiences into believing that it was, hence the outright violation of the Brady-AM&B license, if not the law, on the part of Vitagraph-Edison and the spirit of the law by Lubin. There was little AM&B and Brady could do except engage in a three-way advertising war of words with Edison and Lubin and file costly lawsuits that were unlikely to be settled until long after public interest in the Jeffries-Sharkey contest had waned.

The Jeffries-Sharkey fight motivated a high level of investment, risk, and controversy among motion picture producers precisely because of the vast profits at stake. The most important pattern of industrial activity linking the films considered in this chapter is the amount of intellectual property theft, sharp dealing, legal intimidation, and hucksterism that they inspired. The films of the competing Passion Plays, Pope Leo XIII, many of the key films by the various producers of the Spanish-American War series, and the authorized Jeffries-Sharkey film were all subjected to strenuous efforts by unrelated parties to steal profits from the rightful owners. Some of those efforts came from companies who believed they had a legitimate right, but many more came from those who willfully operated outside the law. However, who knew what the law was? Because the film industry was still so new in 1898–1899 and still evolving so rapidly in all phases of activity, it was difficult to know how the patent and copyright laws applied to the hardware and software of the motion picture industry. These years of the film business fall within the late period of the Robber Baron era, when government regulation was lax and the most admired industrialists and entrepreneurs were those who acted first and explained later.

▨ Summary

The final years of the nineteenth century were a time when people in industrial societies had the first great palpable sense that the technologies of their era were truly conquering time and space. For the first time in 1898–1899 North American audiences saw the pope in lifelike action and received his blessing; through the various Passion Play films, they saw the life of Jesus Christ depicted as a narrative entertainment; over a two-year period they were exposed to hundreds of films about all aspects of an international war; and they were able to see the longest film ever made up to that time, a complete two-and-a-quarter-hour record of the famed championship bout between Jim Jeffries and Tom Sharkey.

In this actuality age, before fictional narrative films began to be more fully developed, insightful people were aware of an important new inter-relationship that developed between newspapers and movies in this period, a relationship that foreshadowed not only the age of newsreels in the twentieth century but also the 24/7 television news coverage of world events taken for granted today. It showed that, by reacting to headlines in major newspapers in a timely manner, producers and exhibitors could profitably capitalize on preestablished audience interest in seeing moving image illustrations that went beyond the limitations of still images and written descriptions. As one prescient journalist observed:

> The magic mirror of romance in whose depths the spectator beheld a recurrence of past and present events, seems almost realized in that modern wonder, the biograph. As in the early days the art of writing was confined chiefly to the making of records of important events for succeeding generations, so the art of moving pictures at first was content to portray events of more or less staple character, in which the element of vital, contemporaneous interest was lacking. This condition is rapidly changing, and now the biograph goes hand in hand with the daily press in presenting to nightly audiences events which they have seen during the day or read of in the evening papers.
>
> With facilities for securing such scenes rivaling the great papers themselves . . . the biograph is constantly exhibiting throughout the leading cities of the world living moving representations of all the great events in which mankind is interested. The quickness of the delivery of this news (for such scenes can properly be termed news) is exceeded only by the telegraph. . . . To such perfection has the biograph brought the manipulation of films and pictures that but a few hours are required after the photographs are taken before they can be presented to the audience.   ("Newspaper's")

In the novelty era, the North American film industry found its niche in the established hierarchy of popular entertainment. During the years 1898–1899 it became more than simply a medium of entertainment and developed into a force of communication that began to transform society.

NOTES

1. "Novelty" is the term generally used by modern historians in reference to the period when motion pictures were generally introduced (1893–1897), and their popularity was largely sustained by public curiosity over a new phenomenon of technology and the attraction of witnessing "in motion" persons, places, and events previously seen only through "still" images presented through other established media, for example, photographs and engravings.

2. Founded as the American Mutoscope Company, the name was changed to incorporate the name of the company's well-known Biograph motion picture camera.

3. Holmes's films were actually produced by his projectionist, Oscar Depue, who obtained a Gaumont 60 mm camera in 1897.

4. See Musser's fuller account of the production activities of Selig, Amet, Lubin et al., relating to the Spanish-American War.

5. Musser's published research on the Edison Company is the model for similar efforts that remain to be done for all North American film companies of the early silent era.

6. White copyrighted the film twice, both versions registered on 4 November. Biograph, hampered by the enormous effort required to develop and process over seven miles of 68 mm film, filed its registrations in a series of claims during 10-15 November. Suspiciously, Lubin's *Reproduction of the Jeffries and Sharkey Fight* was registered almost two months before the fight occurred on 9 September.

1900–1901

Movies, New Imperialism, and the New Century

JEAN-PIERRE SIROIS-TRAHAN

The years 1900–1901 were a time of flux in the new "moving picture" industry (see Musser *Emergence*). The patents war between Edison and the other film companies had cast the industry into a major crisis. At the turn of the twentieth century, the cinema was a relatively modest part of popular attractions and was still no more than an interloper in the world of legitimate art. It responded to current cultural and political events more than it created original stories: historical events are tied up in the development of filmmaking, a fact that receives due recognition in the present chapter. As a mirror of society, this nascent art form was the black-and-white and often ideologically deformed reflection of the horrors of the world.

In the world of arts, Louis "Satchmo" Armstrong was born in 1901, while ragtime, like the blues a predecessor to jazz, was popularized by the black musician Scott Joplin and became the syncopated backdrop of the beginning of the century. This didn't prevent the American Federation of Musicians from issuing a resolution against the music in 1901, calling for the music industry "to make every effort to suppress and discourage the playing, and publishing of such musical trash" (*Brooklyn Daily Eagle*). In literature, the year 1900 saw the publication of the children's book *The Wonderful Wizard of Oz* by L. Frank Baum. Joseph Conrad published *Lord Jim*, while the great French stage actress Sarah Bernhardt embarked on her second American tour.

In 1901, in keeping with the last wishes of the Swedish scientist Alfred Nobel, the inventor of dynamite, the first Nobel Prizes were awarded. Wilhelm Röntgen won the Nobel Prize for physics for his discovery of electromagnetic X-rays, which were to prove of great importance to medicine. The prize for literature was won by Sully-Prud'homme, an academic poet of the Parnassian school justly forgotten today. Sharing the Nobel Peace Prize (with Frédéric Passy) was Henri Dunant, one of the founders of the International Red Cross, the largest humanitarian relief organization in the world. The Edison film *Red Cross Ambulance on Battlefield*, a reenactment of the Red Cross's work in the Boer War, was made by James A. White in 1900. Dunant was also a promoter of the famous Geneva Conventions, which protected hospitals and ambulances from attack during times of war—conventions that would have great importance in the global conflicts that were to rack the nascent century.

An Early Form of Globalization

At the turn of the new century, the whole world entered into an era of rapid industrialization and the gradual application of industrial and scientific technologies by the military. In the year 1900, the world's great powers (England, Germany, France, and the United States) were caught up in the horrors of their expansionist policies, leading to the revolt of several peoples against Western imperialism and to guerrilla warfare, insurrections, massacres, terrorist attacks, religious conflict, and wars of pacification.

Many figures in the American film industry, without exception of European descent, reflected or helped create the New Imperialist ideology then in effect, whether because the actuality views they produced were a means of conveying official propaganda or because viewers were seeing for the first time images of the colonies and the military might of their own country (and that of other countries—a frightening prospect). However, only the most harmless images (mostly military processions and depictions of the exotic beauty of foreign cities and landscapes) were depicted of an immense and otherwise brutal and merciless strategy game on a global scale. The great European powers, and Japan and the United States in their wake, were involved in an aggressive contest of colonial expansion, constantly out-doing the other, particularly in the Dark Continent, the site of a "scramble for Africa." This escalating contest was one of the main causes of the First World War. In 1900, the great U.S. intellectual W.E.B. Du Bois convened in London the first Pan-African Conference, aimed at uniting the people of Africa and their descendants outside Africa against European colonialism.

The most important international event in 1900 was the Boer War in South Africa. The Boers, or Afrikaaners, were descendants of Dutch settlers. Against their resistance, the British tried to annex the Orange Free State and the Republic of South Africa (Transvaal) by force. In January 1900, after several setbacks, the British regained the upper hand against the rebels. The gold and diamond mines in Boer territory were quite ample incentive for war. The film companies the American Mutoscope and Biograph Company

The Edison Manufacturing Company took an interest in the Boer War as film producers, widely distributing actuality views, particularly in Canada, which at the time was a British dominion. (*Duke of York at Montréal and Québec*, a film that incorporates parts of the films from the same series as *The Duke and Duchess of York Presenting Medals to Boer War Veterans at the Unveiling of the Queen's Statue*, Edison, 1900.) GRAFICS collection. Digital frame enlargement.

and the Edison Manufacturing Company (Edison) took an interest in the war as film producers, distributing actuality views somewhat widely and particularly in Canada, which at the time was a British dominion. As a middle power, Canada contributed to the war by sending a regiment of volunteers. James H. White, the Edison Company's principal cinematographer at the time, shot *2nd Special Service Battalion, Canadian Infantry, Embarking for So. Africa* in Montreal. He returned to film the victorious soldiers in *The Duke and Duchess of York Presenting Medals to Boer War Veterans at the Unveiling of the Queen's Statue*. W.K.L. Dickson, the inventor of the cinema camera based on an original idea by his employer, Thomas Alva Edison, left for South Africa to cover the battles for the British affiliate of the Biograph company (he no longer worked for the Wizard of Menlo Park). Dickson published his account of the war in his book *The Biograph in Battle* (1901).

Even though it did not send a film crew to the scene of the action, the Edison Company did not lag behind: James White filmed *Charge of Boer*

Cavalry (1900) in the Orange Mountains—of New Jersey! Unlike our situation today, the prevailing aesthetic of the time made no strict distinction between documentary and fiction, which were often subsumed under the category "miscellaneous views." Views shot onsite and latter re-creations were both called "natural views." James White shot several of these false actuality films in the area around Menlo Park, Thomas Edison's property and laboratory in New Jersey; an important example was *Capture of Boer Battery by British* (1900). Because Americans shared a strong anti-British sentiment, the views in this series were strongly pro-Boer. Great Britain, the turn-of-the-century superpower, was seen in the world the way the United States is seen today, as made clear by this remark in the *New York Clipper*: "If you are foolish enough to applaud English soldiers it would be made so uncomfortable for you that you would gladly leave the theatre" (27). Apart from its politics, the main feature of this series on the Boer War was its depth of field. In the second view of the series, entitled *Charge of Boer Cavalry [no. 2]* (1900), the cavalry move from the back of the frame toward the camera, prompting the Edison catalogue to remark: "Waving their sabres aloft on they come, so that the audience involuntarily makes an effort to move from their seats in order to avoid being trampled by the horses." This kind of reaction, brought on by the illusion of reality, was frequent in early film viewings, especially when large objects (trains, cars, cavalries) moved rapidly toward the camera, and thus toward the audience.[1]

The popular genre of reenactments drew on the tradition of painted panoramas and the illustrated press. The French filmmaker Georges Méliès provided the model of this peculiar genre with *L'affaire Dreyfus* (The Dreyfus Affair, 1899), a re-created actuality film that was banned in France because of anti-Dreyfus sentiment and distributed in the United States throughout the year 1900. Captain Alfred Dreyfus was a Jewish officer in the French army; falsely accused of treason, he was sentenced to a penal colony on Devil's Island in French Guiana. The "Dreyfus Affair" resonated around the world and deeply divided France, which fell into pro- and anti-Dreyfus camps after the matter was brought to the public's attention by Émile Zola, an author of novels known for their naturalism. His letter to the president of the country, Félix Faure, entitled *J'accuse . . . !* (I Accuse!), published in the newspaper *Aurore*, was one of the most famous cries for justice in history and one of the most stirring denunciations of anti-Semitism; it had been inspired by an article written by the anarchist Bernard Lazare.

In September 1900, the British army put into practice in South Africa something that would mark mankind: the concentration camp. Although they had not been condemned for extermination (in this area, the distinction is important), tens of thousands of women, children, and elderly men, both Boer and Black African, died there. To the best of our knowledge, no film producer filmed the British concentration camps. In 1901, a little-known view made by the Edison Company, entitled *Massacre at Constantinople*, was described in the following terms in its catalogue: "Showing a number of ferocious Turks tearing down the doors of an Armenian residence. They drag forth the occupants, consisting of men, women, and little children, butcher them with long knives, and then, after looting the house of all its valuables, they set it [*sic*] fire to it." Newspapers in Europe and North America often reported atrocities of this kind by the Turks, in particular because Armenian Ottomans were a Christian minority in a Muslim empire that Europe and Russia were seeking to carve up for themselves. As if in echo of the film, on 30 August 1901, the *New York Times* reprinted a British report on its front page:

> The Armenian Massacres. Turkish ex-Consul Asserts that the Porte[2] Intends to Exterminate the Race by a Regular System.
>
> London, Aug. 30. — The Daily Mail publishes to-day an article written by Ali Nouri Bey, ex-Turkish Consul at Rotterdam, asserting that the massacre of Armenians by Kurds, which has just recommenced, is part of a regular system of extermination. He says: "The number of Armenians killed will depend upon the outcry raised in Europe and the pressure brought to bear upon the Sultan. The same horrible process will be repeated year by year until all are killed."
>
> ("Armenian Massacres")

In January 1901, Victoria, queen of the United Kingdom of Great Britain and Ireland and empress of India, died at the age of eighty-one. Her son Edward VII succeeded her on the British throne. Thus began the slow decline of the largest empire in human history, on which the sun never set. In time, its hegemony was replaced by that of the increasingly powerful United States of America. Several film companies recorded Queen Victoria's funeral, in the presence of the new king and Germany's Kaiser Wilhelm. Visible in the funeral procession were British soldiers returning triumphant from Transvaal. Biograph made a series of three views entitled *Queen Victoria's Funeral*.

In the United States, lynching and "Jim Crow" laws that legalized discrimination against African Americans increased in number. The turn of the twentieth century has been described by some historians as "the nadir of American race relations," complete with racial discrimination, white supremacy, and segregation. While segregationist laws varied from state to state, in general they imposed the separation of black from white within modes of transportation (trains, streetcars, and buses), hospitals, schools, housing, and restaurants, as well as outlawing mixed marriages. These measures were coupled with iniquitous laws, such as the need to have a grandfather on the electoral rolls, which prevented many African Americans from voting. Lynching did the rest. There was a rise in the number of these "strange fruits" (Billie Holiday) in 1900–1901, with some 100 lynchings per year on record.[3] Films of the day often portrayed African Americans as mentally deficient children, just as a long racist tradition had resorted to stereotypes in minstrel shows—musical performances featuring whites in blackface that were still popular in 1900. Indeed, the famous "Jim Crow" was a fictional and caricatured character in a minstrel song. While it is true that nearly every ethnicity was depicted stereotypically in animated views and vaudeville shows, the consequences of these depictions were not the same for every group. Not all racism is created equal.

In May 1900 the Boxers, a secret Chinese society, staged a rebellion in China. Opposed to Christian missionaries' proselytizing and their Chinese converts, to the Qing imperial dynasty, and, above all, to European and Japanese domination of China, they carried out massacres in Western missions and districts. The Lubin company produced a view on the subject entitled *Massacre of the Christians by the Chinese* (1900). These events set off what has become known as the "55 Days at Peking" episode in which westerners in the embassy district resisted the Boxers. These events were summarized in one of the most important early films made, the British cinematographer James Williamson's *Attack on a China Mission* (1900), also known as *Blue Jackets to the Rescue*. It is hard to say whether Williamson intended the film as a conventional work of fiction or a reenactment. Despite the support of the Dowager Empress Tzu-Hsi and traditionalist elements of the military, the Boxers were defeated by an expeditionary force of 20,000 men, sent by six European countries, Russia, and Japan and led by the British Vice-Admiral Edward Seymour, who rescued foreign embassies and sacked Peking. Beginning in the fall of 1900, and thus after the fall of the Boxers and the taking of Peking, a force of 100,000 men led by the German Field Marshal Alfred Graf von Waldersee was sent to carry out a thorough "cleansing" of the Chinese countryside to "set an example": pillage, destruction, rape, and murder followed, without concern for a person's age or sex, with explicit orders from Kaiser Wilhelm II ("make the name German remembered in China for a thousand years so that no Chinaman will ever again dare to squint at a German," he said).

For the Western European powers, war was a way of doing business by other means. The United States was not left behind, violently suppressing the desire for independence on the part of the Philippines. Biograph (*Dewey*

Parade) and Edison (*U.S. Marines in Dewey Land Parade*) contributed to the propaganda with their films of the return of the victorious Admiral Dewey in early 1900. In February 1901, Cuba proclaimed its independence, but in June the United States occupied it militarily and made it a protectorate, taking control of its economy and receiving Guantánamo Bay, where it built a naval base. The United States was now a major world power, keeping an eye on political and economic developments in Europe and implementing the Open Door Policy, developed by Secretary of State John Hay in 1899–1900, particularly with regard to China: rather than colonizing a country and installing a governor as in the Philippines and Cuba, they allowed the formation of a government friendly to Western interests while enabling unfettered trade with all countries. Unlike the European powers, which colonized distant lands and subjugated their conquered peoples, the United States developed a more subtle version of imperialism, one based on the strength of its economy. In addition, the United States reached an agreement with England (the Hay-Pauncefote Treaty of 1901) to create the Panama Canal, extending their grip on Latin America in strict accordance with the Monroe Doctrine, according to which the entire Western hemisphere was the exclusive preserve of American interests.

In 1901, "Wall Street's man," President William McKinley, made the gold standard for American currency official. It had been in practice since 1873, but the Republican president gave it the force of law in order to counter the populist Democrat William Jennings Bryan's campaign in the American South and Midwest for the silver standard. (Some people believe *The Wonderful Wizard of Oz* was a political allegory of the "bimetallic controversy," with Dorothy taking the "yellow brick road" before returning to Kansas with her "silver shoes.") The gold standard established parity between various world currencies and an ounce of gold. Beginning with Germany, several countries had adopted it, leading to currency stability and the first wave of globalization in international trade, which would be of great benefit to the nascent film industry.

In exchange, the actualities shot by camera operators around the world, along with the wireless telegraph, rendered this globalization more concrete (in December 1901, the Italian Guglielmo Marconi received the first transatlantic wireless telegraph, from England to Newfoundland). Similarly, many European films were widely distributed in the United States, particularly French films by the firms Pathé and Star Film, Georges Méliès's company. Méliès, the world's most popular filmmaker in 1900–1901 and a man imitated by many others in the industry, produced such inventive masterpieces as *L'Homme orchestre* (The One-Man Band, 1900), *L'Homme à la tête de caoutchouc* (The Man with the Rubber Head, 1901), and *Barbe-Bleue* (Blue-beard, 1901). His films were full of anarchic fantasy, something that was sorely lacking at a time when mostly militaristic films were being produced. The concepts of plagiarism and intellectual property were not enshrined in law in cinema's early years and American companies had no qualms about copying Méliès's films, to the extent that he opened a branch office of Star Film in New York, run by his younger brother Gaston, to collect royalties on his films and sell them directly.

■ Modern Style, World's Fairs, and Moving Pictures

While the Impressionist painter Claude Monet was exhibit-ing his work in 1900 in Paris, at the height of his famous "Waterlilies" period, Pablo Picasso was doing the same thing in Barcelona, for the first time, at the age of eighteen. He exhibited his work in Paris the following year, when he began his "blue period"—occasioned, he said, by the suicide of his friend Carlos Casagemas. Although he had been dead for more than ten years, the work of Vincent van Gogh was also exhibited—for the first time!—in a Paris gallery in 1901, the year that his friend, the painter Paul Gauguin, left Tahiti for the Marquesas, where he would die. From an art historical perspective, 1900–1901 can be seen retrospectively as a transition period between the end of Impressionism and the advent of modern art with Cubism, a transition marked by the popularity of Art Nouveau (or Modern Style) in architecture, painting, and design (in the work of such famous artists as Gustav Klimt, Antoni Gaudí, Victor Horta, Hector Gui-mard, René Lalique, and the American Louis Comfort Tiffany). With its flowing, rounded plant forms, Art Nouveau was a clear break with classical tradition since the Renaissance, and can be seen as the first expression of modernism. Some of the most famous works of Art Nouveau are the Park Güell, north of Barcelona, created by the architect Gaudí and the entrance-ways to Paris métro stations by Hector Guimard; the Paris métro itself was inaugurated during the World Exposition in Paris in 1900.

While the United States closed the western frontier, having forcibly subjugated and decimated the indigenous population, global capitalism's need to sell its surplus production in new markets was made clear in major international gatherings such as world's fairs and colonial expositions. The Paris Exposition, which opened in May 1900, attracted various film pro-duction companies, who filmed its attractions and modern-style pavilions. James H. White shot a series of views there: the impressive *Panorama from the Moving Boardwalk*, crowd scenes in *Panorama of Eiffel Tower*, *Panoramic*

View of the Champs Elysees [sic], and *Panoramic View of the Place de la Concorde,* the poetic *Panorama of the Paris Exposition, from the Seine,* and the magnificent and highly cinematic *Scene from the Elevator Ascending Eiffel Tower.* These films are examples of panoramic views, also called panoramas, perhaps the most popular turn-of-the-century genre. Based on camera movement, both panning and traveling shots, panoramic views are similar to the tradition of painted panoramas and dioramas that depicted landscapes or urban scenes, whether in a rotunda or on a moving canvas, on which the landscape unfolded as in a traveling shot.

The camera operators dispatched to Paris took a pass on one of the most troubling features of world's fairs, one that remains largely hidden today even though it is one of the most revealing of colonial mentalities during the period of New Imperialism: human zoos. World's fairs and colonial expositions displayed as "attractions" indigenous people from "exotic" lands, often behind bars or in cages in which their lifestyle amidst wild animals was re-created. Visitors flocked to these zoos to see what was described as these people's "barbarism" and "animalism," particularly of a sexual nature, depicting them as occupying the lowest rungs of humanity according to a racial hierarchy that justified colonialism. During the 1900 Paris Exposition, for example, a "living" diorama from Madagascar was on display. Conditions at these expositions were most often unsanitary, and numerous "savages" caught measles and smallpox. At the Pan-American Exposition in Buffalo in 1901, "Eskimos" were exhibited in animal pens until a "village" was built for them (Rydell 213). When viewing most of the "ethnographic" and "travelogue" views found in film producers' catalogues during these early years of cinema, this Western social conception of the Other, and the Western identity it helped create, must be borne in mind. These views and human zoos, the first massive encounter between the West and nonwestern peoples, had a lasting effect on the West's collective imagination and fantasies about other cultures, which had to be "civilized" and thus colonized. As the authors of a book on human zoos remark,

> The function of zoos, expositions, and gardens was basically to show things that were rare, curious or strange—anything that was unusual and different from a rational construction of the world along European lines. . . . First of all, we might legitimately ask ourselves what these raving masquerades meant. Weren't they all, in the end, the reverse image of the quite real ferocity of colonial conquest? Was there not a desire, intentional or not, to legitimize the conquerors' brutality by animalizing the conquered? No doubt the idea of establishing two distinct racial worlds was central. The world of the conquerors and that of the natives, one a dominant civilization and the other a dominated world. (Bancel et al. 69)

These human zoos must be compared to contemporaneous theories of social Darwinism, anthropometry, and phrenology, which formed the "scientific" basis of racist discourse. We must also compare them to all the "freak shows" (dwarfs, Lilliputians, bearded women, etc.) in fairs throughout Europe and North America whose aim was to create a discourse of normality and monstrous abnormality.

In October 1901, at the Pan-American Exposition in Buffalo, New York, Edwin Porter filmed *Pan-American Exposition by Night*, an aesthetically important and experimental view for the period. A right-to-left pan shows the main pavilions and the esplanade in broad daylight, and then a dissolve shows the scene from the same perspective at night. This was without a doubt one of the first edited sequences with an ellipsis of this sort. The enormous pavilions were illuminated by the "Fairy Electricity": this was how, at the time, electric energy was described. A veritable mania for electricity had gripped the Western world, allegorically depicting this new form of energy as a young fairy woman. At the Paris World Exposition in 1900, an entire pavilion was devoted to electricity, crowned by a sculpture of the fairy woman. This pavilion was filmed by the Edison Company in the view *Palace of Electricity*. Similarly, at the Buffalo exposition, the Electric Tower was the principal attraction, with searchlights at its peak. At the time, using electricity for lighting was still a novelty; cities were lit by gaslight and oil lamp. The Edison catalogue proudly proclaimed about the view *Pan-American Exposition by Night*: "This picture is pronounced by the photographic profession to be a marvel of photography." The enchanting illumination of the pavilions, one of the exposition's principal attractions, also figured in another view featuring a nocturnal pan in the opposite direction, *Panorama of Esplanade by Night*.

The Edison Company also shot President McKinley's visit to Buffalo. Reelected in November 1900, he was assassinated in September 1901 at the exposition (like King Umberto I of Italy the year before in Manza, Italy, in July 1900). Edison shot three views of McKinley's visit to the exposition, on 5 and 6 September, the latter the day he was shot. The first view, entitled *President McKinley's Speech at the Pan-American Exposition*, shows him on a decorated rostrum, surrounded by dignitaries. Perhaps he was delivering one of the speeches we know he made in Buffalo: "Expositions are the timekeepers of progress. They record the world's advancements. They stimulate the energy, enterprise, and intellect of the people, and quicken human genius. They go into the home. They broaden and brighten the daily life of the people. They open mighty storehouses of information to the student." In his essay "Paris, the Capital of the Nineteenth Century," the

The enchanting illumination of the pavilions, one of the Pan-American Exposition's principal attractions (*Panorama of Esplanade by Night*, Edison, 1901). GRAFICS collection. Digital frame enlargement.

philosopher Walter Benjamin delivered another, more critical, verdict on such expositions: "World expositions are places of pilgrimage to the commodity fetish. 'Europe is off to view the merchandise,' says [Hippolyte] Taine in 1855. . . . World expositions glorify the exchange value of the commodity. They create a framework in which its use value recedes into the background. They open a phantasmagoria which a person enters in order to be distracted" (52). We might add that the great international expositions served to justify economic imperialism and colonialism by displaying their products and blessings to the masses, under cover of lofty civilizing values.

The second Edison Company view from the Buffalo exposition, *President McKinley Reviewing the Troops at the Pan-American Exposition*, shows nothing more than what its title describes, apart from a lost kid who passes in front of the president in the foreground. It was common at the time for Edison views to be made up of several shots; when there was nothing more of interest happening in front of the camera, or if the subject was not yet in frame, the camera operator stopped turning the crank. He started turning again when something of interest appeared, sometimes changing the framing to varying degrees. About half the films shot by Edison in 1900 show traces of editing, with an average of five cuts per view. Most of these cuts are what André Gaudreault has suggested we call resumptions ("Fragmentation and Segmentation"). The Edison Company could then edit the shots to eliminate over- or underexposed frames caused when the camera was stopped. In this view of the president and the troops, we can see four shots from the same point of view, with a jump cut between each indicating the editing that took place. The last shot starts with the same framing and then a fine pan sweeps the huge crowd. The camera operator seems to have botched his first two shots: the president is in long shot and the troops walk diagonally in front of him toward the camera, so that we rarely get a clear view of the main subject of the film. In the third shot, an officer appears to have stopped the procession, allowing us to get a clear view of the president.

It must be said that camera operators at the time did not always control their shooting conditions and had to deal with a great number of unpredictable factors. One of the most important documents in all of American film history, the third in this series of Edison views of the Buffalo exposition, shot on the second day, 6 September, is a good illustration of how chance could intrude on the work of the first handle turners. Edison employees were waiting outside the majestic Temple of Music, having found an ideal spot from which to film McKinley's exit from the pavilion and his reception by the crowd. During this time, inside the pavilion, the twenty-fifth president of the United States was shot point-blank by a Detroit anarchist, Leon Frank Czolgosz. McKinley died a week later, on 14 September. No camera was turning when the shooting took place. The Edison employees had to resign themselves to shooting *The Mob outside the Temple of Music after the President Was Shot*. A slow, high-angle pan slowly scans the crowd, watching the door of the pavilion with, one imagines, a mixture of stupor and curiosity. The only person to look our way is a young child in its father's arms, more interested in the camera than in history. The catalogue remarks that "the Pan-American Exposition guards are plainly seen in the background trying to check the frantic multitude as they sway backward and forward in their mad endeavor to reach the assassin."

At the same time as these tragic events were unfolding, Edwin S. Porter began making his first fiction films for the Edison Company after being hired in the fall of 1900. One of his films, the morbid *Execution of Czolgosz, with Panorama of Auburn Prison* (1901), is a heterogeneous collage that appears surprising today. The first three shots are pans of the outside of the Auburn state prison in New York State, the day of the murderer's execution, and can be included in the panorama genre. In the first shot, a train goes by in the foreground, causing Porter to stop shooting and resume when it had passed. A jump cut is visible, even if the two shots match perfectly and create a smooth pan, suggesting a later edit on the movement. The third shot is taken from a different angle and shows the cell windows from a heightened position outside the prison.

Following these pans, the final two shots partake of a completely different aesthetic. They take the form of a re-creation, similar to the staging found in the work of Méliès (theatrical frontality and direct address to the camera), but in a more naturalist vein. Today, on the Internet, some sites present this view as a record of the real execution. It is quite likely that Porter was inspired by the historical tableaux found in the wax museums of the day, which used wax figures to depict political events and bloody crimes. (Also in 1901, in France, Ferdinand Zecca made the film *Histoire d'un crime* [Story of a Crime], showing an execution by guillotine and taking as his inspiration the wax tableaux found in the Musée Grévin in Paris.) Thus in the fourth shot of *Execution of Czolgosz* a dissolve gives way to a prison hallway filmed frontally and, in the background, in a cell on the left, we see Czolgosz waiting. The set seems to be made of papier-mâché. On the right side, a guard waits and then advances, followed by three others. The guard unlocks the cell door and fetches the prisoner, who has withdrawn to the back of his cell offscreen. He grabs hold of him and leads him out to the right. A dissolve opens onto the room where the execution by electric chair will take place. Between this shot and the previous one we might reasonably surmise, following Charles Musser, that there is a temporal overlapping, as if Porter were trying to show two simultaneous points of view of a capital event. Thus, while the guards were fetching the prisoner, four officials were testing the deadly apparatus with a series of light bulbs (another of Edison's famous inventions). Whether it is a real electric chair, we do not know. The guards arrive frame right—meaning that the camera has switched sides, or that the guards made a 180-degree change in direction—and they attach the president's assassin to the chair, who submits without resistance. The executioner checks everything over before an official orders him to proceed with the execution. Throughout all this, the actor playing Czolgosz remains impassive, without apparent emotion (because he appears small in the frame, the actor would have had to exaggerate his terror if he had wanted to convey it). From this we see that Porter was trying to be realistic, not mock-heroic; by amalgamating the staged shots with the outdoor pans, his goal was to present the event as a realistic re-creation.

Then comes the execution. In a doorway in the background, on the left, the executioner pulls a hand lever. The actor goes stiff and rises off the chair. But the subterfuge is apparent in a telling detail: the actor relaxes and falls back on the chair a fraction of a second before the executioner cuts off the current. The electrocution is resumed twice, a couple of seconds each time (in reality, electrocutions take longer). A doctor checks the anarchist assassin's heart and declares him dead—a feeble guarantee, since several people who have been electrocuted have come back to life. To conclude, the official in charge (played by the Edison producer James H. White) speaks to the camera operator (Porter, it would appear), telling him to stop the camera. A clean execution, without mishap.

The reality was completely different. After a brief, eight-hour trial on 23 September, which almost didn't happen so badly was he beaten by the crowd in Buffalo, Czolgosz was sentenced to die. He was electrocuted on 29 October at Auburn state prison. His last words before "riding the lightning" were "I am sorry I could not see my father." Sulfuric acid was thrown on his coffin to disfigure him; his papers and clothes were burned—as if there was a need for nothing to remain physically by which to identify or remember him, as if history had to be erased. The son of Russian immigrants, born in 1873, Czolgosz grew up in poverty and want: at the age of ten, he and his brothers went to work in the American Steel and Wire Company factory owned by J. P. Morgan, like many poor children of the day. From a young age he was witness to many "illegal" strikes, which were violently put down by the state. He became interested in anarchist and socialist ideas. He was particularly impressed by the radical ideas of Emma Goldman and Alexander Berkman, important political agitators of the day. Goldman, a feminist, was arrested after McKinley's assassination but later released when there was no evidence linking her to the assassin. The era was one of violent confrontations between workers and capitalist power. The police and even the army were often called out to put a brutal end to strikes. Czolgosz, for his part, was a loner with incoherent ideas, accused in anarchist circles of being attracted to fanatical violence and of being a double agent in the government's pay (and possibly a member of the Republican Party, the same party as McKinley).

The electric chair was invented by Harold P. Brown, a secret employee of Edison. At the time, Edison was engaged in the famous "war of currents" (between AC and DC) with the entrepreneur George Westinghouse Jr. and the brilliant inventor Nikola Tesla. Edison, although personally opposed to capital punishment, financed the development of a chair electrified by alternate current (AC) in order to garner negative publicity for the competitor to his own direct current (DC) system. To prove the effectiveness of alternate current for electrocutions, and thus demonstrate its dangers, Brown and Edison killed a large number of animals in their laboratory or in front of journalists. This reenactment of the execution of Leon Czolgosz was certainly a way of publicizing his apparatus, which was beginning to be adopted in several states, in particular because this staging was much more expeditious and watchable than a real execution. In many documented cases, the subject survived the execution—not to mention the burnt flesh and smoke. We might hypothesize that *Execution of Czolgosz* served two contrary goals: first, to show that the electric chair was a more humane punishment than hanging; and second, to demonstrate that alternate current could kill, unlike direct current (a misconception maintained by Edison). The electric chair, because of its institutional aspect, would also counter the growth of hasty lynchings.

Edwin S. Porter also made an allegorical view of McKinley's assassination that October, *The Martyred Presidents,* an immobile and solemn tableau vivant. Seated on the steps of the altar of Justice, a young woman dressed as an ancient Greek presides over the apparition on an altar (made possible by the use of a black background) of effigies of the three American presidents assassinated in office: Abraham Lincoln, James A. Garfield, and William McKinley. The young woman, a branch in her hand, represented Columbia, the feminine personification of the United States, as this description in the Edison catalogue spells out:

> We have just finished and now offer to exhibitors a picture which we consider most valuable as an ending to the series of McKinley funeral pictures. The scene opens with a beautiful woman who represents Columbia seated at the altar of Justice. As if from out of space there slowly appears a perfect and lifelike picture of Abraham Lincoln. . . . This in a like manner fades away, and again as out of the dim distance comes the picture of our great martyred President, William McKinley. The tableau is then dissolved into a picture of an assassin kneeling before the throne of Justice. Here the tableau ends, leaving an impression of mingled sorrow and sublimity upon the audience. We predict for this picture a remarkable success, and particularly where it is shown in connection with the funeral ceremonies of the illustrious McKinley.
>
> (*AFI Catalog*)

Because all views were silent, this kind of information was imparted to the audience by a film lecturer in the cinema who would explain the film to the largely illiterate audience, often with the help of texts like these supplied by producers' catalogues.

A New President

Vice President Theodore Roosevelt, a hawk, became the twenty-sixth American president in September 1901. Forty-two years old at the time—still the youngest president in U.S. history—he was immensely popular, in particular because he introduced numerous progressive reforms, such as curtailing the exorbitant power of the trusts. As vice president, he had adopted "big stick" diplomacy, similar to the Monroe Doctrine, that saw the United States take on a new and much more interventionist role on the world stage. Paraphrasing an African proverb, he uttered this famous statement: "Speak softly and carry a big stick, you will go far." A great hunter and fan of safaris, McKinley's successor was mocked in a film shot entirely outdoors: *Terrible Teddy, the Grizzly King* (1901). The first shot shows the president hunting a cougar, which turns out to be a mere cat in a tree, while the second shot shows a kind of victorious parade of the president with his press agents following behind him. This satirical film was adapted from a humorous drawing of the day. Early scriptwriters for films took their inspiration from the mass-circulation press, illustrations, and comics. The film's first shot is frontal, as in a theater, while the second was taken from an angle, like views of military parades. This complex mode of representation, intercutting staged scenes (like the tableaux found in Méliès) with actuality footage like that found in Lumière, would become very important in the years to come. Like most American filmmakers at the time, Porter made short films, often only one or two shots in length, in which he experimented with representational systems he would not necessarily use again.

Porter tried his hand at trick film with *Uncle Josh's Nightmare* (1900), in which he used a technique invented by Méliès to create numerous appearances and disappearances of the devil. Uncle Josh was a famous figure, a rural hick visiting the big city, who was found in comics and circulars as well as the cinema. Growing industrialization drove more and more rural dwellers to the factories of what the poet Émile Verhaeren has described as "tentacle-like cities." Many were European immigrants, landing at Ellis Island in search of the American Dream. These immigrants and rural migrants to the city were stigmatized by "up-to-date" urban residents, who despised them. This attitude is visible in the view *Two Rubes at the Theatre* (Edison, 1901), described in the following way in the Edison catalogue: "Shows two countrymen on their first visit to a theatre. Full of life and animation from start to finish." The film was a remake by Edison of a Lubin film.

The Biograph films *The Downward Path* (1900) and *A Career of Crime* (1900) take the opposite approach, showing the city as a den of vice. In these films, the family, the solid foundation of American culture, stays in the countryside. A multiple-shot film, *The Downward Path* is listed in the catalogues as a series of distinct views, not as a single film. Alongside these edifying melodramas, Biograph also played the other side of the street, making a number of very popular light and suggestive views. At the Edison Company, one of Edwin Porter's views, entitled *What Happened on Twenty-third Street, New York City* (1901), shows a busy street in the bustling city with its vehicles and throngs of people. A young woman, played by the actress Florence Georgie, accompanied by her husband, walks toward the camera in the direction of a subway ventilation grate on the sidewalk. Her long dress is blown up in the air when she walks over it. While Porter's view starts out like a pure actuality, the blend of anonymous people in the crowd and professional actors is remarkable. In addition, while this kind of representation may well be seen as a kind of visual spectacle for a "textually inscribed spectator of male, homosocial entertainments" (Hansen 39), it can also be seen as a brilliant way of playing with Victorian society's censorship of sexuality, given that the mere glimpse of an ankle was seen as erotic.

At the turn of the century, the era of "kine-attractography" (the "writing" of attractions in motion) was in full force (see Gaudreault "'Primitive Cinema'"). This was true both of views depicting circus or vaudeville numbers and of actuality views with exotic or spectacular images. The attraction, a term introduced to early cinema studies by André Gaudreault and Tom Gunning ("Early Cinema as a Challenge to Film History"), following Eisenstein, is used to describe a moment in the film that provokes curiosity, voyeurism, fascination, or horror. One of the most attractive film genres of the era was that of the boxing views, like the fights of the great heavyweight champion Jim Jeffries, one of the best boxers in history (though boxing films were often prohibited because of their violence). Some were actualities. In September 1900, a hurricane leveled the city of Galveston, Texas, causing 8,000 deaths. This was the largest natural disaster in the United States until Hurricane Katrina. The camera operator Albert Smith, of the American Vitagraph compamy, made a series of views of the devastation, as did Billy Bitzer, D. W. Griffith's future camera operator, for Biograph, entitled *Galveston Disaster* (in four parts). The Lubin company distributed the films *Birdseye View of Galveston, Showing Wreckage* and *Taking the Dead from the Ruins*. There we see the complete devastation caused by the hurricane, as if an atomic bomb had been dropped on the city. War and natural disasters were always powerful attractions for film viewers, and remain so today on the likes of CNN and Fox television.

Monopolies

In 1901, Carnegie Steel was sold. Andrew Carnegie, "the richest man in the world," sold the company to John Pierpont Morgan, the financier caricatured on Monopoly money, for the record sum of $480 million. The sale was done without contracts or lawyers, just a manly shake of the hand. Morgan added this to other steel companies he owned, resulting in the United States Steel Corporation, the first business in history to surpass a billion dollars in capitalization. The "steel trust" was also vertical in nature, because U.S. Steel dominated construction in steel (including ships, bridges, and railroads). The "robber barons" (Carnegie, Morgan, and John D. Rockefeller) built colossal fortunes through corruption in the railroads, monopolies in entire industries, and government monetary policies favorable to them. They were also prominent as proselytizing philanthropists who donated fortunes to charity, especially Carnegie, who built thousands of public libraries in the United States and around the world. These not always entirely disinterested gestures established a tradition that lives on today in the charitable work of someone like Bill Gates.

The cinema, like the theater, was not exempt from these monopolistic tendencies. At the turn of the century, American cinema—caught up in the patents war between Edison and the other companies using 35 mm film (Vitagraph, Selig, Lubin, Paley, and so forth) on the one hand, and between the giants Edison and Biograph, the only company using 70 mm film, on the other—was stagnating and showing signs of instability. In 1900–1901, Biograph was the largest American production company, ahead of Edison, although this did not protect it from losses in 1901, resulting in the decision in the final few months of the year not to make fiction films. Edison, trying to create a monopoly, took the other major production companies to court. The patents war seriously undermined the resources and creativity of all involved. At the time, French and British films were more creative. Thomas Edison contemplated selling his company to Biograph, but then changed his mind. In late 1900 he built luxurious new studios, replacing his first studio, the Black Maria, which gave him a decisive advantage over his rivals.

Generally speaking, Biograph films were more original than Edison's product, had less conservative topics, and outclassed his films in quality and quantity. On the other hand, Biograph films had a reputation for being short. According to Paul C. Spehr, in 1900 Biograph produced 374 films:

166 actualities, 194 fiction films, and 14 that cannot be categorized ("Production cinématographique"). "Fiction" is a catch-all category including trick films, playlets, vaudeville, and circus numbers; most Biograph films could be seen as nonfiction. In 1901 Biograph experienced problems, due in large part to the copyright lawsuit that Edison brought against it. The company found it impossible to shoot more than 49 fiction films that year, concentrating on the production of 266 actualities.

In addition to the two giants, Edison and Biograph, numerous other companies were taking off and would become more important in the years to come. At Vitagraph, J. Stuart Blackton tried his hand at animation with *The Enchanted Drawing* (1900), which featured changing "funny faces," a popular genre during the first decade of film's existence. He also made *The Artist's Dilemma* (1901), a remake of Edison's *An Artist's Dream* (1900). Films by Edison Company affiliates (e.g., Vitagraph, Paley) were distributed by Edison. While most films in the United States were shot in New York (the home of Edison and Biograph), Chicago (Selig) and Philadelphia (Lubin) were also major centers, relatively distant from Edison's lawyers. In Philadelphia, Lubin made a large number of actualities, comedies, and re-creations.

Some kinematographers made actualities exclusively for a specific theater. William Paley, for example, went to Montreal, then Canada's largest city, to shoot *Montreal Fire Department on Runners* (1901) for the opening of the Proctor Theatre, a large hall. This view is one example among many of the ever-popular firefighters, who were the subject of many stories afterward. From his vantage point on the side of a major street, Paley filmed the firefighters' horse-drawn fire trucks diagonally as they passed by. This kind of actuality film was often inserted without alteration into later fiction films.

Apart from actuality films, the cinema was greatly influenced by vaudeville. And yet theater people were hardly interested in the cinema directly; they found it vulgar and left the film production companies a monopoly in this new field, which in addition they saw as having no aesthetic value. In these years, the cinema's presence in middle-class or lower-middle-class vaudeville theaters was at its height. Film production companies were contracted to supply large theater circuits, such as Keith. Storefront cinemas—small makeshift cinemas with seating for a few dozen or a couple of hundred people, also derisively called grindhouses—had a precarious existence. Venues devoted exclusively to the cinema would really take off only with the nickelodeons. Many itinerant exhibitors traveled around the country with varying degrees of success. According to Charles Musser, only

Some kinematographers made actualities exclusively for a specific theater. William Paley, for example, went to Montreal, then Canada's largest city, to shoot *Montreal Fire Department on Runners* for the opening of the Proctor Theatre, a large hall (*Montreal Fire Department on Runners*, Edison, 1901). GRAFICS collection. Digital frame enlargement.

Lyman H. Howe, the most important traveling moving-picture showman of the day, worked "in commercial theaters on a regular basis and prospered" (*Emergence* 303).

As Musser explains, early film exhibitors were co-creators of film entertainment, on a par with the production companies, given that they made up the programs, chose the order of the films (*Before the Nickelodeon*), and added verbal commentary where necessary. Around 1900–1901 the production companies began to want to control this aspect. Production was limited to one- or two-shot films, with a few more elaborate multi-shot films whose shots could be purchased separately. Most films were actuality views of vaudeville numbers; a few could be described as "story films"— most often Méliès-like fairy films. There were no films based on the desires or psychology of their characters. Instead, most often there was a series of attractions connected to each other by a very summary narrative line, such as a crime followed by a punishment.

The importance of the strike by the "White Rats" (vaudeville actors) gave American cinema some breathing room in 1901. Films took on the role of scab labor and replaced the actors in theatrical entertainment. The strike brought the film world closer to the owners of New York's theaters, creating a bond of trust between them, although, according to Musser, the effect of the strike outside New York was probably exaggerated. In any event, this helping hand would not be enough: the monotony of the films, seen by viewers as being basically all alike, caused audiences and theater people gradually to lose interest. Views often served as "chasers," indicating to the audience that the theatrical event was at a close. According to Musser,

> To label the early 1900s the "chaser period" is somewhat reductive, and the term can, for that reason, be problematic. The role of motion pictures as "chasers" in vaudeville houses was only symptomatic of the complex crisis that gripped the film industry. This was due in large part to its multiple determinants: patent wars, copyright chaos, technological incompatibility, fee reductions, and too-familiar subject matter that resulted in audience boredom. For many veterans, recurrent commercial instability seemed to be a fact of life in the moving-picture world. Some, like Edwin Porter, contemplated leaving the business.   (*Emergence* 336)

Whatever the popularity of animated views, at this date they were still not independent entertainments that could attract audiences on their own on a regular basis. The fashion for "story films" in the coming years would make it possible to solve, in part, the problem of the films' monotony.

All the same, the American film industry, at the very least unstable in 1900–1901, was a partial reflection, in both senses of the term "partial," of the world's instability at the turn of the century.

NOTES

1. On this topic, see Sirois-Trahan 203–21.

2. "La Sublime Porte" (The Lofty Gate) was the name given to the Ottoman government.

3. The racist mobs that carried out these denials of justice were in the habit of taking photographs of the event and making postcards out of them. An archive of these photographs can be found at http://withoutsanctuary.org (consulted on 15 June 2007).

Translated by Timothy Barnard.

1902–1903

Movies, Stories, and Attractions

TOM GUNNING

By 1902 and 1903 motion pictures had been shown publicly throughout the United States for more than five years. These two years mark a transitional period in which cinema no longer could be considered a novelty, but had not yet achieved an independent identity in terms of regular production modes, set venues of exhibition, or even stable patterns for films themselves. Cinema was evolving an identity as a new form of entertainment beyond the technical novelty or "canned vaudeville" that marked its origins. Most films made and shown in the United States in these years were brief, often no more than a single shot and lasting less than a minute. Rather than telling stories, these brief films usually presented a visual attraction: a performance, a view of a landscape or city site, a camera trick, or a slapstick gag (see Gunning "Attractions"). However, a few longer multi-shot films with more extended story lines also appeared, and their popularity indicated new pathways for filmmaking. It is the interaction between—and the combination of—cinematic display on the one hand and storytelling on the other that characterizes this slice of film history.

New Identities for the United States and for Cinema

The United States was transforming into an industrializing international power, a process closely associated with President Theodore Roosevelt. The U.S. government started antitrust suits against railroad and beef interests, and Roosevelt negotiated an end to a five-month coal strike. In the aftermath of the Spanish-American War, Cuba inaugurated its first elected president and leased Guantánamo Bay to the United States; Roosevelt declared the war against Philippine insurgents officially over (although armed resistance to U.S. occupation continued for at least a decade); and arrangements for the Panama Canal were initiated. Congress extended the Chinese Exclusion Act limiting immigration to the United

States from Asia. Nearly two hundred African Americans were lynched over these two years, which also saw the publication of W.E.B. Du Bois's extraordinary book of essays, *The Souls of Black Folk*. Technology expanded into new horizons. The Wright Brothers completed their first successful (minute-long) flight in Kitty Hawk in 1903; Daniel Burnham's skyscraper the Flatiron Building was completed in New York City; Scott and Shackleton explored Antarctica; and the American Automobile Association was founded. Films presented a number of these events to audiences, since film often functioned partly as a visual newspaper, projecting images of events and personalities of the day.

Competition

Although the Mutoscope and Biograph Company continued to make Mutograph flip-cards for their peepshows (a device that displayed brief motion pictures by flipping a series of cards arranged on a wheel), these were a decided sidelight; films were primarily projected on screens. Films had become a regular feature of the typical vaudeville program, ending most programs and occasionally serving as a "chaser" that encouraged audiences to leave the continuous programs rather than retain their seats to watch them a second time. Occasionally, however, films appeared as a featured act, as did Edison's *The Great Train Robbery*. Although the famous Electric Theater, which showed films as its main attraction, opened in Los Angeles in 1902 (near South Main and Third Streets) as part of a fairly short-lived West Coast group of film theaters,[1] and although there were undoubtedly other theaters that featured films as their primary fare in urban centers across the country, these years preceded the nickelodeon explosion. Vaudeville theaters remained the primary venue for films, but films were shown in a large number of places and situations. Traveling exhibitors offered film shows in opera houses or other local and rural theaters, or in their own tents (sometimes called "blacktops" due to their attempt to darken the interior for daytime showings). While the fairground circuit was never as developed in the United States as in Europe, mobile exhibitors certainly brought films to a broader public. Carnivals, circuses, minstrel shows, amusement parks, travel lecturers, and showboats—indeed, the whole range of popular entertainment included films at one point or another. Since the production companies sold prints of films rather than leasing them, mobile means of exhibition allowed the purchasers of such prints to maximize their investment by offering it to new audiences. Likewise, vaudeville circuits not only changed films frequently but circulated them among chains of interrelated theaters. Vaudeville theaters could also contract for films and projection from film service organizations, such as the service offered by the Biograph Company or by entrepreneurs who acted as middlemen between the theaters and the producers.

Since most films were short (the longest filled a 1,000-foot reel, lasting less than twenty minutes, but few reached this length), film programs typically included several films. The variety format, emphasizing a range of types of films, predominated. In vaudeville, films shared the stage with other acts. Those exhibitors in other venues who featured films also included other forms of entertainment (singers, comics, dancers, or lantern slides). In the vaudeville theaters, musical accompaniment from the house orchestra accompanied most—but, as Rick Altman has demonstrated, not all—films (some film shows were presented silently, as were certain films within a program [Altman]). More modest venues probably offered a range of accompaniment, from single instruments to phonographs, as well as silence. The films shown covered a number of genres. Actualities (films of actual events) continued to dominate film production, although they were not necessarily the most popular films unless they captured a major news event (films of the Boer War were quite popular in these years, whether they were items actually shot in South Africa or more dramatic reenactments shot in New Jersey). Since dramatic real events were unpredictable, most actuality films offered travel views or other curiosities. Staged films were almost invariably comic in tone, whether brief gags consisting of a single shot or the more elaborate comic films constructed by linking a number of gags together around a single character or situation. Trick films featured cinematic disappearances, transformations, or supernatural beings (giants, Lilliputians, transparent phantoms), which appeared as well in the new story films, based on well-known fairytales. Although Edwin S. Porter made a film in this mode in 1902, *Jack and the Beanstalk*, most of the fare came from France, primarily the George Méliès and Pathé companies (or the American film companies who sold pirated duped versions of these films). In this period, especially in 1903, French films began to fill American screens, predominantly the products of Pathé, and most American production companies imported foreign films, legally or illegally, from England and France.

Film production in the United States primarily came from the Edison Manufacturing Company and the American Mutoscope and Biograph Company, bitter commercial rivals locked in patent disputes for years. Edison's motion picture patents and his aggressive legal tactics had discouraged other film producers (forcing Albert E. Smith and J. Stuart Blackton of Vitagraph and "Colonel" William N. Selig to operate as Edison licensees, legally bound to pay him a royalty fee based on his patents). Biograph resisted Edison, believing its own patents, originally designed to evade Edison's specifications, legally powerful. In 1902, a court decision disallowed Edison's film patents as being too broad and demanded they be revised and reissued. Edison complied quickly and resumed his lawsuits. But the breach in his threats provided a breather in the patents war, and encouraged Biograph to expand its production (Sigmund Lubin, who had suspended production, also relaunched his film business). Biograph decided to switch from its large film format of 68 mm to the Edison standard, still used today, of 35 mm and began reprinting its older films. In 1903, it ceased offering its full service of films and projection to vaudeville theaters and only sold prints. The company began constructing a new film studio on Fourteenth Street in New York City, which was illuminated entirely by electrical light in contrast to the standard glass studios that relied on sunlight. Biograph's film production dwindled while the studio was being finished, but went into high gear in late 1903, offering many short comic films as well as a number of longer films such as *Kit Carson*, *A Search for Evidence*, and *The Pioneers*. Edison, operating out of a studio on Twenty-third Street in New York, produced a number of innovative films under the control of cameraman Edwin Porter. The other American producers, such as Selig in Chicago and Lubin in Philadelphia, concentrated more on providing exhibition services and importing or duping the films of their rivals, but they also made a few short comedies and actualities.

Films as Attractions

The majority of films produced and shown in the United States in this two-year period were short films with little narrative development, examples of what I have termed the "cinema of attractions," which dominated the first decade of film history. Attractions displayed tourist sights, camera tricks, vaudeville acts, or brief gags. Naturally, films that seem to anticipate the film styles we are more familiar with, telling stories over a series of shots, such as *The Great Train Robbery*, tend to draw the historian's attention. Likewise, contemporary filmgoers became fascinated by the longer films, whether the fairytales of Méliès and Pathé or the more action-driven films of Porter and Biograph. But film production and film shows were still dominated by the shorter, less narratively driven films (Abel). A close examination of the longer films also reveals their transitional nature, combining attractions with narrative techniques.

An attraction displays something to an audience and does not try either to create an extensive course of action or to develop characters, evoking surprise and wonder rather than suspense. Biograph's (1903) *A Windy Day at the Flatiron Building* filmed pedestrians passing New York's most recent skyscraper on the city's most windy corner. The cameraman A. E. Weed set up his camera framing the sidewalk in front of the building so that passersby appear sometimes framed quite close and sometimes in full figure. The attraction of the film lies not only in showing a busy urban crowd but in the wind, which whips the long skirts of women and against which men and women have to secure their hats. (Martin Scorsese re-created this shot for his period film *The Age of Innocence* [1993].) The wind blows off the hat of an African American gentleman in the foreground while other men struggle to retain theirs. The film records a situation, not a story with a beginning, middle, and end. The viewer's attention moves here and there, attracted by briefly appearing passersby in their struggle with the wind. Some notice the camera and react to it, but most hurry past. We are drawn to individual faces or figures or behavior; then they disappear, a typical experience of the urban stroller, here heightened by the drama of the weather. Although one could describe the film as consisting of a single shot, close examination reveals numerous jumps in the action. These are not the result of damage but of the common practice of stopping the camera briefly in order not to waste film when the action seemed less interesting (a practice often finessed further by editing a few frames out before the film was printed). But here, no editing articulates a drama or varies our viewpoints. The film focuses on display and revelation, addressing the viewer: "Here's an unusual or amusing sight—watch!"

Edison's *Electrocution of an Elephant* filmed the public electrocution of Topsy, a circus elephant that had killed a man (reportedly after being burned by his cigarette). The execution was attended by 1,500 onlookers; Edison, who had frequently stressed the danger of alternating current, the type of electricity advocated by his rival in the power business, Westinghouse, was delighted not only to film a curious attraction but to demonstrate the deadly effect of electricity, even on a huge elephant. The film consists of two shots, one in which Topsy is brought onto the site with a slight pan following the elephant. The second shot, after the elephant has been secured on the metal plate that would deliver the charge, records the smoke rising from the animal's feet as they are burned by the voltage, then the elephant toppling over (the camera reframing slightly and then lingering until the elephant's leg, after twitching a bit, collapses). Again, although time plays an important role here in the unfolding of the event,

Edison's *Electrocution of an Elephant* filmed the public electrocution of Topsy, a circus elephant that had killed a man (Edison, 1903). GRAFICS collection. Digital frame enlargement.

the film basically waits and watches as the attraction unfolds before it, in all its horror.

Attractions could also be of staged scenes shot on sets. Biograph's *Hooligan in Jail* offers a good example. The film features the famous cartoon tramp character created by Fred Opper, Happy Hooligan, with his signature chin whiskers and tin can hat. Hooligan is being held in a set of a jail cell, presumably for vagrancy. Hooligan is given a bowl of food. The cameraman then glides the camera directly in toward Happy as he eats, expressing his hunger and delight with broad facial expressions. The very smooth camera movement suggests it was most likely mounted on rails, a device used at the time mainly for varying camera distance rather than facilitating actual camera movement. This unusual technique does not intensify a dramatic turning point, or reveal any important detail. Rather, true to the cinema of attractions, it intensifies the act of display, enlarging Hooligan's face in a manner difficult to achieve in any other medium, and thus displaying the unique capabilities of the cinema at the same time. Ending with a close view (what today we would call a close-up) of Hooligan, the film recalls a genre of early films that consisted of facial expressions in close framings. Derived from the tradition of drawn caricatures and the fairground and music hall

Hooligan is given a bowl of food (*Hooligan in Jail*, Biograph, 1903). GRAFICS collection. Digital frame enlargement.

tradition of clowns and other performers making exaggerated grimaces, this facial expression genre shows the way the cinema of attractions could encourage filmmakers to explore the visual possibilities of the cinema.

Attraction with Storytelling: *The Gay Shoe Clerk*

The new, longer story films that appeared in 1902–1903 combined narrative tasks with visual attractions. A short 1903 film shot by Porter for the Edison Company, *The Gay Shoe Clerk*, also uses the visual display offered by the enlargement of the close-up, but in a manner that seems more familiar to modern audiences. This three-shot gag film features the erotic display frequently found in the cinema of attractions. A young woman comes to a shoe store accompanied by an older woman. A male shoe clerk helps the young woman try on shoes, and as the pair flirts he kisses her. This makes the older woman furious; she gives the clerk a beating and leaves with her young companion. A close-up of the woman's ankle and foot forms the central shot of the film, literally and dramatically. *The Gay Shoe Clerk* seems to anticipate and perhaps even to originate the later classical practice of the cut-in from the wider view to close-up, so basic to classical film storytelling. However, given how many films are lost from this early period, finding the "first" example of a technique remains futile. A number of films from this period used cut-ins to closer views, especially films by the early British filmmakers such as *Grandma's Reading Glass* (1900) or *As Seen through a Telescope* (1900) (which also enlarges a view of a lady's ankle). But as part of the vocabulary of classical editing, the close-up hardly calls attention to itself, while this shot of the ankle in *Gay Shoe Clerk* does. Rather than being the vehicle of a story—the way to get information essential to the story across to the viewer—this shot delivers the key moment of the film, its central attraction, as much as a means of conveying the key action. As in *Hooligan in Jail*, the shot enlarges a body part and displays it onscreen for the viewer. But differences also intervene between the two films, making Porter's film seem both more familiar and more narratively driven. Instead of the gradual approach and enlargement of Hooligan through camera movement, Porter cuts to a closer view, a technique that is more immediate and, arguably, more invisible, drawing less attention to the act of display. Further, the close-up appears in a more dramatic context. Whereas Hooligan is displayed for the film viewer, the display of the ankle here is part of the fictional action, as the young woman provocatively raises

A male shoe clerk helps the young woman try on shoes (*The Gay Shoe Clerk*, Edison, 1903). GRAFICS collection. Digital frame enlargement.

her hemline displaying ankle and calf (and petticoat)—not only to us, but to the clerk. This act of display has a target within the fictional world. This does not undercut the fact that we, too, are the recipient of this voyeuristic view, but it does embed it more firmly into the film's story. The close-up not only marks the clerk's point of interest (although it could not literally be considered a point-of-view shot), but also the key action of the film of the young woman's flirtation, which leads to the next action, the kiss, which then leads to the next action, the beating. Thus *The Gay Shoe Clerk* demonstrates how early cinema blended display and storytelling, creating a scenario based on the act of display.

The role of cinema as a narrative seems so dominant today that film theorists have sometimes assumed it to be inherent in the form itself. But in fact it is during these years that narrative first shapes cinematic form. The sort of storytelling in the new "story films," as Charles Musser has called them (*Before* 200), however, does not precisely correspond to later classical cinematic narrative forms. In 1902–1903 filmmakers were devising methods of cinematic storytelling, rather than relying on long traditions. They drew on a variety of models, and the patterns to be found in literature and the theater of narrative and drama often played a very secondary role. Visual models came from magic lantern slide shows, comic strips, and cartoon caricatures, illustrated children's books, as well as spectacular stage shows, such as fairy pantomimes, vaudeville sketches, ballets, magic shows, Wild West Shows, and equestrian spectacles, even pageants. Thus, narrative films made in these years drew on sources that already included a strong element of visual display: for example, Biograph's series of short films based on both the *Foxy Grandpa* comic strip by Charles "Bunny" Schultze and the Broadway musical revue inspired by this comic strip (written and starring Joseph Hart, who also appeared in the films). A large number of films in these two years are based on characters, stories, or situations that audiences would find familiar from other forms of popular entertainment, and often from several such sources in combination (as in the case of the *Foxy Grandpa* films familiar from comic strips, musical review, and a variety of ephemera from buttons to postcards). Early films offered other versions of images that circulated through popular culture, endowed with the novelty of motion and projection.

Familiar Narrative: *Jack and the Beanstalk*

Charles Musser has pointed out that in this era, early filmmakers based their films on well-known material not only to take advantage of built-in popularity but also to aid understanding of the story line. Comic strip characters generally possessed a few recurring characteristics and performed recurrent gags (Foxy Grandpa played tricks on his nephews; Hooligan endured being a social outcast with good-natured humor). Everyone (even today) knows the plots of certain fairytales and can follow them with a few visual cues. The Edison Company undoubtedly decided to film *Jack and the Beanstalk* because of the popularity of the longer French fairytale films on the vaudeville circuit. But the Edison Company also recognized that such stories were not only popular with children but familiar to the whole audience. For nearly a century fairytales had been adapted in a variety of highly visual forms. Magic lantern shows presented them in a series of painted slides, children's books illustrated them, advertising cards and other ephemera included images from them, and, perhaps most important, for at least a century fairy pantomimes had presented theatrical versions of fairy tales with music, dance, elaborate sets, and magical theatrical effects, ending with an elaborate tableau known as an apotheosis. Most of the early fairytale films (the fairytale film was primarily a French genre, although British and American fairy pantomimes also appeared on film) drew specifically on this stage tradition in their scenography and visual style. *Jack and the Beanstalk* closely followed this tradition.

As Musser has shown in his detailed and insightful analysis of this film, *Jack and the Beanstalk* was one of the most elaborate productions ever offered by any American production company (*Before* 200–207). The film quite consciously uses the theatrical aspects of the fairy pantomime tradition. The framing of the shots reproduces a proscenium arch, with the actors filling less than half the height of the frame when standing. The scenes are staged frontally, with the camera directly in front of the set at a right angle and with offscreen areas rarely playing important roles except for entrances and exits of characters. The sets use the system of painted flats placed at different distances that nineteenth-century theater had evolved to create a sense of depth and recession out of easily movable two-dimensional elements (see Vardac). Although these sets strike the modern eye as artificial, they create a complex and carefully arranged scenic effect. The opening scene (shot 1) includes not only a flat of a mill on the left (placed in diagonal recession to create a perspective of foreshortening and depth) but a moving three-dimensional mill wheel, a revolving canvas representing a waterfall in the middle background, and beyond it a painted flat or backdrop of a mountain, while to the left a three-dimensional bridge leads off to the left on a diagonal behind a two-dimensional tree. No one would mistake this set for an actual exterior, but the elaborate design impressed viewers with its variety, depth, and motion, while its artificiality does seem out of place in a fairytale. The action of this first scene (the fairy appearing and conjuring the magic beans that a man then trades for Jack's cow) depends primarily on the audience's ability to follow it based on their foreknowledge of the fairytale. The first shot highlights the spectacular attractions: the set; the magical disappearance of the fairy; and the hilarious cow made of two men who comically dance their way through the part and nearly steal the show. But the motivations for the action—the poverty of Jack's family and his mother giving him the mission of selling the family cow in order to sustain them—are present only in the preknowledge of the story or in a lecture that might have been delivered as the film was projected; as Musser has pointed out, the Edison Company's description of the film could form the basis of just such a lecture. This description supplies a motivation— "Jack's mother being very poor, dispatched him to the market to sell their only cow [so] that they may not starve"—that is not otherwise alluded to on the screen. This indicates the challenge encountered by filmmakers telling stories on the screen in 1902. Attractions—performances, elaborate magical effects—could be filmed. But motivations that define and impel character often had to be supplied either from cultural knowledge or from a lecturer standing offscreen. Film lecturers were not infrequent in film shows and certainly could make story films more comprehensible, but they also operated within the scenography of display and attractions, not only pointing out key moments to the viewer but also commenting on the beauty or ingenuity of the attractions. Thus Edison's description for *Jack and the Beanstalk* directs attention to such things as the "beautiful moon light and cloud effects" of the backdrop as the magical bean stalk grows, or the visual presentation of the objects in Jack's dream: "One by one these articles appear and disappear in the picture, coming as if from the dim distance, and as quickly and silently fading away."

Theatrical fairy pantomimes consisted of a series of scenes, often described as "tableaux" or pictures, due to their highly spectacular nature (see Kessler). Thus, this form offered early filmmakers a highly visual scenography that strung together scenes, each usually filmed in a single shot, united by the unfolding of the story. In *Jack and the Beanstalk*, the transition between shots is made by a brief overlap dissolve, a technique already used by Méliès in his fairy pantomime films but derived initially from the "dissolving views" of magic lantern shows, which used an optical overlapping to switch from one slide image to the next. Thus even the cutting between shots becomes a visually pleasant attraction. We dissolve from the butcher leading the recalcitrant cow over the bridge to shot 2, the set of the exterior of Jack's house, as his mother scorns the beans he has just received and dumps them on the ground before they both go into the house. A fade to black and then a fade-in bring on shot 3 showing the same location, only the painted backdrop now shows a moon in a dark sky. The change of set and the fade rather than the dissolve indicate an ellipsis in time to night, as the fairy enters and causes the magical beanstalk to grow (the theatrical device of an "invisible" wire pulls the plant up). A dissolve to shot 4 brings us into the garret where Jack can be seen sleeping.

The fairy appears magically (through stop motion and a substitution splice) and waves her wand over Jack. As she disappears, an image of a painted beanstalk appears in the right corner of the garret. Following conventions of fairy pantomime staging, and of book illustration, we understand this as a visualization of Jack's dream. Illustrations had used such inserts to portray dreams for centuries while theater often opened a section of the set (hence called *découverte*) or used a projection of an image on a scrim to indicate a dream or vision (see Vardac). Filmmaker Porter creates an elegant cinematic equivalent as a double exposure makes the beanstalk seem to float upon the air. Resting at the base of the beanstalk is a horn of plenty from which emerge a variety of objects that, if one knows the story, refer to the treasures that the giant holds in his castle in the sky, reached by climbing the beanstalk. Bags of gold dance about, suspended on strings; a winged harp similarly moves through the air; a white hen seems through filmic manipulation to lay a large egg, which then through a similar manipulation grows progressively larger until it is human size, at which point it cracks in two and reveals a richly costumed princess. The dream vision then fades from view and Jack rises from his bed and rushes to look out the window.

Musser has alertly pointed out a lapse in continuity between the end of this shot and the beginning of the next (shot 5), which again is bridged by a dissolve. This shot returns to the exterior view as Jack looks out the window and sees the towering beanstalk that has grown overnight. Since the last shot ended with Jack looking out the window we assume a continuous time, but Jack, no longer wearing the nightgown seen in the previous shot, is fully dressed. Is this what would later be called an error in continuity? Or should we assume a temporal ellipsis between the two shots, time enough for Jack to get dressed? Musser is almost certainly right to judge that Porter and his audience were most likely unconcerned about precise temporal relations. But he is also right to raise the issue, since this cut faces a situation that films in these years will find challenging. When shots occur in different spaces, temporal relations between them can remain vague.

However, difficulties appear when spaces are brought close together by a cut, such as the interior and exterior views of Jack's home, especially when they are connected by a window or doorway, and—most important—when a continuous action seems to bridge the two spaces. We explore this issue further with Porter's *Life of an American Fireman* and Biograph's *Next!*

Simple movement out of the frame into another, adjoining space allowed a simple and clear narrative progression, as in the dissolve from the end of this shot, as Jack climbs the beanstalk out of the frame at the top, to the next (shot 6), with Jack continuing to climb as the top of the beanstalk reaches into the clouds. Somewhat conventional pantomimic gestures could also substitute for dialogue, as when Jack announces his intention to climb the stalk by miming climbing with his hands, while his mother expresses her disapproval by shaking her fist. But the film continuously balances narrative progression with visual attractions. After Jack climbs the beanstalk out of the frame, a troupe of young children rush in, followed soon by some adults. Although the description explains that they are Jack's schoolmates, the true motivation appears as they join hands and do a dance around the beanstalk. This is followed by Jack reaching the giant's realm and meeting his fairy (shot 7), who must inform him that a giant lives in a castle nearby where he keeps the treasures Jack saw in his dream, and also that these treasures once belonged to Jack's father before the giant stole them. A viewer of the film can only gather this information from her foreknowledge of the story, or from a lecturer or other commentary outside the film. The film, however, comes as close as possible to conveying this information through visual means. The fairy appears magically, first on a crescent moon in the sky and then on the ground next to Jack, and just as abruptly disappears after she speaks to Jack and points off toward the castle. Her information takes visual form as the moon disappears from the dark sky leaving a black void against which a circular insert comes into focus showing a painting of the castle on a cliff. This circular image resembles circular framed magic lantern images, as if the fairy shows Jack a lantern show of her information. Like the dream vision invoked by the fairy earlier, this technique of an inserted vision scene may also come directly from a theatrical model.

The shots that conclude the fairytale follow Jack's physical journey to the castle and back down the beanstalk, but enough space and time exist between shots to avoid the temporal ambiguities that arise with close continuity. The next shot (shot 8) shows a rather elaborate set of the hall in the giant's castle. The giant's wife hides Jack as the giant enters and looks over his treasures. Jack emerges and steals the gold, harp, and hen and is pursued out the door by the giant. With a dissolve to Jack's house (shot 9), the bags of gold drop from above. Then Jack climbs down and sets himself to chopping down the beanstalk, finally causing it to collapse with the giant, who falls to his death. The fairy appears and with a wave of her wand magically turns Jack and his mother into richly costumed royalty. The final static shot 10 re-creates the apotheosis that traditionally ended fairy pantomimes. The mother and son sit within an ornate set of a sailboat led by the fairy, all posed in a static tableau. The only movement in the shot comes from a spinning circular pattern that may represent the sun and a visual effect of ripples on the water. As Musser points out, the Edison description that may have guided a lecturer's commentary "assigns a narrative significance to the last tableau it otherwise lacks," describing it as a voyage to the castle which will be their future home. However, the tableau brings the film to a close less through narrative completion than through a visual climax, its pictorial nature emphasized by its frozen pose.

Story Time

Creating a consistent and continuous sense of time posed a new frontier for story films. As films began to follow actions over more than one shot, the models of practices that filmmakers drew on (such as the succession of magic lantern slides or the layout of a comic strip) did not exist in time in the same way that motion pictures did. In 1902–1903, films tried out ways of dealing with time that differ from later practices. Both close continuity of action and simultaneity posed problems. A Biograph film, *The Story the Biograph Told*, portrayed the simultaneity of a telephone call in a manner that was ingenious but obscure. The shot shows both a man in his office and his wife at home as they speak to each other, but they appear in superimposition overlapping visually so that neither of them is clearly seen. Temporal relations are clear—if one can make out the action in the image, which in fact is very difficult to do. Later films portray phone calls with a split screen, showing both ends of the conversation, but each restricted to a separate part of the screen, thus avoiding the visual obscurity of the superimposition.

Another Biograph film from 1903, *Next!* consists of two shots, showing the problem of portraying continuity of action. Based on a comic strip by Frederick Burr Opper, the film featured two overly polite Frenchmen, each of whom repeatedly indicates that the other should go first as they enter doorways or vehicles ("After you, Alphonse"; "You first, my dear Gaston"). A burly man becomes infuriated with the delay caused by these two and tosses the pair out a window. The second shot switches to the exterior of the window, which initially appears intact. Then the two men come crashing through successively. The action is clear and the spatial relation between the two shots (inside and outside) is also clear. However, to a modern viewer, something seems strange. Most modern films maintain a rather strict continuity of time when an action continues over contiguous locations joined by a cut. We would see the man starting to toss out the hapless Alphonse and Gaston, and then, as they were propelled toward the window, the cut would follow the action seamlessly and continuously. Here, however, Alphonse and Gaston crash through the window once, seen from inside the room, and then we switch to a view from outside in which we see them crash through again. The film certainly does not indicate that this action happens twice; rather, we see it twice from two different viewpoints. But from a modern viewpoint it seems that time stutters and repeats itself. Film historians refer to this form of editing as a temporal overlap. In the 1920s, filmmakers like Sergei Eisenstein would return to it to create elaborate rhythms, and editors in the 1970s occasionally used it as well (e.g., Walter Murch in *Apocalypse Now* [1979]). But for 1902 such a repetition should not be considered as a violation or mistake (since rules of temporality were not yet in place), nor was it an artistic flourish. Indeed, one might see it as a compromise between the desire that story films showed for continuity of action over several shots and variance of point of view, and the logic of display that here gives the viewer two spectacular crashes through the window instead of just one.

A more extended example of temporal overlap occurs in a longer film that Porter filmed for the Edison Company in 1902 and released in 1903, *The Life of an American Fireman*. The film demonstrates the way a series of shots could be strung together to create a longer narrative, by focusing on process more than characters. The film includes very disparate shots. Shot 1 shows a man in uniform apparently dozing at a desk (the painted backdrop behind him actually includes a lighting effect: beams coming from a lamp painted over the desk). On the right, a circular "dream balloon" (much like the dream visions in *Jack and the Beanstalk* and drawing on similar stage and magic lantern traditions) shows a woman putting her child to bed. This balloon vision fades out and the fireman rises and exits. This highly theatrical shot with its painted flats dissolves to a very close shot of a fire alarm on an actual city street. The alarm box fills most of the frame, a rather unusual enlargement of an object that serves purely to trigger dramatic action; here we have a close-up clearly designed to deliver story information. An unidentified hand enters the frame and twists the handle, sending the alarm that triggers the fire rescue through a series of closely interrelated and action-dominated shots.

We dissolve from the alarm close-up to a long shot (shot 3) of the firemen's bedroom as they rise from their beds, donning clothes in a single action and sliding down the poles. The next shot (shot 4) follows this action, showing the lower floor of the fire station as men hitch horses to the fire engines and the firemen (after a brief delay that represents a slight temporal overlap) come sliding down the pole and mount their engines, which then charge out of the frame. The following shot presents the exterior of the fire house as the large doors open and the engines emerge (again a slight overlap in time appears). The next shot (shot 5) shows a crowd gathered on a city street to watch the fire engines, which enter charging from right background to left foreground, steam pouring from their boilers, the horses galloping. The next shot (shot 6) shows a more suburban street as the engines enter from the distance on the right (maintaining the same screen direction as in the previous shot). As the last engine passes, the camera pans to the left, settling in front of a house from which smoke pours, as firemen attach and unroll hoses. A cut inside to a set of a bedroom (shot 7) shows a woman asleep as smoke fills the room. She awakes in alarm, then collapses on the bed. A fireman enters through the doorway on the right, smashes the window, and picking up the unconscious woman climbs out the window carrying her over his shoulder. He then reenters through the window and picks up a child (only slightly visible before this) from the bed and carries her out the window as well. Then two firemen enter with a hose and spray the set. Porter then returns to the previous exterior view of the house (shot 8). A fireman rushes in the door. A woman appears in a nightgown at the window. Some firemen raise a ladder to her as others hose down the other side of the house. A fireman emerges from the window carrying a woman down the ladder. Once placed on the ground she makes broad pleading gestures and the fireman mounts the ladder again, emerging this time with the child. The mother watches anxiously and then embraces her child, as other firemen mount the ladder toward the window with the hose.

Life of an American Fireman follows an overarching action, forging a number of shots into a continuous dramatic danger-and-rescue scenario. But what type of story and what type of storytelling is this? As Musser has pointed out, the fire rescue was a familiar topic: it was the subject of lantern slides, a topic of amusement-park reenactment ("Fighting the Flames" became an attraction at Dreamland and other amusement parks), and a familiar "sensation scene" in stage melodramas since the nineteenth century

(*Before* 218–23). Fire and rescue formed a spectacle, an attraction, even more than a narrative situation. *Life of an American Fireman* straightforwardly follows a process rather than creating the narrative enigmas and delays we associate with storytelling. From the alarm to the arrival of the firemen at the house, the film follows a sequence of preparing and racing to a fire that any urban dweller would find familiar. Physical action moving through the frame (the firemen down the pole, the engines out of the station, down the street) also propels the film, even overriding apparent inconsistencies. Besides the temporal overlaps that stretch out actions between shots, lapses in continuity indicate little concern for the consistencies that later Hollywood practice would try to preserve, as the number of vehicles and the colors of the horses vary from shot to shot. Actions rather than characters carry the film. The firemen are not individualized and even the woman and child, undoubtedly stirring audience sympathy, remain distant figures whose actions remain clearer than their faces. The opening shot of the fireman thinking or dreaming of his family may gesture toward creating a character, and the catalogue description rather cautiously states, "The inference is that he dreams of his own wife and child" (see *Before* 215–18). Later viewers may assume that the fireman in shot 1 is the same man who rescues the woman and child in the end and that they are his own family. However, although this is one possible way to approach the film (and lecturers might have supplied this reading), the Edison description does not claim it and the film remains unspecific about who these people are other than rescuers and rescued. Rather than characters we have actants, figures who do things. Who turns on the alarm? A passerby? Someone from the burning house? A repentant arsonist? These would be relevant questions in a character-driven story. But here the significance of the unidentified hand lies in its action of turning the alarm and setting the rescue (and the film) in motion.

The most widely discussed aspect of *Life of an American Fireman*, brilliantly analyzed by Musser (see *Before* 212–34), Noël Burch ("Primitive Mode"), and André Gaudreault ("Detours") decades ago, involves the rescue climax. Building this climax by intensifying and then resolving suspense and concern shows the film's strong narrative impulse. But the way this resolution is cinematically portrayed in terms of time shows again the different regime of filmmaking to which this film belongs, a regime far from later classical storytelling. The last two shots of the film show the rescue twice, once from inside the house, once from outside, thus providing the most extensive example of temporal overlap we have in early American cinema. Because of its length, this example has attracted attention for years, due in part also to the controversy over an alternative version of the film circulated for years by the Museum of Modern Art that eliminated the temporal overlap by intercutting the two views of the rescue continuously. Research by Musser and Gaudreault established that the theatrical prints from the period contained the temporal overlap during the rescue. As Biograph's *Next!* demonstrates, such overlap was no anomaly but a recurrent editing practice in the era. To have two presentations of an especially dramatic scene was an advantage within a cinema still based primarily on a strategy of display rather than on linear and continuous storytelling.

The Great Train Robbery

The most widely known American film from these years is Porter's *The Great Train Robbery*, made for the Edison Company in 1903. The film gained great popularity on its release (and was shown for years to come). Often incorrectly identified as the first western story film, nonetheless this film deserves close attention. The sources the film drew on reflect the usual range of popular culture: a stage melodrama of the same name; the recent news event of a train robbery by the Wild Bunch gang; films about railroads; dime novels of western bandits. Richard Abel has even discovered an advertisement billboard of a western bandit with his gun drawn that may have been the source of the film's famous close-up of the outlaw leader firing his six-gun at the camera (Abel). Since at this time the western gang belonged less to a nostalgic past than to current criminal activity, *The Great Train Robbery* could be considered a contemporary crime film (or even, as David Levy has claimed, a reenacted news item [Levy]) as much as an early western. However, the iconography of the West, from the bandana-wearing outlaw to the cowboys making the dude dance by firing at his shoes, formed part of the film's appeal. Like *Life of an American Fireman*, *The Great Train Robbery* links together shots by following the progression of a larger action, in this case a robbery (including its preparation and execution), an escape, and finally a capture. With a greater consistency than he showed in *Fireman*, Porter interweaves the interiors of the railway station, the railway mail car, and the dance hall with location exteriors of a railway water tower, the track, and the woods into which the robbers escape and are pursued. The bandits, although not individualized, are easily identifiable in their broad-brimmed cowboy hats as they move from shot to shot carrying out the robbery (indeed, a common objection to this and other early crime films was that they detailed the means by which crimes could be committed). Porter integrates his interior sets with exterior locations through quite sophisticated matte work. In the first shot, as the robbers hold up the telegraph operator in the interior of the station, through the window we can see a locomotive arriving, an effect accomplished through a careful double exposure. Likewise, in the set of the mail car, Porter cinematically inserts a landscape whizzing past the open doorway. As Philip Rosen has claimed, this concern for creating a realistic background may be as important as the progression of action to what became known as the Classical Hollywood style (Rosen).

The robbery of the train is a more complex action than the rescue in *Life of an American Fireman*, involving a number of subsidiary actions that Porter interweaves with great clarity. The stationmaster is subdued (shot 1). The train is boarded by the bandits surreptitiously as it takes on water (shot 2). The baggage car is invaded and the safe blown (shot 3). The bandits invade the locomotive and force the engineer to stop the train (shot 4), then climb down and uncouple the locomotive from the rest of the train (shot 5). The passengers are made to disembark and are robbed of their valuables (one man is shot when he tries to flee) (shot 6). The robbers then make a getaway on the uncoupled locomotive (shot 7). Stopping the locomotive some distance away they climb down a hillside, carrying their loot (shot 8). Moving through a wooded area and crossing a stream the bandits then mount their tethered horses (shot 9). In these two shots, the camera follows the outlaws by panning and tilting to keep them in the frame. However, after this clear and basically linear progression, the next shot (shot 10) performs an abrupt about-face and returns us to the location of the opening shot, the station, as a young girl enters, finds a man tied up, and releases him. He rushes out. As Gaudreault has shown, this picking up of another action thread (initiating a counter-action to the robbery, capturing the thieves, and recovering the loot) breaks the clear temporal succession of the previous shots. Exactly when this shot takes place remains rather vague, as do the temporal relations of the remaining shots of the film. After the stationmaster rushes out, the film cuts to the interior of a dance hall (shot 11) as men and women execute a square dance and a dude is given a dancing lesson. This dance and the dude gag basically stall the narrative progression in favor of a bit of spectacular entertainment. In the surviving tinted print, this scene, like the blowing of the safe and the concluding close-up of the gun firing into the audience, has the most striking coloration, emphasizing these shots as attractions even when they also play a narrative role. If the dance serves any narrative purpose, it is simply delay. At the end of the number, the stationmaster rushes in and apparently tells about the robbery; men rush out at the end of the shot carrying rifles. A striking shot (shot 12) of a chase on horseback shows the posse close behind the outlaws, firing at them, with the gun smoke brightly tinted. One of the outlaws is shot and falls from his horse. The next shot (shot 13) shows the outlaws dismounted, going over their loot in the forest while the posse creeps up from behind and kills them, then gathers up their ill-gotten gains. The final shot (shot 14) shows the close-up of the gang member firing his pistol directly into the viewer's face. The climax of the film is more ambiguous in its narrative and temporal structure than the first two-thirds. After the scene at the dance hall, the posse is shown suddenly close on the heels of the outlaw gang. Then in the next shot the gang members have rather unaccountably dismounted and let their pursuers sneak up on them. My point here is not plausibility, but rather that the final scenes show a more random linkage in terms of time and action. The action runs more smoothly if one eliminates the horseback chase, but clearly Porter recognized a good scene when he saw one. Spectacle took precedence over consistency.

Action, rather than individualized characters, holds the film together. Actors rarely appear to fill more than about half the frame. This distant framing shows people moving through space instead of individualizing them. The film does not use its single close-up of the bandit (as later narrative filmmakers would) to create a recognizable character, convey emotion through enlarged facial expressions, or create empathy. This shot remains outside the course of linked actions. In fact, the description of the film in the Edison catalogue indicated this shot could be placed either at the end or the beginning of the film, as exhibitors wished. As Burch has indicated, the shot seems to wander around the periphery of the film rather than embed itself at its core ("A Primitive Mode of Representation"). The shot functions very much as a semi-independent facial expression shot. The direct firing at the audience corresponded to that genre's use of direct address to the audience (nods, winks, and laughs at the camera often appear in these films), acknowledging itself as an attraction, a moment of display. The gunshot at the camera, with its smoky explosion, adds to the shock and impact of this direct address. (Musser claims the shot fired at the audience creates antipathy toward the bandits, a reading I find plausible but more ingenuous than convincing, and by no means an exclusive interpretation [*Before* 256].) As sophisticated as we can find its mastery of action, *The Great Train Robbery* still bridges two modes of filmmaking that can at points interfere with each other.

But one could find similar examples in later films even during the sound era. American cinema was not only a narrative form but a spectacular one, and although the narrative increasingly served as a dominating integrating force, one can see from these films of 1902 and 1903 that if American cinema possesses an enduring tradition, it lies in the balancing of showmanship with storytelling. In these years, display often outbid narrative consistency.

NOTES
1. I thank Paul Moore for this information on West Coast Electric Theaters.

1904–1905

Movies and Chasing the Missing Link(s)

ANDRÉ GAUDREAULT

As far as the development of motion pictures is concerned, 1904 and 1905 could be seen as years of revolution and, at the same time, of consolidation of production and exhibition. As far as production is concerned, these are the years when the chase film came on the scene; it would play a key role in the evolution of what we call "film form." With respect to exhibition, these are the years in which itinerant exhibition gave way to fixed-venue exhibition. These two developments were the most emblematic of the transformations—mutations, we might say—taking place in the newborn world of kinematography in the early years of the century.

The importance of the chase film has by now been well established. Charles Musser even makes the audacious claim that, with the 1904 chase film *Personal*, "the Biograph Company was the first in the United States, if not the world, to make the decisive shift toward fiction 'feature' films— headline attractions that filled at least half a thousand-foot reel" (*Emergence* 375). This claim is indicative of the capital importance for film historians of the chase film at this crucial point in film history. Establishing its structure as indispensable, as an inescapable model, the chase film encouraged film-makers to conceive of animated views as a series of juxtaposed tableaux in need of stronger links between them. For several years, the first multi-shot films (in contrast to single-shot films) had been presenting the viewer with a significant narrative challenge: the large gaps that the narrative left between tableaux made understanding the film difficult in the absence of adequate links. Viewers had to fill in these gaps if they were to grasp the gist of what they were seeing, although a well-placed intertitle, a benevolent lecturer, or familiarity with the story being told sometimes made this challenge less insurmountable.

Generally speaking, the chase film is the essence of simplicity. It poses no such problems of comprehension, if only because its structure is based on repeating the same basic set-up, shot after shot. An initial shot shows an event that sets the chase in motion, and the tableaux that follow almost invariably show the same action: a character (or sometimes several characters) runs toward the camera (and thus toward the viewer) and then leaves our field of vision, at which point several (rarely just one) characters appear in the background in pursuit, following the same route. This is how *Personal* unfolds, as do the following American films, some of the best known of the entire period: *The Bold Bank Robbery* (Lubin), *The Escaped Lunatic* (Biograph), *How a French Nobleman Got a Wife through the New York Herald "Personal" Columns* (Edison), *The Lost Child* (Biograph), *The Maniac Chase* (Edison), and *The Suburbanites* (Biograph), all from 1904; and *The Counterfeiters* (Lubin), *Stolen by Gypsies* (Edison), *Tom, Tom, the Piper's Son* (Biograph), and *The White Caps* (Edison), from 1905.

In the exhibition sector, the transition from itinerant to fixed-venue exhibition came about, in particular, through the introduction of another kind of link (a "missing link" in this case) between the film producer and the exhibitor: the film renter (known as film exchanges). Somehow, films had to make their way from the producer to the exhibitor's projection facilities in an economically sensible way. The mere presence of this new intermediary between the producer and the exhibitor, with its built-in predictability and regularity of operation, made possible, late in this period, the appearance of a specifically American institution: the nickelodeon, the first form of specialized moving picture theater. As I explain below, the creation of links, even tenuous ones, between the tableaux in multi-shot films and the rise of the missing link between film producers and exhibitors transformed the emerging world of kinematography.

The very nature of the chase film fits quite well with the project of creating specialized moving picture theaters. We might even say that chase films and the nickelodeon were two sides of the same coin: both are clear signs of the predominant role that stories were beginning to take in films, or, put a little differently, of the predominant role that story films were beginning to take in cinema. In order to grow and spread, nickelodeons needed narrative films such as chase films, which depicted fairly breathless adventures and comic incidents and made it possible to introduce unexpected situations. This raised the likelihood of the viewer's keen interest with both what passed across the screen and what came to pass on it. It also made it possible to install these viewers in a relationship of duration with the screen. The mere fact that an ordinary chase film was much longer than the usual "snap shot" (as was another genre in fashion at the time, the sensational melodrama) made screenings of animated views less heterogeneous. Access to a variety of longer films provided the exhibitor with fewer elements with which to create a program of films. This also contributed to changing viewers' expectations with respect to the length of the show and that of its component parts, the films themselves. In these days it was not unusual for films to be three or four times longer than the "prescribed" two- to three-minute length at the turn of the century (and ten to twenty times the length of the first Edison and Lumière film strips, which were less than a minute long). Thus, to mention only a few examples, *Personal* was 371 feet long, giving a projection time of six or seven minutes, and *Meet Me at the Fountain* (Lubin, 1904) was 465 feet, for a projection time of about eight minutes. Some films even reached hitherto unseen heights: the Biograph film *The Moonshiners* (1904, 960 feet) would have run for about fifteen minutes.

Gradually, with the growth of specific venues like the nickelodeons, where one could take part in the new practice of going to the cinema that was taking hold in society, a faithful audience was created for the new entertainment by presenting views that were more complete, more complex, and more finished than what viewers had seen before.

That said, the world of kinematography was still in an in-between state, as the caterpillar "kinematograph" began to transform itself into the butterfly "cinema." This was true because, in particular, despite a few moves toward narration, attraction still ruled animated views. The principle of the attraction in cinema is well known: it is a mode of representation that privileges the spectacular quality of what is in front of the camera rather than its potential for narrative development. An attractional view shows spectacular events that startle viewers, an action that suddenly grips them, or an effect that astonishes and amuses them more than it tells a story capable of moving or captivating them (on this topic, see the previous chapter in this volume by Tom Gunning). This is the mode of representation that holds sway in what I have recently suggested we call "kine-attractography" (Gaudreault "Primitive"),[1] wherein the attraction is the principal paradigm. Indeed, as we shall soon see, it was only very timidly that the attraction began in these years to yield to narration. Most films on offer to exhibitors, and which were offered in turn to viewers by exhibitors, remained subject to the principles of attraction—even in the case of the increasingly numerous multi-shot films such as chase films or sensational melodramas which, at the same time, made use of cinema's various narrative faculties. In chase films, for example, what people saw, and were captivated by, were objects and people racing about, repetitively following one another in the same space, and the thrust of things toward or away from the camera. In short: movement itself. The fact that a film is what I have called, following Eisenstein, "pluripunctiliar" (made up of a series of shots rather than a single tableau) (Gaudreault *From Plato*) is not a guarantee of absolute adherence to the narrative principle because, as I discuss below, a great many "pluripunctiliar" films display no interest in the prospect of narrative development.

These years are pivotal years, a period that defines the borders of two worlds. On one hand is the world—now in the past—of the medium's minor beginnings (the invention of cinema, the first films, the arrival of the very first permanent exhibition venues, and so forth), and on the other the world—yet to come—of major changes (cinema's development as an art form, the amalgamation of commercial interests in the production sector, and the medium's institutionalization).

A World of Major Changes Full of Minor Beginnings

The world itself is both a witness to and actor in the minor beginnings and major changes that announce great upheavals. In Moscow, Czar Nicholas II was confronted with the first Soviets during the first, and unsuccessful, Russian revolution (of 1905), when the Battleship *Potemkin* (the real one!) made its remarkable entry into history. While docked at the port of Odessa in June, the ship was the site of a famous mutiny that would be a source of inspiration for the Russian revolutionaries of 1917. What the mutiny of these Russian sailors announced was that the world would soon be separated and divided into two great spheres of influence. At the other end of the world, in America, the earth itself, in a sense, was divided in two when the United States purchased France's equipment and installations to continue digging the Panama Canal, leading to a quite empirical separation of the Americas. And yet this division was conceived not to isolate peoples from each other but rather to bring them together by shortening the distances separating them by sea. On one side lay Europe and Africa; on the other, Asia. Even the east and west coasts of the United States would be joined, as ships would no longer have to travel around Cape Horn at the southern tip of South America. Excavations were also under way during these years, but this time on terra firma, in New York, where on 27 October 1904 the first underground line of the New York City subway was opened. The city of St. Louis hosted both a World's Fair and the third Olympic Games of modern times. Theodore Roosevelt was elected president. In the Far East, the Russo-Japanese war began, ending with Russia's defeat in 1905. The year 1905 was also when two important works were published: Albert Einstein's special theory of relativity and the novel *The Clansman* by Thomas Dixon Jr.

Naturally, most of these events were depicted on the screen. The *Potemkin* mutiny was seen around the world thanks to the French firm Pathé, whose re-created actualities were one of its specialties (*Revolution in Russia*, 1905). This genre was equally popular with American producers of animated views, who were quick to produce, on imitation sets thousands of miles from where the events really took place, re-creations of scenes from the Russo-Japanese War. Biograph produced *The Battle of the Yalu* and Edison made *Skirmish between Russian and Japanese Advance Guards* (both 1904). Edison was one of the companies to depict the inauguration of the New York subway, featuring it in a "news story": *Opening Ceremonies, New York Subway, October 27, 1904*. A few months later, interest in the subject appears not to have abated, because Biograph offered its own version: *Interior New York Subway, Fourteenth Street to Forty-second Street* (1905). This film's production involved a number of technical feats. The camera was placed on a platform at the front of a subway train behind another train on the same track, with lighting provided by a device specially built for the purpose and mounted on a car traveling on a parallel track.

The tendency of films to act as extensions of newspapers was confirmed and consolidated. Until recently, it was common to say that the number of actualities fell below that of staged films only after 1907, but today it is generally agreed that the transition occurred around 1904–1905. This was when story films began to dominate the market, preceding the nickelodeon craze of late 1905 and not, as was previously believed, its consequence.

From Itinerant to Fixed-Venue Exhibition

Film production and exhibition were thus beginning to take on a degree of stability. Animated views had now been on the market for ten years, in all kinds of venues and circumstances. The situation was ripe for change. Some of these changes would be major ones. With a very few exceptions, there were still no fixed venues dedicated to projecting moving pictures alone. Films were obliged, therefore, to go to the viewer—by way of itinerant exhibitors—rather than having viewers go to see films. During this period animated views were shown, intermittently and spontaneously, by small-scale showmen in amusement parks, carnivals, community halls, opera houses, and sometimes in major theaters. People had not yet adopted the habit of "going to the cinema." Animated views were generally shown "by invitation" or, in any event, at the invitation of a showman passing through town who put out the word of his presence by means of newspaper ads or handbills. This relationship was about to be reversed, however, because of the role that moving pictures were beginning to take on in vaudeville theaters and because of the rise of the nickelodeon. As Richard Abel remarks, "The trade press reported that moving pictures for the first time [the fall of 1904] had become a regular vaudeville feature in several major cities" (25). The situation was changing and films were occupying an increasingly important place amongst popular entertainments. As Musser reports, in September 1905 George Kleine commented that "we know of no vaudeville house in the United States which does not fill one number of its programme with motion pictures" (*Emergence* 371).

In vaudeville houses, animated views were but one attraction among others and normally had the same status as a vaudeville number, shown between the trained dog act and the contortionist. Nevertheless, this introduction of moving pictures into fixed venues on a regular basis, which had begun in high-class vaudeville houses in the larger cities and in family vaudeville houses in smaller cities, created enormous pressure on the supply of animated views and forced film production companies to step up their production.

This, however, was nothing compared to what was about to happen. The widespread adoption of films in vaudeville houses throughout the fall of 1904 was soon followed, the next summer, by the opening of the first storefront moving picture theaters, the "nickelodeons," which were small venues dedicated to screening animated views. It was not long before this new form of film exhibition cast a shadow on the use of films in vaudeville. As Abel remarks, "George Kleine later singled out December 1905 as a turning point, when nickelodeons began *competing* with vaudeville houses as the primary venue for moving pictures" (80–82).

Historians tell us that nickelodeons were launched in Pittsburgh by a certain Harry Davis when he opened a hall under that name, but it is not certain that this isolated event had any real influence on the course of events. What is certain is that the name of this establishment (a combination of the Greek word "odeon" ["theater"] and the word "nickel," which was the price of admission) quickly entered into the language and became the common term for the very first specialized moving picture theaters. The nickelodeon's emergence was of capital importance: it was now possible for viewers to go to films on their own in permanent venues whose raison d'être was film exhibition. This was a reversal of the relationship between the audience and the film and one that was to prove crucial to subsequent events. Before finding a home in vaudeville houses and nickelodeons, films had no fixed address: they wandered the land, appearing in places that were not their own. And "going to the cinema" was not yet a part of the normal routine of the average person. The cinema could not yet reign over the entertainment world because it had no kingdom from which to do so.

The arrival of nickelodeons was a capital event for cinema's growth because it completely reversed the relationship between film producers and exhibitors. It also brought about an equally radical reversal of the relationship between exhibitors and viewers. The new paradigm required exhibitors to renew their stock of films on a regular basis, something they never had to do before. As John Collier insightfully remarked, the nickelodeon became a neighborhood institution, "cheap amusements" (qtd. in Abel 75–76), which is why the showman who presided over its fortunes needed to attract the same viewers back again week after week (if not more frequently). This was undoubtedly a new kind of exhibitor, with needs completely different from those of the traditional exhibitor who, by virtue of the itinerant nature of his trade, found new viewers (every time he arrived at a new location) rather than acquiring new views. Now, however, market conditions clearly favored itinerant exhibitors over those who wanted to find a home in a fixed venue. One reason is that film producers, at the time, offered only one way to acquire views: by purchasing copies outright, something that required an investment on the part of the exhibitor that could only be paid off by exhibiting the same films over a long period of time.

The Renter as the Missing Link

Since the market itself didn't encourage the establishment of fixed venues, there arose in the United States the missing link that would make the nickelodeon boom possible: the film renter. Thanks to this intermediary, the fixed-venue exhibitor no longer had to pay large sums to purchase films he would show for only a few days to his neighborhood audience. Exhibitors now rented films and returned them immediately after use to the renter, who, to amortize his own costs, would rent out the same (still barely used) films to second-run exhibitors, and so on down the line. This new state of affairs, which reversed the relationship between film exhibitors and producers, also brought about changes in the exhibitor's relationship to the films he showed. Before the film rental system, the films exhibitors showed belonged to them. They had been the property of the film producer who, by selling them, granted all rights concerning them to the exhibitor. The exhibitor thus acquired films that could be used in any way he saw fit: once purchased, they became his property. Film producers were well aware of this situation and even consciously encouraged the idea that the films they sold were, as film historians today remark, semi-finished products. It fell to the exhibitor to polish the product according to his own needs and taste and thus to complete their conception just before projecting them on the screen. The exhibitor was not at all hesitant to "touch up" the views he bought and to play a role in editing them and deciding how they would be shown. It was the exhibitor who decided whether or not to provide a particular view with musical accompaniment and/or a lecture. He showed what he wanted to show, how he wanted to show it, and film producers had no say in what form their products were seen.

The establishment of a film rental system turned everything topsy-turvy. A new era was under way, one that saw exhibitors purchasing not products but rights (to project), rights, moreover, of limited duration. The reversion of property rights to film producers changed everything, and some production companies would soon claim all rights over the ways in which their films were projected (the films were theirs, even if the establishment showing them was not). Within production companies, some people (actors, scriptwriters, directors) began to conceive as their own some of the property rights to views, given that these "works of art" were made by them, with their talent. The time when the exhibitor of views—the showman—would be relegated to the rather limited role of mere theater manager was not far off. That's another story, but it began here, with the various upheavals and sudden reversals that took place in the world of film exhibition.

Near the end of this period, there thus began to appear a growing number of establishments showing animated views on a regular basis. These establishments were also required to change their program relatively frequently—in some cases, as often as once a week. The nickelodeon craze was really taking off. With this sudden increase in demand came a very curious—even unique—phenomenon in the history of American cinema with respect to both film production and exhibition. There were so many exhibitors in need of new films that American producers couldn't keep up with the demand, to such an extent that most of the views shown in the United States were not American. Various French companies, led by Pathé, dominated the nascent film industry at this time, and many European producers grew to such an extent that they had a greater production capacity than their American rivals. Moreover, American producers, caught short for several years, resorted to the unfortunate habit of pirating—simply making duped copies of—European films already on the American market. The French firm Pathé Frères was the only company able, during these years, to promise "to fulfill [the] expectation [to provide a wonderful creation each week], with every possible kind of story film" (Abel 29). American companies such as Edison and Biograph simply could not meet the growing demand.

Nevertheless, two factors helped offset this imbalance. First, the Lubin company began increasing production in the summer of 1905. Second, the Vitagraph company returned to the scene: "Moving into fiction filmmaking during the later part of 1905, Vitagraph promptly established itself as a major American producer" (Musser, *Emergence* 412). And yet not a single American company had more than one film production studio (unlike some of their French competitors, Pathé in particular). To meet this increased demand for films, two American companies, Edison and Vitagraph, began construction of new studios.

The solid place of moving pictures in vaudeville houses would appear to be one of the major factors in the decision to set up theaters specializing in projecting animated views, which were almost exclusively present in them. "Almost" because, in fact, nickelodeons always featured another genre of projected images (another kind of screen practice) in addition to moving pictures: illustrated songs, which always went hand-in-hand with moving pictures in these years. Illustrated songs, as their name suggests, were songs accompanied by the projection of a series of lantern slides. These songs were usually performed live by a flesh-and-blood singer right there in the theater, but they could also be recorded. The songs were illustrated by images, most often still images. In the earliest nickelodeons, therefore, fixed and moving images lived together without shame. The fixed images were invariably accompanied by a musical performance (singing and music), while the moving images were accompanied by a range of sounds (music, singing, sound effects, and/or a lecture). Or there was complete silence: it has recently been discovered that the piano in nickelodeons was not necessarily there to provide musical accompaniment to animated views but may also have been used primarily to entertain viewers between films, or to fill the silence of their arrival or departure (Altman).

A Tiny Genre with a Brilliant Future: The Chase Film

It is not easy to identify which exactly were the first chase films in film history. One might even ask oneself if it is possible to delineate the boundaries of a genre with such precision. Many early films include the beginnings of a chase sequence that is aborted, develops over a very restricted number of shots, or represents only an unimportant part of a story whose main focus lies elsewhere. The classic chase film is in a comic vein and emphasizes the thrills and spills that occur between the event that sets the chase in motion and the end of the film (the initial situation is normally quite simple and can usually be summed up in a single shot), rather than any action that preceded the chase sequence itself, a sequence that often develops over fewer than a dozen shots. Most historians agree that the very first American example was *The Escaped Lunatic*. In the United States, Biograph set the pace for chase films, with this and many other titles that had considerable influence on the entire nascent film industry, notably *Personal* and *The Lost Child*.

The critical importance of the chase film to the development of filmic expression lies in the fact that its basic story line required the use of editing and, as a result of this, that it was pluripunctiliar. The chase film genre found a home, by necessity we might say, in the multishot film. This pluripunctiliar quality, however, was very limited in nature, because the basic structure of the chase film required only a minimum of continuity between the shots it linked together. Such films generally take the following form:

> They open with an initial tableau, revealing a peaceful scene that a character suddenly disrupts (by committing a misdeed of some sort or by some other disruptive action); at the end of the tableau, the offending person takes flight (becoming in the process the pursued).
> The opening tableau is followed by a series of tableaux in the course of which the victims of the misdeed set off in pursuit of the pursued (thereby becoming the pursuers).
> The chase ends when the pursued is caught and punished.

The shots or tableaux in a chase film are so loosely connected that the order in which they appear is interchangeable (except when, in some films, the number of pursuers increases from one shot to the next, in which case for reasons of consistency the shots must be screened in a predetermined order). *Personal*, whose story line maintains the same number of pursuers from beginning to end, is a case of a film in which many shots could be inverted without much effect on its meaning. The film recounts the misadventures of a Frenchman recently arrived in the United States who places an ad in a newspaper in search of a woman to marry. When he arrives at the advertised meeting place, a woman approaches him, immediately followed by several other pretenders to his affections who had also seen the ad. He then takes flight, down streets, across fields, and over streams, pursued by the horde of women. In the end, one of them catches up with him and, brandishing a gun, forces him to agree to marry her.

A Genre Midway between Attraction and Narration

Although the chase film is in some respects a fundamentally attractional genre, it is just as much an essentially narrative genre, telling a rudimentary story: what is an early chase film, in the end, if not the narration of a series of attractions? This means that, as a genre, the heart (so to speak) of the chase wavers between attraction and narration. For this reason, we might say that the chase film, historically speaking, was probably the ideal genre for moving from a paradigm in which attraction was the principal element around which views were conceived and produced to a paradigm in which narration took over. And this is exactly what happened in these years when chase films ruled the roost.

In *Personal*, the chase extends over eight shots basically showing the same thing: a man running away from a group of women chasing after him. There are eight shots of this, although there could have been two or three had the idea behind the film been essentially narrative or if the point of the film was something other than the chase itself. While the eight shots don't contribute much on a narrative level (apart from repeating the same idea), piling them one on top of the other makes it possible to prolong the action, to add detail, and to insist upon the film's attractional aspects or developments. For this accumulation of shots to contribute something on the narrative level, it would have to advance the action. But here, it is not the action that advances (there are no new developments), it is the characters (literally, as the chase proceeds). The film provides the viewer with a series of "acts," each one as spectacular as the last. Underlining the attraction aspect of the spectacle, the Biograph Bulletin makes the following remark: "A neat little lady with white stockings also attracts attention as she lifts her fluffy skirts and chases the Frenchman." Here are a few examples drawn from the film:

> In tableau 6 (of the copy held at the Paper Print Film Collection of the Library of Congress), an obstacle appears in the form of a fence, which the women either climb over or slip through.
> In tableau 8 the obstacle is a steep embankment, which the women must jump down in one or two leaps (sometimes falling down), their skirts blown by the wind, revealing their ankles to the viewer.

In tableau 9, the only obstacle is one of the women, who has unfortunately fallen down, causing her rivals to trip over her, creating a spectacular pile-up of bodies.

The Chase Film: Tableaux with Few Links between Them

With *Personal* we are still closer to the tableau than we are to the shot. For there to be "shots," there have to be "fragments"; the film has to be assembled out of bits and pieces. None of the segments here is a fragment: each is an independent tableau, containing and conveying a self-sufficient micro-narrative recounting the thrills and spills of an event (jumping the fence, descending the embankment, falling down) that make up the macro-narrative of the chase as a whole. There is very little connection between the tableaux. The shots are rather loosely joined, separated by a temporal ellipsis and a spatial break that are significant enough for there to be no problem in matching the shots. Each shot shows us what is happening to the characters "a little further on" (in a later spatial segment) and "a little later" (in a later temporal segment) in the story. Because the elements of each shot are unconnected to each other and are not contiguous, the links between them are clearly distended and there is therefore no problem in matching. Thus, in these years, with this and many other films of the same kind, audiences paid to be entertained by moving pictures that didn't have the kind of narrative rise and fall they found in literature; didn't have a central story that developed from one point to another; and still managed to be thrilling because of the movement, the space, the zaniness, the beauty, or the excitement they reproduced. In chase films, there was an excuse to concentrate on movement itself.

Personal is the prototype of a genre that played a fundamental role in the development of editing. The linear progression inherent in the chase theme contributed to changing the way "tableaux" were seen at the time (tableaux which were about to become "shots"). The earliest films consisted of no more and no less than a single picture (a single tableau, or "scene"). The regular recourse to punctiliarity, which seemed self-evident then, lasted several years and left traces in the pluripunctiliar films of a later era. Even when kinematographers made a film composed of several tableaux in this era, they often understood the shots they took as self-sufficient units, independent of adjacent tableaux.

A film such as *Personal*, despite the fact that it pertains in some ways to what we might call the narrative paradigm, also subscribes to the rule of the autonomy of the tableau. This is one of the consequences of the domination of the attraction paradigm at this point in film history. The autonomy of tableaux was the decisive factor in their possible interchangeability, but it also made the camera operator feel obliged to record the entire action depicted within each, right to the bitter end when the field of vision had been emptied of all the characters who had occupied the frame.

This conception of the shot as an autonomous tableau also led kinematographers to see tableaux as centripetal units. When staging a scene, actors avoided sudden departures from the field of vision, and there was a strong tendency always to bring the action back to the center of the frame so that the tableau might contain (and show) every element relative to the event being depicted. It was this view of the frame that the chase film undermined, because it broke up the well-framed (and highly controlled) profilmic space to which the viewer (and actors) had become accustomed. Most tableaux in chase films are clearly no more than transitory spaces; everything we see in these spaces must, of necessity, exit the frame. With the chase film, the frame initially appears empty (or almost) and is filled with someone being pursued and then with pursuers, who enter from offscreen (usually from the back of the frame) one after the other a few yards apart, moving toward the camera before finally exiting the field of vision (usually in the foreground). And this same chain of events repeats itself in its entirety, in each tableau, tableau after tableau. Offscreen space thus begins to take on value and meaning for filmic expression. Centripetal *tableaux* were in the process of becoming centrifugal *shots*. And the camera would soon respond with greater frequency and greater ease to what we might term the "call" of offscreen space. This was the contribution of the chase film's basic structure to the development of cinema.

Another constant of the chase film is that pursuers and pursued are invariably shown in the same shot and that they are never (except in highly rare cases) isolated in separate shots. Thus while the genre encouraged the growth of editing, this was a relatively linear editing.

■ An Age-Old Problem: Pirating Pictures and Ideas

What I have just said about *Personal* also applies to the numerous remakes the Biograph film directly inspired and especially to the remake that was virtually an exact copy of the original, *How a French Nobleman Got a Wife through the New York Herald "Personal" Columns*, made by Edwin S. Porter just a few weeks after the release of the Biograph film.

This remake was virtually an exact copy of the original, *Personal* (*How a French Nobleman Got a Wife through the New York Herald "Personal" Columns*, Edison, 1904). Digital frame enlargement.

Some of the shots in this remake were even made in the same locations as the original film, such as Grant's Tomb on Riverside Drive in New York, where in each version the man meets the women responding to his ad. What is more, Porter imitated the initial film's structure almost shot for shot. His only seemingly original contribution was a medium close-up as a prologue to the action, showing the main character reading a newspaper to make sure that his ad appeared. When he sees the ad, he puts a bouton-niere of violets in his lapel so that the women who reply to his ad will be able to recognize him.

Remakes were a new pirating strategy adopted by American producers in their ongoing plagiarizing of their competitors' catalogues. In *French Nobleman*, Porter didn't even try to distinguish his film from the Biograph film. All the Edison Company wanted to do with this film was to create a cheap copy of a competitor's latest hit and to add it to their own sales cata-logue. In previous years, competitors had simply duped prints that they bought on the market for that purpose, shamelessly selling them as their own. (Clearly, the pirating of audiovisual works of art is not a new prob-lem, but an age-old one!)

This new strategy of exact replicas was adopted by Edison because of Biograph's new policy of restricting the release of some of its new films to its own exhibition circuit. The *Biograph Bulletin* of 15 August 1904 spells this out: "'Personal,' like 'The Escaped Lunatic' . . . and other great productions of our own manufacture, is restricted to our own use and not for sale. We are the only concern in America prepared to supply an exclusive service." It thus became impossible for Edison to obtain copies of some of its principal competitor's major films in order to dupe them. The only option open to them, in their commercial battles with Biograph, was to market its own version of their rival's most successful films. Naturally, this entailed certain legal risks, if Biograph were to drag the Edison Company before the courts. And this is what they did, precisely for the film *French Nobleman*. And so the chase film gave rise, appropriately enough, to companies (pur)suing each other through the courts.

Clearly, the film world in these years was still in a fairly lawless state. "Respectable" companies, led by "respected" people like Edison, gave themselves over without regret and in plain view to illicit (and not especially legitimate) activities such as the barefaced pirating of a competitor's films. It would seem, in such a context, that necessity made its own laws. The extraordinary growth of fixed-venue exhibition had an effect on the demand for films, forcing American producers to do everything in their power to meet market demand. "To do everything" meant not hesitating to sell dupes or exact remakes of other companies' films.

Very few companies escaped the pirating saga untarnished. In Edison's January catalogue, nineteen of the thirty-four pictures being sold were counterfeit; in September, the same company was offering for sale fifty-two films, of which thirty-six were pirated (see Musser, *Before* 277). As Richard Abel explains: "In September [1904], both Edison and Eugene Cline, for instance, featured either Pathé dupes or 'originals.' . . . In October a Lubin ad in the *Clipper* listed a half dozen Pathé titles . . . as his company's own product. This duping was so extensive that, in a December *Billboard* ad, J. A. Berst, the [Pathé] company's New York manager, could turn the practice to Pathé's advantage, declaring that 'the best advertising for our films is the fact that so many concerns dupe them'" (28). Copyright legislation was vague enough that this sort of behavior was possible, especially since the victims of pirating were French and British companies, not all of which had yet established a sales representative in the United States to protect their interests. In addition, many foreign firms did not copyright their films, leaving them without any protection.

This new form of piracy, the exact remake, was quite in vogue now. *Personal* alone, which was made in June, gave rise to at least four pastiches in less than nine months. Porter's *French Nobleman*, made in August, was followed a few months later by *Meet Me at the Fountain* and—the reputation of *Personal* (and/or one of the early remakes, perhaps) having crossed the Atlantic—by *L'Hereu de Ca'n Pruna* (made by Segundo de Chomón in December for the Spanish firm Macaya-Marro) and by *Dix femmes pour un mari* (produced by Pathé, seemingly in March 1905).

With *French Nobleman*, Porter thus retailed the Biograph film—outrageously, we would say today—purely and simply by copying its story line, all its thrills and spills, and everything having to do with what I have proposed elsewhere that we call the "field of cineastic intervention": putting in place, putting in frame, and putting in sequence (Gaudreault *From Plato*). Porter's film is so close to the original that one has to place the two films side by side to be able to tell them apart. A detailed comparison reveals the following differences:

> Porter's film begins, as we have seen, by a seemingly brand new "scene" that isn't found in *Personal*: "The first scene shows the young 'Nobleman' in his dressing room. He picks up the 'Herald,' and finally locates his 'ad' with evident satisfaction" (*AFI Catalog*).
>
> In his version, Porter adds a touch of parody to the action; this is visible particularly in the acting of the man playing the French nobleman, which is more labored and exaggerated than in *Personal*.
>
> Porter's version outdoes the original: there are no longer nine women chasing after the man in single file but eleven, which slows down the pace of the editing because the tableaux are generally longer in the Edison film (the Biograph film is 371 feet long, the remake more than 600).
>
> The story's endings are a little different, because in Porter's remake it is not by brandishing a gun that one of the pursuers wins her man but rather through her courage: she is the only woman brave enough to throw herself into the water in the middle of a pond to join the pursued where he has taken refuge.

Even by the standards of the day, these minor differences were not enough to keep Biograph from becoming a (pur)suer and dragging the Edison Company before the courts, making it the (pur)sued in this legal chase. In Porter's defense, it must be said that, throughout this period, the institutional rules governing the production of remakes were not yet established. By initiating a court battle, Biograph was trying, in fact, to convince law-

Lubin took a certain number of precautions in order to avoid legal problems. Two weeks after the release of his own version of the film in 1904, under the title *A New Version of Personal*, he decided to rename it *Meet Me at the Fountain* and to add a supplementary scene of 75 feet in length, in order to head off possible lawsuits. Digital frame enlargement.

makers to regulate the practice. The launching of this lawsuit had immediate effect: Lubin took a certain number of precautions in order to avoid legal problems. Two weeks after the release of his own version of the film, under the title *A New Version of Personal*, he decided to rename the film *Meet Me at the Fountain* and to add a supplementary scene of 75 feet in length, in order to head off possible lawsuits.

In any event, this new pastiche had already distanced itself somewhat from the original. As the title of the film suggests, the protagonist asks his prospects to meet him at a fountain (since Lubin was not based in New York, the idea of using Grant's Tomb for the rendezvous probably didn't cross his mind). This new copy of *Personal* was also, to an equal degree, a remake of *French Nobleman*; like the latter film, Lubin's film opens on a medium shot of the "Frenchman" getting ready to go out. And Lubin's finishing touch, in a parody of the original version, is to have the woman who succeeds in trapping the man played by a stage actor recognizable to most viewers of the day as a well-known female impersonator.

Chases and Discontinuity:
The Case of *The Firebug*

As we have seen, the chase film was the ideal genre for kine-matographers to begin thinking more closely about editing and what we might call "continuity exercises," given that the genre typically constitutes a "chain" of loosely connected fragments that can easily accommodate the presence of gaps and breaks in the action. The chase film was no doubt a school for editing and also a school for narration, but it was a liberal school, where continuity was not yet the rule. Although chase films did not have continuous links, they taught kinematographers to make links nonetheless, even if these were not binding. The chase film brought editing into play in a sustained manner, first because its characters are by definition engaged in what we might call a "continuous trajectory" that "programs" them to leave the frame quickly and move on, tableau after tableau, to another setting; and also because the camera would soon have to take a step sideways or a leap ahead, spatially or temporally. Once the film was shot, kinematographers were called upon to place this series of sequential scenes end to end so that the action might be transferred from one to the next, in order to form, through editing, a narrative chain in which each tableau is one of the links.

Nevertheless, what had to happen did: as time went on the chase film developed in a way that brought kinematographers face to face with new parameters, new questions, and new issues, particularly with respect to linking tableaux. This was the case, in rather spectacular fashion, with *The Firebug*, which joined the chase film and the abduction drama. *The Firebug* confronted its makers with immense challenges with respect to the spatio-temporal linking of shots. The film opens on an emblematic medium shot showing a pyromaniac against a neutral background, holding a torch and looking threateningly out at the viewer. This shot is placed on the film's periphery and outside its narrative. We are introduced to the pyromaniac in an imprecise setting performing an activity indicative of his unique nature; he is shown to us abstractly, outside time and in a nonfigurative space.

Beginning with the second tableau, which shows the interior of a well-to-do home, the film tells the story of a little girl who discovers that a shady character has gained entrance to the house. She follows him into the basement, where he has gone to set the house on fire. The third tableau takes place in the basement, after he starts the fire. The firebug grabs the girl and takes her with him as he escapes out a basement window. A servant comes on the scene, sees the pyromaniac escaping with the girl, and

The Firebug opens on an emblematic medium shot showing a pyromaniac against a neutral background, holding a torch and looking threateningly out at the viewer (Biograph, 1905). Digital frame enlargement.

sets off in pursuit, also through the basement window. At that moment the father also arrives and tries to put out the fire; his wife appears and faints; then the maid does the same; and the man carries his unconscious wife upstairs. The next tableau (the fourth) takes the viewer out of doors for the first time, while the front door of the house and the basement window remain clearly in view. Accustomed to a certain kind of continuity, anyone viewing the film today assumes, at this point in the story, that this fourth tableau will continue on where the previous tableau left off—with the father exiting the frame as he carries his wife upstairs in his arms. Unexpectedly, however, the film takes us back to the firebug escaping through the basement window with his hostage and taking flight, seen this time from outside the house. Then the servant exits the window and sets off in pursuit. Barely has the servant exited the frame to the left—we're still in the fourth tableau—when the man exits the house with his wife through the door giving onto the front porch. He sets her down and goes back inside, returning with a gun and setting off after the pyromaniac. There follows a sequence of four tableaux showing an atypical chase, to which we return below.

There are two major incongruities in this film with respect to the standards that would be adopted later as part of what we call "institutional
mode of representation" (for a discussion of this concept, see Burch *Life*).
First, there is the long episode repeating the action that occurs in tableau 3
(the firebug exiting the basement window with the little girl, followed by
the servant). The agent responsible for this film had problems working with
simultaneous action, problems that were not yet resolved: it felt the need
to show the same action twice from different points of view. This is the
same problem that led Porter to show a similar kind of repetition in the rescue sequence of *Life of an American Fireman* in 1902. Both films show characters exiting a building through a window. In such cases, there is no more
efficient way of depicting such action than systematic alternation between
two adjoining spaces, but this was not yet a spontaneous option for kinematographers. Here we are still working within a system in which attraction rules, and the prevailing paradigm is that of the autonomy of the
tableau. This explains, among other things, why there is resistance to any
interweaving of the shots taken from the two points of observation. Each
autonomous tableau shows us one of two points of view (first inside and
then outside the house) and, because of their autonomy, it is the job of each
to show the entire action—even if this means making the pace of the action
crawl and the narrative time of the second tableau (no. 4, outdoors) considerably overlap that of the first (no. 3, indoors). The rule dictating the
autonomy of tableaux not only requires the camera operator to record the
characters' movements until they have left the field of vision; it also
requires that each tableau be a complete unit that cannot easily be divided
or fragmented.

The Firebug, however, would break this rule in its final two shots—it is
preferable in this case, I think, to speak of "shots" rather than "tableaux"—
and create a fine example, quite rare at this time, of a precise matching
shot without any overlap. The father's fight with the firebug, whom he has
managed to catch, is seen first in an establishing shot and then in a cut to
a medium long shot. My analysis of a large number of films of the period
prompts me to hypothesize that the principle of the autonomy of the
tableau began to lose ground mostly because of the repeated joining of
shots analyzing the *same* spatial segment, like here. Cuts and matches
between shots showing the same action from different points of view led
kinematographers to see that the film could follow the continuous unfolding of the action. It was as if the only purpose of a change of shot (that is,
of the point of view) was to enable the viewer to see the action from a better angle. This action, despite the change of perspective, inexorably con-

tinued its course according to a strict chronometric and chronological logic.

Let's return for a moment to tableaux 3 and 4, because it is in the relationship between them that the second incongruity found in *The Firebug* appears. These two tableaux not only present a repetition of the action; they are also the site of a major discrepancy in the sequence of narrative events they relate. In fact, tableau 4 contradicts in a sense what tableau 3 says, at least on the level of the logic of the story line. The viewer, watching tableau 4, in which events are shown from outside the building, can only be surprised by the brief lapse of time—five seconds at most—between the moment when the servant exits through the basement window in pursuit of the pyromaniac and the moment when the father arrives on the porch, his wife in his arms. This lapse of time is completely out of kilter with the length of time it took for the same events to be told in the preceding tableau—a little more than fifty seconds. This is how long it took for the father to arrive in the basement and try to put out the fire, for the mother and the maid to arrive, for them to faint in turn, and, finally, for the father to carry his wife back upstairs. The ratio (fifty seconds to five) is ten to one! Of course, the later tableau could not show this rapid sequence of events, because it was quite simply beyond the camera's field of vision, now located outside the building. To show what was going on inside the house at the same time as what was going on outside, it would have been absolutely necessary for each tableau to transmute into a number of short shots. In addition, the editing would have had to constantly transport the viewer from inside the house to the outside and back again, systematically alternating between the two observation posts. This is the path that institutional cinema soon took with the various forms of alternation it developed, including a device that would become canonical: crosscutting, a technique that was not yet in fashion. It would not be long before it was, however; in fact, just a few months after Biograph's release of *The Firebug* in August, Edison released a film containing one of the rare prototypes of crosscutting at this early date. *The Watermelon Patch* is little known today (or, more accurately, underappreciated) and is the last film we examine here.

Let's begin by returning briefly to the unusual temporal construction of *The Firebug* and its atypical chase scene. As we saw, the duration of the off-screen events in tableau 4 was literally compressed, elided even. This was done without any editing (there is no cut anywhere in tableau 4). Rather, the filmmakers employed mise-en-scène to achieve this effect. Rather than cutting the film to produce an ellipsis, they chose to manipulate the pro-filmic action in order to shorten its duration, thereby concealing the length of events taking place beyond the camera's field of vision. Between maintaining the unity of the point of view and temporal coherence, most often filmmakers in the days of kine-attractography chose the former. Spatially anchoring the action usually prevailed over temporal logic. The stability, persistence, and singularity of the point of view were still so important that they made filmmakers fear neither anachronism nor parachronism.

The atypical nature of the chase scene in *The Firebug* following from tableaux 3 and 4 is noteworthy for two reasons. Right from the beginning, it is clear that the film will not adhere to the rules of the genre and that it has quite different concerns. In a sense, the film's firmly dramatic tone already suggests this. *The Firebug*, in fact, is not a chase film but a dramatic film with a chase sequence. This sequence, moreover, occupies only two tableaux. Each of these tableaux respects the sacrosanct rule that the camera record the scene as long as there are characters still in its field of vision. What they do not respect, however, is the other convention of the chase film, which holds that the pursued and pursuers follow a continuous, linear path, normally toward the camera, until every character has exited the frame in the foreground. In *The Firebug*, neither of the two tableaux of the chase sequence conforms to this rule, nor limits itself to being a mere transitory space. Each of these tableaux also shows events one would not expect to see in a chase film. One of them even gives rise to a kind of sudden reversal of the situation or, at the very least, to a sudden reversal of direction. I refer to the first of the two tableaux, which the *Biograph Bulletin* describes as follows: "The Firebug conceals himself and the little girl behind a group of bushes while his pursuers are beating the thickets on every side. He is unobserved as they pass him and finds his way back in the same direction from which he came. He is discovered just about as he is disappearing in the distance." Here the setting is more than a mere transitory space ("The Firebug conceals himself . . . and finds his way back in the same direction from which he came") because it frames actions unlike those found in ordinary chase scenes, which involve simply running in a straight line in an attempt to cover as much ground as possible.

The second tableau in this chase sequence functions in a similar manner when it depicts an exchange of gunfire between the protagonists: "Using the little girl as a shield against the shots of his pursuers, the Firebug runs swiftly down the rough path until he comes to an intersection with another path where for a few moments he holds his pursuers at bay with his revolver. Finding that he is being surrounded he abandons his position and again taking the child hurries on to a wooden barn." As should be apparent, *The Firebug* is a film that subverts the genre of the chase film and scorns its conventions.

An Unusual Chase Film with a Bonus Feature: *The Watermelon Patch*

The Watermelon Patch was made by Edwin S. Porter and Wallace McCutcheon for the Edison Company and used the chase film genre in just as unconventional a manner. This little-studied film is of great importance because it is no more and no less than the very first known occurrence of crosscutting in film history. That would make this rare pearl one of the missing links between kine-attractography and institutional cinema.

It would be ironic if the first documented example of crosscutting were to be found in a chase film, given that this genre's narrative program has absolutely no need of technical virtuosity. Chase films employ two groups of protagonists who are generally located not far from each other. This is what makes it possible to film each group's movements within a single tableau. Hence the fact that the chase film, almost invariably, is nothing more than tableaux of the same kind laid end to end, as we saw above. The chase film thus normally uses a completely linear form of editing, without losing any sleep over the matter, whose segments are simply joined end to end to create an almost statutory series of temporal ellipses and spatial gaps.

The Watermelon Patch threw quite a wrench into the genre's conventions, because the film's chase turns into a tracking game, a completely different narrative program than a chase, even if it is not that far removed. The film's story line is quite simple, if not simplistic. A small group of Blacks is caught stealing watermelons from a field and is chased by two white men. After two or three fairly classic tableaux showing the latter running after the former, we see the Blacks hide behind some trees and their pursuers run by without seeing them, exiting the frame in the foreground. The Blacks then retrace their steps and exit the frame in the background, the direction from which they came. This tableau thus subverts a convention of the chase film by creating a radical change of direction in the movements of one of the groups of protagonists, just like one of the tableaux in *The Firebug*. Here the move is even more important, however, because this tactic enables the pursued to shake their pursuers, something that was *never seen* in chase films of the day. The Blacks thus succeed in returning with the watermelons to their folk in a wooden cabin somewhere in the woods. A sequence of them eating the watermelons is then shown in three sequential shots (an establishing shot of a group of Blacks seated at a wooden table interrupted in the middle by a cut-in close-up). Despite having certain properly narrative features, the film often, indeed mostly, adheres to an attraction paradigm. Thus the first of the three shots of the watermelon-eating sequence (inside the cabin) begins with a long series of short, fully attractional dance numbers having absolutely nothing to do with the action. It is only when this "attractional pause" (which is, in a sense, a true bonus feature) is finished that the watermelon thieves make their appearance.

This sequence, moreover, is so long, and its action so secondary to that of the film's earlier tableaux, that the viewer becomes somewhat lost when the tableau following the watermelon eating appears. The film's narrative thread has in fact been lost, and the dead-end chase is now no more than a faint memory. This next tableau shows a group of white men arriving with dogs at the site where the original pursuers had lost all trace of the Blacks. As the tableau unfolds, the viewer comes to understand that we have returned to the first line of the action to recap what has happened in the meantime: realizing that they have been fooled, the white pursuers have alerted some companions and called for their help to form a posse to track down and punish the thieves.

The return of this initial line of the film's action shows that the film's "narrator" is following through on its ideas, but it is not very easy for viewers to follow these ideas, to the extent that they are required to do some of the narrator's work and envision the missing elements after the fact. This creates a certain amount of confusion, which is apparently why this film is not well known and very little commented upon by scholars today. (Indeed, to arrive at my hypothesis concerning this film's importance in the history of crosscutting, I had to screen it a great many times and analyze it in detail.)

Once the dogs go into action, the posse succeeds in finding the thieves' trail back to the cabin in which they took refuge. The white pursuers block all the exits to the cabin, including the chimney. We then see from the inside that the growing amount of smoke forces the Blacks outside. The film cuts back outside, where the posse helps the Blacks get out of the house, taking advantage of the opportunity to deal them a few minor blows.

Here, then, is a film extremely little known until now but one that demonstrates a degree of narrative planning and sophistication quite rare for its time. It is the true prototype of crosscutting, for which film historians of every generation have been searching for many years. And it is the prototype of crosscutting despite the fact that it is just as much a worthy representative of kine-attractography.

NOTE

1. I use the term "kine-attractography" here to translate the French expression "cinématographie-attraction" found in an early work of film history (see Coissac 359).

Translated by Timothy Barnard.

1906

Movies and Spectacle

LAUREN RABINOVITZ

New institutions that staged grand displays, impressive performances, or "spectacle" characterized turn-of-the-century modern life. Department stores featured magnificent architecture and fabulous displays of material goods. Grandiose international expositions provided immersive catalogues of culture. Dime museums dramatized and sensationalized topics and celebrities of the day. Traveling panoramas offered large-scale depictions of history and landscapes. Newly built electric amusement parks (early exhibition sites for cinema) provided a carnival of noise, light, and motion. But the definitive mode of modern spectacle was the motion picture and, in this year, new approaches to movies secured the status of motion pictures as spectacle.

The social conditions for the invention of modern spectacle began well before this year and well before the beginning of the movies when intense industrial growth in the late nineteenth century changed European and American societies. In the United States, immigration and country-to-city migrations responded to new manufacturing and commercial jobs and resulted in massive population and employment shifts that remade the physical spaces and institutions of U.S. cities. By the turn of the century, urban inhabitants were themselves transformed as they adjusted to changing ideas about speed and distance and to the assaults on their senses from the noise, congestion, and visual bombardments in the modern city.

Cultural critic Walter Benjamin has written convincingly that early twentieth century urban spectacles, including motion pictures, transformed modern social consciousness and modified the institutions of mass society. His ideas build on sociologist Georg Simmel's concerns about mob psychology and about nervous overstimulation in modern city life, examining a variety of novel spectacles (such as expositions, shopping arcades, and movies) for how they transformed modern social consciousness, modified the institutions of mass society, and radically reframed what counts as modern knowledge (Benjamin *Arcades*; Simmel). Benjamin grasped that modern spectacle is central to what matters in modern societies. Anxiety about new lived experiences required innovative reassurances in the forms of spectacle that perceptual knowledge would assume. Movies served their audiences by adjusting them to contemporary features of city life, its modernization, consumerism, and alienation.

Movies became transformed into spectacle in three ways. First, motion pictures sensationalized chief events of the year: the 18 April San Francisco earthquake, the 25 June murder of architect Stanford White by wealthy playboy Harry Thaw, Mafia activities in New York City, and the passage of food reform legislation on 30 June as a result of public outrage over conditions in the Chicago meatpacking industry. In all these examples, movies depicted horrible *urban* excesses of national crime, scandal, and disaster with simulated tourism and voyeurism as the means for overcoming anxiety about different kinds of catastrophes of modernity. Second, movies that predominantly played at new nickel theaters and at amusement parks participated in larger programs of theatrical, architectural, and kinesthesiac spectacle; movies were always experienced in combination with illustrated songs, band, or orchestral music, live animal or human acts, thrill rides, or technological feats of electric, water, or mechanical displays. Third, the new fad of simulating travel in "virtual voyage" installations (such as Hale's Tours and Scenes of the World) was a novel kind of cinematic spectacle that extended the pleasures of well-known moving panorama "rides" like the Trans-Siberian Railway by turning the theater space into a bouncing, breezy sightseeing conveyance and by projecting the thrilling destinations onto the screen.

The Spectacle of Current Events

On 18 April, a devastating earthquake struck San Francisco, and fires subsequently swept the city. The U.S. government reported 700 deaths, although this figure has been continually revised upward throughout the twentieth century and may be closer to 3,000 direct or indirect deaths in a city whose population was around 400,000. Approximately 225,000 people, or more than half the city, were left homeless due to the destruction. The quake and subsequent fires destroyed more than 28,000 buildings in a five-square-mile radius that included downtown San Francisco and Chinatown. The damage and loss of life made this one of the worst natural disasters in U.S. history.

The nation rallied to aid San Francisco in its effort to rebuild. While newspapers reported the destruction in words, motion pictures provided grand, detailed illustrations of the ruins, fires, and relief efforts. Motion picture manufacturers either sent itinerant camera operators to San Francisco to capture the scene as soon as possible, or they restaged the annihilation for more immediate release to audiences. For example, Lubin Company's *The San Francisco Disaster* and American Mutoscope and Biograph's *San Francisco Disaster* are essentially the result of static cameras set up in front of miniatures of San Francisco set ablaze. The motion picture practice of such re-creations in order to sensationalize and capitalize on timely events was already a well-established convention and had been done for great audience effect and profit since the Spanish-American War.

Throughout April, May, and June, however, numerous motion picture companies released actuality or newsreel films of the streets of San Francisco. Many of these contained panoramic or sweeping left-to-right and right-to-left camera movements, often lingering on significant landmarks. *Scenes in San Francisco, No. 1* (American Mutoscope & Biograph), for example, depicts ruins downtown along Mission and Market Streets as shot on 9 May. This particular film even includes a camera operator in the foreground shooting another earthquake ruins film. *Panorama of the Ruined City*, also a Biograph film, edits in sequence left-right pans of downtown streets and scenes in refugee camps set up for those made homeless by the earthquake and fires.

Another extant film depicts panoramic views of five downtown streets and the refugee camps, probably in late April (*San Francisco after the Earthquake and Fire of 1906*, manufacturer unknown). It also includes a "homeless" family, who appear to eat a meal staged for the camera. Edison Manufacturing Company's *Dynamiting Ruins and Rescuing Soldiers Caught in Falling Walls* is a panoramic view of downtown ruins and of police and male civilians cleaning up debris. Edison's *Exploded Gas Tanks, U.S. Mint, Emporium, and Spreckel's Bldg.* is a panorama of buildings south of downtown Market Street. This 240-degree pan is quite spectacular, since the camera's point of view is low to the ground and aims at a vista of tall, ruined buildings. Edison's *Army Pack Train Bringing Supplies* is a parade in both medium and long shots of relief troops on horseback with supply wagons.

A different kind of catastrophe that also preoccupied the nation was the Thaw-White scandal, the much talked-about murder of Stanford White on 25 June. White was arguably the country's most prominent architect and a partner in the country's leading architectural firm of McKim, Mead, and White. He designed opulent, private residences for the rich and famous (including the Rockefellers, the Astors, and the Vanderbilts) and important public buildings like the Boston Public Library, the New York Herald building, the Washington Arch, and Madison Square Garden. His lavish, highly decorated buildings in imitation of Italian Renaissance architecture well suited the temperament of the Gilded Age and the pretensions of his millionaire clients.

At the summer opening of the rooftop garden "nightclub" of his own building (Madison Square Garden), White was shot by wealthy playboy and railroad heir Harry K. Thaw. White had been having an affair with Thaw's wife, chorus girl Evelyn Nesbit. There was never any dispute that Thaw killed White since he shot him three times in the face before the crowd at Madison Square Garden.

The appalling crime fascinated the country and made front-page news everywhere because it revealed a darker side to the life of one of New York's richest, most successful men. White's wild parties, nighttime debauchery, corruption of a string of chorus girls, and his love triangle with Nesbit and Thaw made for titillating reading in the press. Evelyn Nesbit's climb from childhood poverty to a theatrical career and wealthy marriage because of her sexual charms contained those ingredients of scandal, promiscuity, and the downfall of the rich and famous that generally were found only in dime novels.

Awaiting trial, Thaw was incarcerated in the famous New York jail, the Tombs. Even this event provided grist for both newspaper stories and motion pictures. They said that his wealth and position allowed him to bribe guards, who carried in catered meals from the famous Delmonico's restaurant. The *New York Times* reported on 5 July that Thaw had treated all the male prisoners to ice cream and cake in honor of the Fourth of July holiday. Newspapers enumerated other material comforts and services extended to Thaw, and they even described regular visits by both his mother and wife. Motion pictures like *Thaw White Tragedy* (released in July) and *In the Tombs* (released in August) reenacted the murder, the scene of the affair, and the "luxuries" of Thaw's imprisonment. (The scandal's public notoriety and role in motion pictures would continue in the following year when Thaw went on trial, most notably in *The Unwritten Law*.) For example, *In the Tombs* offers a static studio interior shot of the front of a prison cell; a young man in prison garb paces back and forth behind the bars. A policeman brings in a well-dressed matron, who embraces the man through the bars. She cries and exits. Another younger, fashionably dressed woman enters and goes through the same motions. Such single-shot films themselves were not sensationalistic; rather, the sensation was the event to which they referred.

The Thaw-White scandal films followed similar movie successes at pictorializing New York City crimes and newspaper headlines. *The Black Hand:*

The True Story of a Recent Occurrence in the Italian Quarter of New York (American Mutoscope & Biograph) likewise capitalized on dramatic events reported in the newspapers. On 17 February, local newspapers reported that police detectives had captured "Black Hand" Italian gangsters by staking them out in the meat locker of a local Italian American butcher. The detectives were responding to the butcher, who had sought police protection when "the Black Hand" tried to extort money from him.

Less than a month later on 29 March, Biograph released *The Black Hand*, directed by Wallace McCutcheon and shot by Billy Bitzer. It is a fictional story about "the black hand" or Mafia-connected gangs of southern Italian immigrants who extorted money from other immigrants with threats of kidnapping, murder, and arson. In short, "the black hand" was a protection racket in urban immigrant neighborhoods.

The Black Hand capitalizes on the notoriety of the well-known urban immigrant gangs as well as the February headline while appealing to new immigrant Italian audiences in its portrayal of the good Italian immigrant butcher. The film opens with an intertitle: "Writing the letter." Two thugs are seated at a table and writing a letter. Their status as Italian "thugs" is reinforced by their appearances. They have dark complexions, thick dark moustaches, stereotypically and comically Italian hats, and working-class garb. They drink alcohol and act like drunken caricatures. A close-up of the letter reveals the threat: pay $1,000 to the Black Hand or they will kidnap the victim's daughter and burn his shop. An intertitle precedes the next shot: "the letter received." In the next shot, also a studio interior of a shallow space with a flat painted backdrop, the victim is introduced: Mr. Angelo, the butcher, is in his shop waiting on a customer. With a wife and daughter by his side, he represents the good, hard-working immigrant. The postman arrives and delivers a letter to him; he reads the letter and reacts in horror. He shows the letter to his wife, puts on his coat, grabs his gun, and exits. The young daughter and her mother embrace fearfully, clutching each other closely.

"The threat carried out" introduces the next section of the film. In contrast to the earlier studio interior shots, what follows is a long shot of an actual New York City street, busy Seventh Avenue. As traffic and pedestrians pass by, the young daughter in the center of the frame stops to help a gentleman look for something on the sidewalk. A horse-drawn carriage pulls up and a man leaps out and grabs her. Onlookers run over to the spot where she "disappeared." In this section, the film relies on a familiar melodramatic trope (one often used at Biograph)—the kidnapping of a child—in order to set up the peril of the situation and to solidify the Black Hand's criminal activity as the most heinous possible. (While the actual case on which the film was based did not involve a child kidnapping, there are other newspaper reports from this time period of Black Hand kidnappings.)

The film cuts to another outdoor street scene. The horse-drawn carriage arrives and gang members pay the driver. The film cuts to an interior studio shot: a man rises from a mattress, goes over to the door, removes a wooden bar across the door, and allows a woman followed by two men and the kidnapped daughter to enter the room. The woman puts the child to bed and leaves. The male gang members replace the wooden bar and then drink more alcohol. While they are preoccupied, the daughter tries to sneak out of the room. But the gang members catch her at the door. One moves as if to strike her, but the other two thugs stop him.

An intertitle that describes the succeeding actions and alludes to the real-life event introduces the penultimate section of the film: "Levying the blackmail. A clever arrest. Actually as made by the New York detectives." In this sequence, two detectives arrive at the butcher shop. They hide in the meat locker in the corner of the store, then return from the meat locker and indicate that it is quite cold. But they jump back into the room when the wife warns them a Black Hand member is at the door. The armed thug demands payment. The wife responds by trying to open the door to the meat locker. The thug pushes her away from the door. The butcher shows the gangster his money, giving his wife time to free the detectives from the other room. The detectives emerge and arrest the thug.

An intertitle "Rescue of Maria" announces the film's climax: back in the room where the child is held captive, the gang members now drunkenly stagger to the door. One of the gang readmits the woman. She gives a drink to the child and leaves. While the men are barring the door again, a note appears pushed through the window frame. The child snatches the note, reads it, and tiptoes past the drunken gang members to unlock the window and remove the bar from the door. Three policemen immediately enter the room and arrest the men. The child's mother and father enter and the film ends with the family reunited.

The Black Hand is typical fare insofar as it reproduces melodramatic conventions that rely upon kidnapping, an imperiled child or young woman, and a rescue that results in a final climactic reunion. Even McCutcheon had earlier used this formula in *The Pioneers*, a 1903 Biograph drama supposedly about scout Kit Carson but that utilizes an Indian raid on innocent settlers, the kidnapping of their daughter, and her rescue by Carson as its plot line. The popular, well-known ingredients employed by McCutcheon in *The Black Hand* include a drama provoked by a fatal threat (kidnapping), a "sensation" scene like the physical violence posed to the innocent victim by evil gang members, and the final rescue scene that results in the reunification of the family. Just like the tabloid newspapers and dime novels, *The Black Hand* balances the spectacle of re-creating a violent crime with a family drama that pits social transgression against moral goodness, pure evil against the ultimate triumph of virtue.

As if the forces of nature, kidnapping, and celebrity murders were not enough violence for a single year, public indignation and anger rose over another type of specifically modern disaster, the horrors of working conditions in the meatpacking industry and the threats to public health now that food was industrially processed and packaged. The publication of Upton Sinclair's novel *The Jungle*, a fictional exploration of the conditions of the Chicago meatpacking industry, stirred public opinion for food reform. Sinclair's novel, originally serialized as a "muckraking" story in a socialist magazine in 1905, is the story of a Lithuanian immigrant family that tries to live the American Dream in Chicago's Back of the Yards neighborhood while working in the meatpacking industry. But in the novel, hope gives way to despair because the family members are victims over and over again of a corrupt system manipulated by evil, greedy capitalists. The protagonist eventually sees salvation at the novel's end when he joins with a socialist political party and dreams of workers uniting and taking over industry. Less compelling as a socialist diatribe, the novel's force lay in its vivid, graphic depictions of the horrific ways in which hogs and cows are butchered and processed, of the flagrant factory violations of city ordinances, and of workers brutally maimed and killed due to unsafe work conditions. The novel's descriptions of the meatpackers was so awful and apparently legitimate, since Sinclair had spent time in the stockyards, that President Teddy Roosevelt commissioned an independent investigative team on the matter. His commission verified Sinclair's descriptions of abysmal factory safety and health conditions, infractions of city ordinances, and deliberate use of tainted meat. Throughout the spring, Congress debated legislation to reform the meatpacking industry and, by 30 June, passed both the Pure Food and Drug Act and the Meat Inspection Act.

In Chicago, William Selig's motion picture company capitalized on the issue's timeliness. Selig re-released a series of films showing the stockyards that the company had made for Armour and Company in 1901 (e.g., *Interior of Armour's Power House* and *A Busy Corner at Armour's*) when the meatpacker was his chief client and when he made more than sixty short films for the company. Although most of these films no longer exist, their titles describe their subjects: stockyard exteriors and railroads, herds of animals

in the pens, assembly lines and meat-cutting operations in the plant, can-
nery machines and processes, various rooms within the Armour plant, and
shipping activities. Since these were industrial films made for the city's
largest meatpacker, none of them actually depicted any of the horrors
vividly portrayed in Sinclair's novel. Based on extant images, they simply
illustrated the highly rationalized order and environment of the meatpacking plant and pens. Selig's company, about to go bankrupt, made enough
profits from the footage of the meatpacking plant that it achieved a new sol-
vency. Despite the fact that the Armour films provided little "evidence" to
support or rebut the controversial claims surrounding the meatpacking
industry throughout the spring, they provided national references to a
larger set of political issues.

While motion pictures had capitalized on timely events and provided a
kind of "living newspaper" service for several years, they had not before so
assiduously exploited sensationalistic news events for visual drama and regularly recurring profit. Movies reached a new height of spectacle now that
they regularly and repetitively restaged or replayed the violence of national
modern life. The "violence," however, that these films depicted was not so
much graphic, violent action onscreen as tableaux that alluded to and provided pictorial information and details about notorious current affairs.
What made these movies sensationalistic and spectacular was not so much
any "aesthetics" in the images themselves but their context—the actual
events to which they made reference. In this manner, movies focused on
the three biggest events of the year so that anyone could achieve the status
of a witness to the most disturbing events of the day.

The Spectacle of the Nickelodeon

With cheap prices, easy accessibility on main commercial
thoroughfares, and continuous schedules that allowed passersby to drop in
throughout the day and evening, small nickelodeon theaters were wildly
popular. "Nickel madness" overtook major U.S. cities, and the number of
nickel theaters climbed from a dozen or so theaters apiece in cities like New
York City, Philadelphia, Chicago, or Pittsburgh to hundreds in each place by
the year's end.

Nickel theaters or nickelodeons were typically plain, long, dark rooms.
Interiors were undecorated boxes with only a muslin screen at one end of
the room or a cloth behind a small stage. A piano and drum set might be
below the screen and off to the side for musical and sound effects accompaniment. Rows of wooden or camp chairs seated 200 to as many as 500,

Nickelodeon exterior, unknown location, ca. 1906. Collection Lauren Rabinovitz.

depending on the theater. In some cities, where local theater ordinances required "bigger" amusements to pay higher licensing fees, theater owners might well limit the number of seats in order to qualify for a cheaper license—in many cities, including Chicago and New York City, the maximum was 299. Visitors and journalists alike, however, frequently reported on crowds standing (illegally) in the aisles and at the back of the room throughout the program. Because city authorities were concerned about both fire and public safety, they often regulated not only the number of patrons in a small space but also the number of exits. They also often required some lighting, fans, and separated lead-lined projection booths to avoid fire spreading should the highly flammable nitrate film stock explode.

The exterior of the theater might be as simple as an unadorned storefront with the theater's name printed in block letters, or as fancy as electrical illumination allowed. Typically, a ticket-seller booth sat adjacent to the front or side of the entrance, and posters advertising the program might be pasted onto the front walls or on sidewalk billboards. Most theaters employed "barkers" to stand on the sidewalk and cajole potential customers while gramophones or phonographs blared out popular music to attract attention.

The composition and size of the audience varied depending on the time of day. During the afternoon, audiences more often included female shoppers and children. In early evening, audiences included both white- and blue-collar employees who dropped in for the shows after they left work. As the evening wore on, nickelodeons competed with nearby and even adjacent saloons for the same audiences of working-class men and women. But, from the beginning, immigrants (especially in northeastern and midwestern cities) made up an important part of the audience.

Nickelodeons almost immediately drew the unwelcome attention of social reformers who expressed concern both for the immoralities expressed in the movies as well as for the unwholesome atmospheres of the venues themselves. Reformers were especially concerned that nickelodeons encouraged young women, especially immigrant women, to engage in immoral exchanges and liaisons with strange men in the darkened spaces. Others feared that the lure of the nickel theater would corrupt minors, leading them to steal nickels for admission as well as learn immoral habits and behavior watching overstimulating movies in unsavory environments.

In addition, many nickelodeons made audience participation and crowd conviviality part of the show through sing-alongs and amateur acts. The program of movies was interspersed with illustrated songs, piano accompaniment, and live entertainment. Indeed, the live entertainment in many immigrant neighborhood nickelodeons played specifically to the denizens of that neighborhood and often provided opportunities for local amateurs to sing or dance for small sums of money.

Nickelodeon programs were quite varied and included several motion pictures that had no programmatic coherence. Audiences attended for "the show," not necessarily in order to see specific films. Indeed, nickelodeon proprietors infrequently advertised individual film titles and, when they did advertise, their ads were just as likely to emphasize the entertainment in between the short films as the films themselves. That said, individual films

Nickelodeon interior, unknown location, ca. 1906. Collection Lauren Rabinovitz.

could achieve a measure of popularity and draw audiences, especially since popular titles might be played until the print wore out. Advertisements for individual films, in this case, more often consisted of graphic posters and sandwich boards located on the sidewalk outside the theater.

Origins of Animated Films

Among the most popular of individual film titles had been earlier "trick films" and especially Georges Méliès's imported French films. (*A Trip to the Moon* [1902] had spawned many imitations.) *The Dream of a Rarebit Fiend* (Edison Manufacturing Company) by Edwin S. Porter and Wallace McCutcheon has generally been credited as an important American-produced antecedent of animated film, whereas *Humorous Phases of Funny Faces* (Vitagraph) is a landmark American animated film, relying upon frame-by-frame cinematography. The former is more accurately a "trick film" imitating a long line of Méliès films as well as those by Gaston Velle and Segundo de Chomón, both of whom directed current successful trick film fantasies for Pathé Frères. *Rarebit Fiend* relies on fantastic special effects through wires and stop-action substitution, as do other trick films. *Humorous Phases of Funny Faces*, on the other hand, "animates" the vaudeville act of an illustrated lecturer so that the pictures appear to move on their own.

The Dream of a Rarebit Fiend was a popular comic strip series by illustrator Winsor McCay. A regular feature in the *New York Telegram* from 1904 until 1914, McCay's most successful cartoon strip always began the same way: with a portly gentleman who had overindulged in a dinner of Welsh rarebit, a kind of cheese fondue over toast. The combination of grated cheese, beer, butter, and seasonings led to rarebit-induced nightmares of epic proportions. In McCay's strip, the first frame depicts the diner getting into bed or falling asleep, and the succeeding frames are filled with remarkable dreams beautifully drawn about phobias and anxieties, ones often attendant on modern urban life featuring cityscapes, skylines, and skyscrapers. The strip ends with the dreamer awakening.

The Edison film *The Dream of a Rarebit Fiend* emphasizes instead the illusion that inanimate objects move of their accord (e.g., the bed hops up and down, shoes move by themselves) and that the dreamer in his bed flies through the night sky. The film borrows more from Gaston Velle's 1905 film *Rêve à la lune* (Pathé) than it does from McCay.

Dream of a Rarebit Fiend took longer to produce and was a more elaborate production than most films of the time. Increased sales at Edison gave Porter and his collaborator Wallace McCutcheon (who left Edison for Biograph shortly after this film was released) the ability to work more painstakingly, using miniatures, scripts, and the unheard-of length of two months' time to develop the elaborate effects in this movie (Musser, *Emergence* 458). As the manufacturer's catalogue said, "The picture is probably best described as being humorously humorous and mysteriously mysterious, and is certain to make the biggest kind of a 'hit' with any audience. Some of the photographic 'stunts' have never been seen or attempted before, and but few experts in photography will be able to understand how they are done" (*AFI Catalog*).

The movie opens with a medium shot of the gentleman-diner drinking alcohol and eating rarebit. But immediately after this conventional emblematic shot, Porter begins to employ tricks. The second shot is a double exposure of the gentleman, a swinging lamppost set in an exterior cityscape, and a background of panning, blurring New York City streets. As Charles Musser has written, "It suggested the subjective sensation of the fiend's predicament without being a point-of-view shot" (Musser, *Before* 342). After cinematically establishing the fiend's inebriated state, the film depicts the man's drunken adventures in his bedroom, a studio interior. First, his shoes appear to scamper across the floor and then the furniture disappears—the result of stop-camera cinematography.

The film technically shifts again to employ another method for depicting a subjective state and introduces a split-screen effect that portrays both the sleeping man and his dreams. In the lower half of the screen, a cap-clad man snores in his nightgown in medium close-up. In the upper half of the screen, actors in devil's costumes and an oversized tureen of rarebit not only occupy his thoughts but prod and poke his head with pitchforks and axes. Returning to a view of the bedroom interior, the bed now hops up and down and spins around.

Then, in another use of split-screen action, the bed with the fiend in it flies across the New York City skyline: the upper half of the screen is the sleeper in his bed against a black background; the lower half of the image is an aerial panorama of New York City. The velocity of the trip wreaks havoc on the bedcovers, and even the sleeper is forced to hang on for dear life to the bed frame. In the last part of the fiend's imaginative journey, the dreamer is flung from the bed and skewered on the top of a church steeple. In the final scene, the interior of the bedroom reappears as the fiend crashes through the roof and finally wakes up. Musser describes the overall effect: "The changing tricks and discontinuities disorient the spectators in ways analogous to dream, particularly the dreams portrayed in Winsor McCay's comic strips" (Musser, *Before* 342).

Humorous Phases of Funny Faces, now well known as an early animated motion picture, was the work of J. Stuart Blackton, a famed lightning sketch artist who had a vaudeville act known as "The Komical Kartoonist." Lightning sketches were vaudeville routines wherein an individual artist rapidly drew a series of caricatures and cartoons set on an easel before the live audience. Several motion picture animators began their careers this way, entertaining audiences with topical caricatures and whimsical series and sequences of drawings. Blackton had teamed up with Albert Smith and formed Vitagraph Motion Picture Company, a partnership that afforded him the opportunity to bring together his former lightning sketch artist career with his new career as a movie manufacturer. He soon began to make trick movies with stop-camera cinematography.

Humorous Phases begins with its title forming into letters out of bits and pieces. The first shot is a close-up of Blackton's hand and arm drawing a chalk figure on a blackboard, excerpting his famous vaudeville act. Once the drawn figure outline of a gentleman is completed on the left and the artist's hand is withdrawn, a companion female figure on the right appears to draw itself. Through stop-camera techniques, the pretty young woman smiles and winks back at the much older balding gentleman. He smiles and grows hair with tufts that form a dollar sign in a magic version of what surely was a stock gag that Blackton drew in his act. The gentleman smokes a cigar that puffs out billows of smoke to the pretty young woman's dismay. When the billows of smoke cover her in a cloud, the artist's hand reappears and rubs out the entire scene.

Next, a full-figure drawing of a gentleman appears in side profile. He tosses his umbrella and lifts his bowler hat. A new shot of chalk smudges "reverses" itself back into the drawn features of a man and woman in profile, and then the lines of their profile disappear inch by inch. A chalk-drawn clown lifts his hat and juggles it with his hands and then with his feet. A chalk dog appears and the clown has him jump and then leap through a hoop interspersed with occasional glimpses of the arm flashing before the chalkboard. At the completion of their act, the hand erases the left half of the drawing. The right half continues to perform until the entire arm of the artist wipes the slate clean. Blackton continues with racist and stereotyped caricatures of an African American ("Coon") and a Jew ("Cohen"), caricatures that would have been recognizable to contemporary audiences. Although the rapid-fire sketch technique was central to the vaudeville act, it is transformed here into a trick that makes the pictures come alive. The film sets a precedent for early animation in revealing the hand of the artist so that the film is as much about the self-revelation of the trickery as the trick of animation itself (Crafton 35–58).

The Spectacle of the Amusement Park

At this time there were approximately one thousand amusement parks in the United States. They evolved out of the amusement areas of turn-of-the-century international expositions, the seaside bathing resort, the country fair, and the European pleasure garden. Amusement parks were so widespread because new electric streetcar and interurban railroad companies across the United States built the parks at the end of their rail lines. These traction companies, as they were called, did not need to make a profit at their parks so long as the parks encouraged excursions on their railroads, especially in evenings and on weekends. Big cities like New York and Chicago each had half a dozen parks operating at a time. Medium-size cities like Cleveland, Pittsburgh, or Washington, D.C., had more than one. Even small cities in rural states almost always had at least one amusement park on the outskirts of town.

Amusement parks, sometimes also called electric parks or trolley parks, featured mechanical thrill rides, games of chance, dancing, roller skating, band concerts, disaster shows, live acts, and ethnographic displays, fireworks shows, food, and swimming, as well as movies. The architecture of the parks often provided fanciful, exotic backdrops with ornate electrified towers, boldly painted facades, brilliant flags waving, and vividly colored gardens. Barkers attempting to lure customers to different attractions, gramophone music, bands, and mechanical pianos and orchestras filled the air. Practically all these parks featured movies, especially since urban houses tended to go dark in the summer due to the heat. They either had nickel theaters or free outdoor screenings in airdomes and, with the introduction and rapid popularity of *Hale's Tours and Scenes of the World* this year, they had rides that featured movies as well. The movies that the parks showed, therefore, were always in the context of an atmosphere of visual and auditory excitement, kinesthesia, a showcase of new mechanical technologies, and crowds of diverse peoples.

The Spectacle of Virtual Travel: *Hale's Tours and Scenes of the World*

George C. Hale had introduced *Hale's Tours and Scenes of the World* at Kansas City's Electric Park. Its success there led him and his business partner, Kansas City magistrate Fred Gifford, to license and grant territorial rights for the installation at other amusement parks and at nickelodeon storefronts. Hale and Gifford sold the rights east of Pittsburgh to William A. Brady of New York and Edward B. Grossmann of Chicago and the southern rights to Wells, Dunne & Harlan of New York. They sold additional licenses to C. W. Parker Co. of Abilene, Kansas, for traveling carnival companies, and the Pacific-Northwest rights to a group of men who incorporated as "The Northwest Hale's Tourist Amusement Company" in Portland, Oregon. Hale and Gifford immediately retired with their profits, leaving the regional entrepreneurs to run Hale's Tours installations at storefront theaters and amusement parks with, at first, dramatic success and then, in succeeding years, with financial reverses.

There were more than 500 Hale's Tours at both amusement parks and storefront theaters in all major cities in the United States and Canada. The figures represent a quick, high saturation rate among sites for cheap commercial mass entertainment. In downtown and ethnic working-class commercial strips, storefront Hale's Tours installations sat adjacent to nickelodeons, dance halls, cheap vaudeville, and saloons. At amusement parks, they quickly became among the top-grossing park concessions. Even though the fad lingered for several years, the popularity of the attraction reached its peak this year. In all likelihood the increased systematization and consolidation of the movie industry made it first difficult and then al-together impossible to obtain new phantom train ride movie products (what we today would call the software for the enterprise).

Hale's Tours consisted of one or more theater cars, each seating sixty to seventy-two passengers. Admission for a ten- to twenty-minute show was ten cents. The moving pictures that showed out the front end of the car offered a filmed point of view from the front or rear of a moving train. The goal was to create the sensory illusion of movement into or away from a scene, accentuated by mechanical apparatuses and levers that simultane-ously vibrated, rocked, and tilted the car—an early version of today's motion simulators. They offered subjective point-of-view journeys to scenic spots in the United States (including Niagara Falls, the Catskill Mountains, the Rocky Mountains, northern California, and the Black Hills); to Canada, South America, and Europe; and to foreign lands that were especially remote or pre-industrial (China, Ceylon, Japan, Samoa, the Fiji Islands, Borneo), and even to urban centers via trolley or subway. Representative new film titles included *A Trip on the Catskill Mt. Railway* (American Muto-scope & Biograph), *The Hold-up of the Rocky Mountain Express* (American Mutoscope & Biograph), *Trip Through Utah* (Selig), and *Trip Through the Black Hills* (Selig). While steam whistles tooted and wheels clattered, air was blown into the travelers' faces.

Hale's Tours made spectators into travelers on journeys to consume the exotic, whether that was the city for the country "rube," the "primitive" for the westerner, or picturesque nature for the urbanite. The subjects of travel films assumed a series of oppositions already in place about nature and civ-ilization and the function of tourism for flirting with those oppositions. Hale's Tours thus offered up picturesque nature as an antidote for the over-stimulation of city life; it romanticized colonial outposts as quaint pre-industrial relics in need of Western civilization; it glorified the city as a technological wonderland. It allowed the spectator-passengers to pretend that, as railway tourists, they could master and take pleasure in those envi-ronments to which society was claiming new access. By emphasizing the commercial nature of railroad travel into scenic rural, often western, reaches of the United States and by extending its model of idealized railway tourism to both remote and urban destinations, Hale's Tours defined a new kind of traveler, for whom "Manifest Destiny" meant inevitably possessing a geographically expanded playground.

Imitators and variants capitalized on Hale and Gifford's success: Palace Touring Cars, Hurst's Touring New York, Cessna's Sightseeing Auto Tours, Citron's Overland Flyer, Auto Tours of the World and Sightseeing in the

Principal Cities, White & Langever's Steamboat Tours of the World, and Hruby & Plummer's Tours and Scenes of the World.

Hale's Tours capitalized on and extended the popular phantom train ride films made from the late 1890s (some films were even used in Hale's Tours installations). The films shown in Hale's Tours and other motion travel cars typically featured the landscape as the vehicle picked up speed, so that details accelerating into the foreground were the featured information. The films employed both editing and camera movements but usually only after presenting an extended shot organized by the locomotion of the camera. The initial effect, then, was a continuous flow of objects rushing toward the camera, the same cinematographic practice as the earliest phantom train ride films.

The camera, usually mounted at a slightly tipped angle, showed the railroad tracks in the foreground as parallel lines that converge at the horizon, an important indicator of perspectival depth. Telephone poles, bridges, tunnels, and other environmental markers in the frame also marked continuous flow according to the lines of perspective. Passing through tunnels created a particularly dramatic difference of darkness and light, moving image or no image, and interruption and flow. There were also ambient sounds associated with the visual movement forward into the landscape—wheels clattering, paddlewheels churning—punctuated by the announcements of whistles for braking and stopping, and bells or horns that served "as fictional warnings" timed to coordinate with the visual appearances of pedestrians or animals on the street or tracks.

The films specially manufactured for Hale's Tours, however, did not always maintain a strict cowcatcher point of view: they employed various kinds of editing and camera movement, although usually only after that lengthy opening travel shot. For example, *Ute Pass from Freight Train* (Selig Polyscope) depicts in turn an engineer and fireman at work on a train up ahead on the tracks, Pike's Peak, and the view out the back of the train from the caboose. In another example, one of the earliest Hale's Tours train travel shows reported at Coney Island was rather incongruously "A Trip in a Balloon," an "imaginary sky voyage" that featured aerial cinematographic views of New York made during aeronaut Leo Stevens's recent balloon trip ("Dreamland" 6).

Moreover, they often expanded the travel format with views of tourist attractions or with comic and dramatic scenes that typically featured mingling between men and women, one class and another, farmers and urbanites, train employees and civilians, ordinary citizens and outlaws, and so on. A Hale's Tours advertisement in the *New York Clipper* listed five "humorous railway scenes" that could be included in Hale's Tours programs (Edison Manufacturing). Therefore, it was not unusual for the films to cut regularly to the interior of a railroad car, producing a "mirror image" of the social space in which the Hale's Tours' patron was seated. These films were not purely travelogues, then, but were also about the social relations and expectations connected with the experience of travel. They suggest that what was fundamental to the event was not merely the sight of the "destination" and the sensation and sound of immersion in it, but the experience, both physical and social, of being in that place.

The Spectacle of Drama and Travel

Like *The Great Train Robbery* (1903), *The Hold-up of the Rocky Mountain Express* was likely an adaptation of a popular stage melodrama. A stage play by the same name by George Klimt and Frank Gazzolo circulated in the first decade of the century and, even if this film was a loose reworking of the play, it capitalized on the play's popularity to garner audiences. Made to be shown expressly in Hale's Tours cars, *The Hold-up of the Rocky Mountain Express* begins with a long shot of the train station platform, and then the camera slowly and smoothly moves forward. The point of view is the front of a departing train. As the train/camera picks up speed and leaves the station, people on the tracks jump out of the way. The train/camera passes through a town and then into the scenic rural landscape. The voyage through the picturesque snow-covered fields and past trees continues for a few minutes.

Then there is an abrupt cut to the inside of a coach, obviously a studio set of a passenger car. This is the first shift of address that the film effects: it changes the point of view from the cowcatcher to the backseat of a railway coach. Inside the coach, two men sit across from two women. Behind the women, another woman tries to flirt with the men. Oblivious to her efforts, one of the men trades places with the woman opposite him so that the four become paired off in two couples. The frustrated flirt instead hits the porter (an actor in blackface) over the head and knocks him down. The conductor arrives and intervenes. Both railroad employees exit.

Next, a tramp crawls out from under the seat behind the couple on the left. Unobserved by the passengers, he sits down next to the lone woman (in effect, producing a third coupling and realizing her goal, although the humor here resides in the impropriety of this pairing). She reacts in horror and attacks him until the conductor reappears and throws him out of the car.

Shots from *Grand Hotel to Big Indian* (American Mutoscope & Biograph, 1906). Paper Print Collection, Motion Picture, Broadcasting, and Recorded Sound Division, Library of Congress.

At this point, the film returns to the cowcatcher point of view. But the camera/train soon stops moving because a log is laid across the tracks. Two railroad men enter from the foreground to move the log but instead are held up by outlaws. The film then returns to the interior of the passenger car. Travelers looking out the window to see the cause of the delay are disturbed by one of the thieves entering the car. He lines up the passengers and robs them, and one of the women faints.

The film returns to the point of view of the tracks and depicts the criminals getting away on a handcar; the train starts up and pursues them. Here the point of view of forward locomotion serves narrative rather than picturesque purposes. As the vehicles approach a station, the bandits are apprehended and the film ends. In this way, the film conjoins narrative closure and the end of the "trip." The station is the scenic destination, the dramatic story is concluded, and the spectator who has been made over into a traveler has reached the end of the "journey." When one considers as well that Hale's Tours installations were just as often at amusement parks as in downtown storefronts, the virtual voyage and visceral experience may be understood as a novel motion picture variant consistent with the rhythms and subjects of the park's other thrill rides.

Grand Hotel to Big Indian (American Mutoscope & Biograph) is a variant of *The Hold-up of the Rocky Mountain Express*. Its title depends upon familiarity with well-known summer resort landmarks in the Catskill Mountains of New York. Like *The Hold-up of the Rocky Mountain Express*, the film begins with an extended shot of a cowcatcher traveling point of view along the famous Horseshoe Loop on the New York State Ulster and Delaware Railway.

The film then cuts to the train interior, where men and women are seated on opposite sides of the aisle. The conductor walks through the car while mattes of traveling landscape "flow" through windows on each side. A porter enters and seats a well-dressed man in a place just vacated by another passenger. The newcomer (the *New York World*'s comic strip character Mr. Butt-In come to life) tips his hat to a young girl across the aisle; she gives him the cold shoulder and tells her papa, who crosses the aisle to give the masher a hard time. No sooner has that action been completed than the man who initially vacated his seat returns and wants his seat back. A fight in the aisle ensues; it is broken up by the conductor and the porter, and everyone is sent back to his seat. The film then cuts back to the cowcatcher point of view.

Other such narrative interruptions of the continuous flow of locomotion in this film include a man who cannot get his horse to move off the tracks. Similar to the shot of the train men entering the foreground in *Hold-up of the Rocky Mountain Express*, the engineer and fireman alight in front of the train and try to help the man pull his horse off the tracks. The engineer squirts oil from a can onto the wheels of the wagon and onto the horse's legs! Mr. Butt-In, the gentleman who caused a comic struggle in the interior, arrives and another fight ensues. The railroad employees carry off Mr. Butt-In, and the man in the wagon urges his horse off the tracks. After a pause, the train starts up again and continues on its voyage.

Hale's Tours thus offered its customers vicarious long-distance railroad journeys compressed into ten minutes while it poked fun at tourist travel. Primarily the domain of the affluent, the famous Pullman railroad car like the ones depicted in *Hold-up of the Rocky Mountain Express* and *Grand Hotel to Big Indian* was advertised as "a steamship on rails" that signified luxury travel and class status. The railroad trip and the advent of train tourism, moreover, may be said to have initiated men and women into their new standing within the system of commodity production, converting them from private individuals into a mass who consumed machine, travel, and nature alike. In this regard, Hale's Tours supported this process, transforming the status of a mechanical conveyance into a spectacle of pleasure and excitement.

Grand Hotel to Big Indian improves upon the formula of *The Hold-up of the Rocky Mountain Express* to the extent that it mixes vicarious scenic tourism with dramatic social intercourse *and* the fantasy of the newspaper comic strip come to life (as earlier demonstrated in *The Dream of a Rarebit Fiend*).

The space of the Hale's Tours car provided the spectator-travelers the pleasure of a fantasy born out of modern life. It allowed the movie spectator to become immersed in a spectacle that combined worlds of fiction and the real and, in the process, to blur the distinction between the two.

If Hale's Tours movie installations put a novel "thrill" into motion pictures by making movies a visceral multi-media experience, in many ways they simply extended the work of movies in general. By establishing a link between movies and the spectacular, the excesses, and the sensations of modern urban life, movie spectacles provided sensory and especially visual verification of the mayhem increasingly associated with modernity, the new century, and urban life. Movie spectacles were cultural artifices that managed the social violence of city streets (often insinuated as a consequence of massive immigration); the chaos and mess attendant on poorly planned, rapidly swelling industrial neighborhoods; and the changing rhythms of life that required leisure to be an antidote to and escape from alienating modern labor.

1907

Movies and the Expansion of the Audience

EILEEN BOWSER

The economy verged on a depression that climaxed in a run on the banks in October known as the Panic of 1907. Immigration reached a peak of 1.3 million new Americans, chiefly from southern and eastern Europe, an infusion of culture distinct from earlier German and Irish immigrations. Concerns about the ever-larger waves of immigrants led to the Immigration Act of 1907, which tightened the restrictions on those who could enter the country. During the summer, the San Francisco streetcar strike by the Carmen's Union split the city known for its strong municipal political support for organized labor. The strike ended in violence. In New York, Richard Strauss's opera *Salome* opened at the Metropolitan Opera House on 22 January. It was a scandal, both for its musical dissonances and for its shockingly erotic scenes. And in France, Pablo Picasso's *Les Demoiselles d'Avignon* opened eyes to a new way of seeing the world and launched the art movement known as Cubism.

The Nickelodeon Craze

The rapidly increasing number of nickelodeons across the nation made its mark on the social fabric. Here was a cheap new amusement, a new public space for the masses to gather, and a new entrepreneurial profession. In large cities, such as New York, Chicago, Philadelphia, Pittsburgh, and Los Angeles, storefront theaters that first appeared in the established entertainment districts, sometimes several in the same block competing with each other, now began to spread further out into residential areas. They began to reach into smaller cities and towns across the country. The business of opening storefront movie theaters required only a small investment and proved to be a profitable way for ambitious immigrants to take their place in American life. The competition for customers in large cities led to more frequent changes of the program, from every week to two a week and now a new program every day. The programs were usually about a half hour in length and repeated all day. Spectators could easily take in more than one show in an afternoon or evening. Many shows included live performances of popular songs accompanied by slides while reels were being changed (almost all theaters had only a single projector), and some of them presented lecturers with the films. The more successful among the entrepreneurs soon owned more than one nickelodeon. Harry Davis, who opened the first nickelodeon in Pittsburgh, had built up a far-reaching chain of twenty-five nickelodeons.

The public attending the nickelodeons, in contrast to the middle-class audiences at earlier amusement enterprises such as music halls and vaudeville theaters, now included large numbers of the poor immigrant and working classes for whom the nickelodeons offered affordable entertainment. The shows could even be enjoyed with little knowledge of English. In small towns, however, where there might be only one or two nickelodeons, the audiences tended to include all classes. It is difficult to characterize the nickelodeon audience with accuracy because it was changing rapidly day to day. Joseph Medill Patterson's "The Nickelodeons: The Poor Man's Elementary Course in The Drama," which appeared in the *Saturday Evening Post* in November, provided a brave attempt to describe the people attending the storefront shows but was limited by the few nickelodeons that the author visited and their urban locations.

The urban nickelodeons in the entertainment districts and nearby tenement districts were viewed by a paternalistic society as threatening to the forces of social order. The new freedom for women and children to mingle promiscuously with men in crowds, the unfamiliar ways of the new immigrants from different areas of Europe, and the darkened conditions inside the storefront theaters were considered likely to lead to immorality and disorder. Some people deplored the moral tone of the films, acceptable in upper- or middle-class vaudeville houses, as not suitable for the women and innocent children in the nickelodeons, who, in many areas, now made up the bulk of the audience.

The opera *Salome* was almost immediately fodder for the nickelodeons. On 9 February, Lubin Film Manufacturing Company released *Salome, The Dance of the Seven Veils* and the Biograph Company filmed a "Salome dance" for *If You Had a Wife Like This* in February (released in May), while another *Salome* was made by Gaumont in France and released in the United States in May by George Kleine. The biblical story of Salome, the dancer who so pleased Herod at his birthday feast that he promised to give her whatever she asked, whereupon she requested and got the head of the imprisoned prophet John the Baptist, was treated in the movies as comedy and sensation. Strauss's dissonant music was replaced in the nickelodeons by ragtime and other popular tunes. It was the notoriety of the opera performance and suggestive posters placed at the show's entrance that drew public attention. Conservative society did not even need to go inside to see these obvious signs of the dangers of the cheap new entertainment sites. More advanced reformers thought that the new venues might provide opportunities to educate and uplift their audiences, or to Americanize the new flood of immigrants, if the quality of films and the unsavory conditions inside the nickelodeons could only be upgraded.

In Chicago, Jane Addams of Hull House opened an "uplift theater" on Halstead Street in June, a three-month experiment in the exhibition of educational and wholesome films for the children of the slums. In the same city, home of the nation's largest chains of film exchanges, censorship made an appearance in November, when the city council empowered the chief of police to issue licenses for each film to be exhibited.

Efforts to Organize the Movie Business

Uncertainty, even chaos, characterized the new motion picture industry. Film production was far from increasing at the same rate as exhibition venues. There were not enough films to meet the demand for a daily change of program. About twelve hundred films of less than one thousand feet—the maximum length held by a single reel, and most of them much shorter—were released in the whole country and only about four hundred of them were produced in the United States (*AFI Catalog*). The future of this business still looked uncertain and the financial backers of production companies were reluctant to invest the large sums needed for studios, laboratories, and equipment for the expansion of production. The economy was one factor in this unease: the financial crisis was only to be resolved late in the year through the personal intervention of the powerful financier J. P. Morgan. Another factor is that Thomas Edison remained engrossed in trying to control the market with his patents. Film production at Edison slowed to a trickle of ten fiction films.

As the number of exhibition venues increased, and as films were shown for shorter runs in nickelodeons, it no longer made sense for theater managers to buy prints of films from producers. The number of film exchanges grew. William Fox, an exhibitor, started a business called Greater New York Rental Company in March. By that same month some fifteen Chicago exchanges controlled the largest part of the rental business in the whole country. Vitagraph and Lubin set up their own rental divisions. William Swanson, who entered the distribution business this year, became president of the United Film Services Protection Association. This group was formed on 16 November in Pittsburgh at a meeting called by the major producers. Those present agreed that exchanges were to be limited to buying prints only from the producers licensed by Edison and the exchanges agreed not to make copies. This last provision was needed to protect the producers, but it was also desirable for reasons of quality: a good duplicating stock was not yet manufactured. In a meeting held in Chicago on 14 December to ratify the agreement, the efforts to unify the whole industry under this head collapsed because Biograph dropped out. Biograph decided to issue its own licenses to various importers of foreign films, including George Kleine in Chicago, a very important distributor.

The great popularity of the fiction film had its effect on production: the ratio of story films to actualities reversed. Comedies, chase films, and trick films now predominated. Dramas, however, were as yet comparatively few in number. For example, Biograph produced thirty-one films (not counting those made for the Biograph mutoscope). Of these, only two were non-fiction, twenty-five were comedies, three were dramas, and two films were classified as fantasy, one as a novelty (Biograph production records). During the summer, the Empire Trust bank, worried about its investment in Biograph, sent Jeremiah J. Kennedy to decide Biograph's future. He remained to become the company's president and a leader in the efforts to organize the industry. Although Vitagraph films may have been the most popular and influential, Lubin appears to have been the more prolific American production company, with the release of about one hundred and fifteen films, although some of these were illegally duplicated foreign imports. Vitagraph released about seventy-five films. Selig, Kalem, and Essanay together accounted for around eighty films. Two of these companies were new: Kalem was founded early in the year by two former Biograph men, Samuel Long and Frank Marion, and George Kleine, the Chicago exchangeman. Biograph's loss of two key men to Kalem, followed by Sidney Olcott, who became Kalem's director, and Gene Gauntier, the actress and scriptwriter, seriously weakened Biograph and precipitated the arrival of Kennedy, the man from Empire Trust bank. The first Kalem film was released that spring. In December, Kalem released an unauthorized version of the stage play *Ben Hur*, chiefly consisting of the famous chariot race filmed on the sands of Coney Island with scenery and "supers" (extras) supplied by Pain's Fireworks Company, costumes from the Metropolitan Opera House, and the chariot race by the 3d Battery (of the Brooklyn Volunteer Artillery, U.S.

Army). In Chicago, Essanay was founded by George K. Spoor, exhibitor, and Gilbert M. Anderson, formerly of Edison and Selig, later known as "Broncho Billy." Essanay released its first film on 31 July.

As a result of the paucity of American films, French and English films filled most of the gap on the nation's screens. The Paris-based Pathé Frères' dominance grew rapidly. Pathé, which distributed films worldwide, now found America to be its largest market. And as Richard Abel has shown, the experience of cinema at this time in America was altogether more French than American (Abel). Edison's attempts to control the burgeoning film industry by issuing licenses based on his patents for motion picture equipment took an important step forward after he negotiated all summer and finally convinced Pathé to accept an Edison license late in the year. As Edison anticipated, most of the producers followed. Another French firm, Gaumont, distributed in the United States by George Kleine, was second to Pathé in number of American releases, while Urban Eclipse, a new British-French company founded by an American who had become an important British producer, Charles Urban, was third. After French films, British films made up the largest number of imports. Pathé's dominance led to anxieties about the influence of French morals on the American public.

Film Styles

In the last days of December, D. W. Griffith found work at the Biograph studio as an extra in *Falsely Accused*. One of the major questions of this year in film history concerns the characteristics of films and methods of production as they appeared to Griffith and his colleagues when they arrived on the scene and began to transform film narrative style. The efforts to meet the demand for story films and the increase in the number of multi-shot films soon led to problems of narrative clarity, a condition commented on by the critics in the new trade periodicals *Moving Picture World* and *Show World*. As the complexity of stories told by the movies grew, viewers could be confused about relationships between people and scenes or events. They might even not know where to look within the image and thus miss the significant action. Existing forms were found to be too limited to relate a more complex story. Lecturers could be employed to make the plot clear, but as the numbers of nickelodeons grew and spread out across the country, the expense of the lecturer was a factor: a more self-sufficient film would be found useful. Producers looked for narrative solutions in the relationship of one shot, or one space, with another, in the need to create a spatial geography in which a continuous narrative takes place. A concept of time is an essential element of a narrative. Magic films and object ani-mation films that played with notions of time were frequent in this year, inspired in part by popular foreign imports. Linked episode films were found particularly useful in the fast-changing exhibition setting because the length could easily be changed to suit local conditions, with episodes dropped or added as needed. Chase film comedies, similarly adaptable, con-tinued to be important to the development of the fiction film because they suggested ways to link shots by movement of the actors within the frame and ways to draw the spectator's attention to the center of the action.

One of the solutions to narrative problems turned out to be alternating editing. A few examples of this technique, usually restricted to an under-standing of the relationship of two adjacent spaces, can be found in films of this year. These films were on the edge of cinema's transformation from an amusement spectacle (or attraction) to continuity cinema. With alternating editing, the story could move back and forth between two locations where related action was taking place. In *The Trainer's Daughter* (Edison), for ex-ample, a scene in the racing stables is interrupted by an alternate scene of a man blowing the horn that signals the start of the race, and the next scene is again in the stables, where the characters react to the (unheard) sound. The reason for the reaction is made clear, the simultaneity of the shots is inferred, and suspense has been built into the narrative.

Fairy Tale Meets Political Satire: *The "Teddy" Bears*

President Theodore Roosevelt was in the middle of his sec-ond term. The well-known story of the hunting expedition when he was said to have declined to shoot a bear cub after killing its mother had become so embedded in the popular imagination that it was now represented by a furry stuffed toy known as a "Teddy" bear, selling by thousands a week (Musser, *Before* 349). Teddy bears became a nationwide fad. The image of the president as a rugged outdoorsman, a manly man with a tender heart, is imbued with the idealism of the age. The teddy bear may have started out as a political symbol, but some part of the image of the teddy bear, shed of its political meaning and perhaps tinged with nostalgia for a world before the cataclysm of the Great War, remains even today as a symbol of comfort for children and adults.

The "Teddy" Bears, made by Wallace McCutcheon and Edwin S. Porter for Edison, was meant, according to its advertisements, to be a satire on the teddy bear craze. The first part of the film is a recounting of the very popu-

An animated sequence showing a group of toy teddy bears of assorted sizes putting on a kind of acrobatic display. It is seen through a peephole by Goldilocks as she snoops around the house (*The "Teddy" Bears*, Edison, 1907).

lar fairy tale of Goldilocks and the Three Bears, told in sequential scenes and in a variety of indoor and outdoor spaces, with vestiges of the temporal overlapping that characterized Porter's early films. Originally a tale of bears eating an intrusive female fox, now changed into the story of a curious girl-child who escapes harm by jumping out the window after being discovered by the bears in their house, the story featured a heroine who comes from who-knows-where and tries out identities as she samples the porridge and the beds of Papa Bear, Momma Bear, and Baby Bear. In the Goldilocks character, we might find an unconscious reflection of the immigrant who attempts to find a role in the new world and is regarded as an object of suspicion by established society. The fairy tale is ambiguous on the question of where its sympathies lie. In the film, the cruelty of the hunter who shoots the pursuing bears (clearly human beings in furry costumes) as they chase Goldilocks through the woods hands over our sympathy to the bears. In a direct reference to the Teddy Roosevelt mythology, Goldilocks pleads with the hunter to spare the life of the bear cub. He does so, and Goldilocks goes in the house to collect the toy teddy bears; the hunter then emerges with Baby Bear, a chain around its neck, an orphan and a prisoner.

The third element in this mixture of fairy tale and contemporary political life is an animated sequence showing a group of toy teddy bears of assorted sizes putting on a kind of acrobatic display. It is seen through a peephole by Goldilocks as she snoops around the house. Bruno Bettelheim reads this tale as a prepubescent search for sexual identity (215–24). In Bettelheim's psychoanalytical terms, this sequence can be read as a comparison of Goldilocks's voyeuristic gaze to the child's fascinated peek at the forbidden sights behind the bedroom door.

Typically for this period, there is not a lot of narrative logic for the animation sequence, even if it does serve to underline the Goldilocks role as an outsider looking in. It is there to provide an attraction for the audience. It is a spectacle outside the narrative continuity. Porter was often drawn to the time-consuming technical work that provided wonder and entertainment. According to Charles Musser, the animated sequence took eight days of work, moving the teddy bears between each shot (Musser, *Before* 331). This is a period of significant achievements in object animation: the genre is discussed later in this chapter.

While producers searched for means to relate a narrative with clarity, stories known in advance to the audience were a great help to understanding what a film was about. The enjoyment for the audience lay in the familiar scenes illustrated in lifelike moving pictures. The illustration of fairy tales held a prominent place in the earliest years, here and in other countries. Fairy tales are especially important in the most ambitious productions of the French artist George Méliès, whose films were so often illegally duped by the Americans. On the one hand, fairy tales tell a well-known story, and on the other participate in the magic that held audiences spellbound in the early years of cinema. At the same time, however, *The "Teddy" Bears* references contemporary events also known to the audience, such as the tale about President Roosevelt and his bear hunt. The change from fairy tale to contemporary event is marked inside the film by a change from artificial painted sets for outdoor scenes to the actuality of snow-covered woods for the chase sequence. The traditional chase film makes use of outdoor locations to obtain a variety of spaces for the participants to run and tumble through. Discrepancies like these, between photographed reality and an obviously faked imitation of it, do not appear to have had great importance in the era before the story film became dominant, but at this transition point it begins to be noticed by critics. The reviewers for *Variety*, for example, just beginning to cover films late in the year, frequently used the word "fake" to describe some scenes—sometimes in a pejorative sense, seeming to assume that all films should be actualities, sometimes only to indicate that the scene is an artificial construct. Along with the development of new styles of filmmaking that endeavored to find ways to deal with the complexity of the story, the concept of film as an illusion of reality was becoming more significant. The change from cinema as presentation (an attraction) to representation (the realistic expression of the drama and emotions of a story) is only in its early stages at this time, and is characterized by the inconsistent but growing realization that for a film to enlist the spectator in the narrative, it should avoid as far as possible inconsistencies that might break that illusion.

As the audience of new immigrants grew, the common cultural elements could no longer be considered universal. For that reason, and for the lack of stylistic means to relate a more complex narrative, some of the films of this year were not always clear to all of the audience. As noted, some exhibitors explained the film as it was being shown and others hired a professional lecturer to perform this role, which added another element to the exhibition format.

Selling Scandal: Lubin Film Manufacturing Company and *The Unwritten Law*

Sigmund Lubin was a German immigrant, an early exhibitor and producer in Philadelphia, and the only Jew in the establishment of the major film producers who would constitute the Motion Picture Patents Company. Notorious for duping the films of Pathé and Méliès, he was, in fact, far from the only one to do so, but he may have been given such a reputation in order to make him the scapegoat for the others. He was highly successful, however, in understanding his audiences and was a prolific film producer, releasing more films this year than any other American production company. Edison could not ignore Lubin Film Manufacturing Company when it tried to organize the industry by licensing the major producers.

The trial of Harry K. Thaw for the murder of the celebrated architect Stanford White created a journalistic sensation early in the year. Day after day the yellow press gave lurid details of the dissolute life lived by the rich and famous. Long before the fate of Thaw was finally settled by a court of law, the Lubin Film Manufacturing Company of Philadelphia made *The Unwritten Law*, which renders its own verdict: Thaw is acquitted with the defense that he had to defend his wife's honor, "the unwritten law" of the title. This case is cited even today in legal circles as offering a definition of "the unwritten law." While White had allegedly compromised the honor of the young showgirl Evelyn Nesbit, it was before she met and married Thaw.

The real-life trial that finally determined Thaw's fate would find him not guilty by reason of insanity and send him to an institution for the criminally insane. The press ate up the shocking details about the scandalous way that a famous and highly respected architect like White led a life of lechery, entertaining and seducing young chorus girls, and, equally titillating, the high-society status and great wealth of the Thaw family. Far from uninteresting, as it turned out, was Thaw's own unsavory past.

The Unwritten Law is a prime example of the kind of film that drew the attention of progressive and establishment forces to the new cheap amusement sites where working class people, immigrants, women, and children gathered to socialize. The disapproving spectator did not need to attend the show to know about its sensational nature: outside, advertising posters made it clear. It was the real-life events related and exaggerated in the daily press that provided the excitement. The press continued to give coverage while the trial went on, and while Thaw's mother fought to obtain his release. Later on, Evelyn Nesbit Thaw and her son would have brief screen careers on the basis of her notoriety. The film itself, barred in some cities (in Chicago, it was banned by the police), continued to play in places where censorship was not strong, even though its film style quickly became old-fashioned. Its notoriety kept it in demand. Its fame remained alive through the many efforts to suppress it.

The majority of the surviving films of this year are made in the presentation style of early cinema, and only a few show signs of a coming change. The Lubin Film Manufacturing Company did make films that are more forward looking, but *The Unwritten Law* definitely belongs to the old school. It is told by means of a series of tableaux that illustrate the newspaper headlines of the Thaw/White scandal. Scenes are announced by intertitles drawn from the newspaper headlines. There are thirteen such intertitles listed in the Lubin promotional materials, which may at the least provide us with the concept intended at the time of the original release:

"The Artist's Studio" (Stanford White first sets eyes on Evelyn Nesbit.)
"Preparing for the Stage" (She is in a dancing class when White enters and invites her to go out.)
"The Young Millionaire" (White and Nesbit are in a café when Thaw enters with two companions and observes White's insistence that she drink.)
"The Fight" (In the café, Thaw gets into a fight with White.)
"The Room with the Velvet Swing" (Nesbit plays in White's studio.)
"Drugged" (In an upper room, White puts a substance into a glass.)

"A Fiendish Deed" (She drinks and faints; White carries her to a divan and places a screen to hide the scene.)

"The Wedding" (The wedding party of Thaw and Evelyn Nesbit exits a church.)

"The Thaw Home" (The happy couple are invited by a friend to visit the Madison Square Roof Garden.)

"The Tragedy at the Roof Garden" (The party arrives and watches the show, seen by the film audience as well, while White sits nearby and tries to send a note to Evelyn, enraging her husband, who shoots and kills White.)

"The Tombs Prison" (Thaw receives his mother and his wife.)

"On Trial for Life" (Evelyn Nesbit is on the witness stand, the lawyer presents his case to the jury.)

"The Unwritten Law" (The jury gives its verdict and Thaw goes free.)

(AFI Catalog)

The above description does not exactly match the surviving copies of the film. That is a condition of many films of the time. For one thing, a film such as this could be shown in shortened versions, omitting whole scenes, without making a lot of difference. Further, the in-house publicist who wrote the advertisements for the company releases could often be inaccurate. Or a film as popular as this one might be worn out through the countless trips through projection machines, the release prints sometimes damaged and even the negative incomplete when printed too many times. Given the long life of *The Unwritten Law*, it could even have been necessary to remake scenes, leading to more than one version. At any rate, the original description fails completely to mention one of the more interesting events: Thaw revisits his crime in his prison cell by means of a vision superimposed on the wall. The vision scene of *The Unwritten Law* recalls to Thaw the visits of his mother and his wife. The superimposed vision is a device used to show what a character is thinking, most frequently to show memories. Superimposition is in keeping with the efforts of filmmakers to complete an action within a single shot, instead of editing together one shot showing the character thinking and another shot showing what he is thinking about. There is a certain efficiency in the portrayal of this episode in one shot, but it must be compared to the amount of technical work needed to achieve that shot by the superimposition of another scene.

Each shot in the film shows a completed action: Stanford White visits the artist's studio where Evelyn Nesbit is posing; Evelyn is in her dancing class when White comes in pursuit of her; in a café, Thaw observes the behavior of White offering a drink to Nesbit. The wedding party (Thaw and

Nesbit) is shown exiting the church in one shot, and in the next the newly married couple is at home, receiving a visit from a friend. The only connection is that the same characters appear in each shot. In any case they are separated by an intertitle to announce the following scene. The exceptions are few and subtle: in the studio where Nesbit sits in the swing and points her toes, a painted staircase on the set hints at the next scene, which takes place in the upstairs room, but here too an intertitle separates the two shots.

Object Animation: *The Tired Tailor's Dream*

Magical object animation films were popular at this time. J. Stuart Blackton produced a number of them for Vitagraph, and one of his best, *The Haunted Hotel*, was released in February. Edwin S. Porter made several varieties of object animation films: his trick work is notable for his cleverly animated titles. Elsewhere in this chapter I discuss two examples of Porter's object animation: *The "Teddy" Bears* and *College Chums*. The American Mutoscope and Biograph Company also followed the vogue. During the brief time in the spring that Joseph Golden served as the Biograph director he made at least three films using object animation, *Crayono*, *Dolls in Dreamland*, and *The Tired Tailor's Dream*. Golden produced the latter film at the end of May but it was not released until the end of August, after he left the company. In this film, a customer in a tailor's shop demands that his suit be ready in an hour. While the overworked tailor sleeps, he dreams that the overdue suit of clothes assembles itself. When the customer returns to claim the clothes, they arrange themselves on his body.

A big wall clock is dominant in the middle of the set. The clock hands, while not moving continuously, are changed to suit the lapses of time. Sometimes early filmmakers included a prominent clock in the set but did not seem interested enough in its function to make the hands move during the entire film, for instance, the static clock in Edison's *Lost in the Alps*. By changing the clock hands in *The Tired Tailor's Dream*, the filmmaker showed an understanding of the need to make the time lapse clear to the spectator, time being of key importance to the suspense of this film, which is driven by a deadline for completing the task of making the suit.

Object animation creates the illusion of objects moving by magical means. It is done by the stop-camera technique: every few frames the camera is stopped and the objects (or living beings) are moved between each shot. If one observes the stop-camera films of the period very closely, it is possible to see the occasional use of "invisible" strings to move the objects, and then, of course, it is no longer, strictly speaking, stop-camera filming.

In the use of stop-camera, all the shots in the sequence bear a relationship based on the movement from shot to shot. The cuts between shots are supposed to remain unobserved by the spectator: the joined shots appear to be one shot. In *The Tired Tailor's Dream*, there are cuts to close-up to show the scissors, needle, and thread at work without human hands. These close views may have two purposes: to make the action clear to the spectator and to make a presentation of the astonishing display. Biograph cameraman Billy Bitzer said that everybody who operated a moving picture camera for the first time played with this fascinating effect. Stop-camera plays its part in the structure of a scene in this period when the completion of an action within a single image is still important, but in object animation the action is only *seemingly* completed within the single image. The magic works because the cuts are unnoticed by the spectator: the shots seem to be one continuous action, yet the filmmaker understands that there is a relationship between each shot and the next. The use of this illusion may have opened up the filmmaker to the possibilities of editing shots together based on parts that add up to a whole action.

Trick films are often portrayed as dreams. Sometimes dream sequences are shown in the same scene with the dreamer, in the form of a matted-in scene on the wall, as in *The Unwritten Law*, with the idea that two actions depicted in the same frame must be related. In *The Tired Tailor's Dream*, a dissolve within the dream smoothes over the cut to close-up, but no dissolves set off the dream itself from the dreamer. A direct cut from a sleeping tailor to the object animation scene is understood to show his dream.

The Tired Tailor's Dream is a comedy as well as a trick film. Imagine the delight of exhausted working-class spectators sunk in their nickelodeon seats after a hard day on the job to see labor performed by magic; imagine the laughs when the demanding customer returns and finds himself dumbfounded by the new suit clothing his body all by itself. In a time when underpaid and overworked labor suffered from repetitive and monotonous work and protest strikes were often brutally repressed, in a time when organized labor struggled against a largely unsympathetic society, this little film allowed the working-class spectators to relieve frustration with laughter.

Surrogate Voyeurism:
The Boy, the Bust, and the Bath

Poor immigrants lived in overcrowded tenements, while large portions of the urban rising middle class lived in rooming houses and boarding houses. The people of the theater who were now beginning to find work in films when other employment failed lived in such quarters. Apartment houses were relatively new on the scene and were built primarily for the fashionable and the well-to-do, the same class of people who had lived previously in private homes and row houses, some of which were now being turned into rooming houses.

Sharing bathrooms, telephones in the hall, and other facilities in boarding houses fed the voyeuristic urges that are one of cinema's basic appeals, the joys of watching people without being seen. In Vitagraph's *The Boy, the Bust, and the Bath*, directed by J. Stuart Blackton, a mischievous boy plays a joke on the residents of a boarding house: he places a bust of the woman of the house (played by Florence Lawrence) in the bathtub and waits to watch as, one by one, the male roomers come to peer in the keyhole under the illusion that it is a real woman in the bath. The bad boy sticks pins in the unsuspecting voyeurs and laughs heartily, slapping his knees, at the embarrassment of each new victim. The bad boy creating mischief is a well-established comedy motif, very common in this year's films and extending well back into the previous century. In this film the boy, because he looks at the camera when he laughs, may serve as the surrogate for the spectators—at least, until the victims of his joke get together at the end to dunk the boy in the tub as an act of revenge. Yet the gleeful voyeurs also freely act to the camera, as though to enlist the spectator in the jokes and pleasures of voyeurism. There is the acknowledgment in both cases that the spectator is present and is implicit as a voyeur. Each episode is varied by the nature of the particular boarding house resident. One man uses a kind of spyglass, as though to bring the view closer, while another man is wearing a clerical collar: he has the most dignity to lose when he, in turn, is caught out.

The composition is that of the linked-episode film. Each episode is connected to the next only by the repetition, with variations, of the basic concept. Nevertheless, within this format, the filmmaker has chosen to use a repetitive series of two shots, between the hallway and the bathroom door scenes, using carefully matched cuts. Each pair of shots resembles the last pair in construction, composition, and action, as each new character arrives to fall victim to the joke. This results in a smoothly continuous narrative within the two-shot episodes, and the overlapping action of earlier films is eliminated. Overlapping was used as a means to relate two shots in different spaces, that is, an action in one shot may be repeated in part in the next shot. The simplest way to comprehend this idea may be to think of a person opening a door and exiting the scene, followed by an exterior shot, in which the same person opens the door and enters the scene. As filmmakers and their audiences began to understand a more direct relationship between two shots, overlapping was no longer used. Surprisingly, there is no use of keyhole point-of-view shots in *The Boy, the Bust and the Bath* when the men gaze at the bathing "woman," as we might have expected. Examples of the point of view of the voyeur expressed through matte shots in the form of peepholes are common enough in other films of the year, however, as in *The "Teddy" Bears.*

The film is shot closer than usual for its time, the actors approaching so close to the camera that their legs at mid-calf disappear below the frame, and therefore close enough for us to appreciate their facial expressions. The end of the film shows an even closer view of the bad boy splashing in the water. Close views at the introduction or the end of the film are a frequent strategy: they serve as an emblematic image representing the film's subject, existing to a greater or lesser degree outside the narrative. In the case of a linked-episode film, which this film is, it may serve as a closure, signifying the end. The linked-episode format, almost always used for a comedy, is not sufficient to portray a complex drama.

The titillating subject of the comedy, too, means that it belongs more to the past when films were seen in the music halls. Naughty jokes such as men looking through keyholes at naked women who turn out not to be naked women would not really be thought suitable by the social reformers for the new audiences filling the nickelodeons.

Action at the Center of the Frame: *The Mill Girl*

The Mill Girl, another Vitagraph film, is a melodrama. The subject matter must have been an attractive one for the new audiences drawn from the working class. It would have been of interest as well to the reformers because it presented social problems they were concerned about, specifically, the perils that the working woman faced as she moved freely about man's world and safety standards in the workplace. These issues are explored within the framework of the traditional melodrama of the touring shows, a type of drama familiar to audiences everywhere. Such dramas depended on stereotypical characters and exaggerated situations: in the end tensions between good and evil would be resolved in the defeat of the latter. The narratives were neither subtle nor complex. The heroine of *The Mill Girl*, a young girl working in a textile mill, suffers from the unwanted advances of the mill owner. She is rescued by a fellow worker who attacks the boss and knocks him down. The boss hires two ruffians to beat up her rescuer, who defeats them on two occasions by his superior strength and wit but is then dismissed from the mill. Free of the worker's interference the boss again forces his attentions on the young girl but is interrupted by a horrific fire in the mill, which brings about his death. The girl is rescued a second time by her hero, this time from the fire that has trapped her inside the mill. A working-class hero is provided for a working-class audience.

This is a useful film to illustrate the stage at which filmmaking had arrived. I would like here to examine the means by which it narrated a more complex story than the chase films and linked-episode films. It is by no means the earliest example of its style of editing nor is it typical of films of its year, but *The Mill Girl* may be seen as a signpost to the future. Vitagraph films were frequently at the forefront of the expansion of film style at this time.

The Mill Girl has one intertitle and thirty-one shots, a high number. It is filmed at the same "stage distance" that most films were at this time, with the floor showing in front of the actors' feet and inactive space above their heads at the top of the frame. The distance between camera and actors is narrowed a bit more in the climactic scenes. When the actors enter and exit the frame, however, they often move on the diagonal to the axial plane, thus appearing much closer to the camera, at what we call a "three-quarters shot." At this point, the actors' knees are near the bottom of the frame and their heads are near the top. This kind of position for entering or leaving the frame would have been familiar to audiences from the structure of the chase comedy. However, the significant action of the scene takes place only when the actors reach the center of the frame. The movement into center frame has the effect of leading the spectator's eye to the significant action. The movement internalizes a narrative function that might otherwise have been fulfilled by a live lecturer. Such seemingly slight alterations in film style were part of the project to make a self-contained unit of the film itself, making distribution to a growing variety of exhibition venues more efficient, as well as giving more control over the presentation to the producer.

The diagonal entry and exit contributes more than a directional arrow, however: it also serves as a system for linking shots and outlining the geography of the action. The first two shots of *The Mill Girl* may be used to illustrate this. The film begins with a shot of a gate set into a hedge, representing the home of the heroine, where the hero joins her in the morning to accompany her to the mill. The hero enters from the spectator's right, stops at center to meet the girl at the gate, and they continue together forward to the left side of the frame, approaching the three-quarters position as they exit. The following shot, in front of the mill, shows groups of workers entering from the same three-quarters position at left, going into mid-distance and entering the factory gate at center. The young couple from the previous shot is among them. By following this direction principle with a fair degree of consistency, the filmmakers keep the action flowing continuously in a kind of synthetic space.

The Mill Girl contains a sequence that exemplifies alternating editing in its basic original form, that is, action taking place inside and outside a building. This occurs when the thugs hired by the boss come to the helpful worker's home during the night:

1. Exterior: the hero enters scene from left and goes through gate to his house.
2. Interior: in bedroom, the hero enters from right foreground, goes around the bed, yawns, closes window, and sits on chair to remove his shoes.
3. Exterior: another view of house, followed by the employer leading his thugs into the scene, then sending them back out of frame while he stands and waits.
4. Interior: a slightly closer view of the bedroom, with the hero now in bed. Hearing a noise, he puts hand to ear, goes to window, and looks out.
5. Exterior: the thugs come back with a ladder and place it against the house so that the top disappears from sight, while the boss gestures a command of silence.
6. Interior: the hero is at the window, then he turns away and makes up a dummy shape in his bed, gets a stick, and crouches below the foot of the bed in the foreground.
7. Exterior: the thugs climb the ladder while the boss holds it.
8. Interior: the hero cups his ear, listening, while the thugs raise the window, enter, and attack the dummy. The hero jumps up, knocks one man down as the other flees, then throws the first man out the window.
9. Exterior: the man who has been thrown falls down on the man at the bottom, the other having already fled the scene.   (Bowser 60–61)

Between shots 4 and 5, we might note that the cut between shots is motivated by the pretence of hearing a noise, one example among several in this period that shows such a motivation for a cut to another scene and back again. In the interior/exterior scenes of *The Mill Girl* there is simultaneity and/or an ellipsis of time between the shots (there is no overlap of time or repeated action from interior to exterior). By now, there were few films other than those of Edwin S. Porter to contain such repetition.

▰▰▰▰▰▰▰▰ Episodic Comedy in Black and White: *Laughing Gas*

Laughing Gas is another example of the linked-episode comedy, this one from the Edison studio and directed by Edwin S. Porter. A basic premise is established: a woman is given gas at the dentist that makes her laugh uncontrollably and, in a series of episodes in varying urban settings, her laughter sets off the chaotic laughter of others. Episodes could be dropped or extended, and the joke remains the same. Laughing gas, or N_2O, discovered in 1793 by Joseph Priestly, was used as a recreational drug for a long period before its acceptance as an anesthetic in dental practice. Medicine shows and carnivals sold it to customers to inhale as a cheap high. The joke of the nonstop laughter that spreads like a contagion can be found in vaudeville acts and minstrel shows.

The woman in *Laughing Gas* is black. She is performing at a time when ethnic stereotypes were commonly used in cinema as an aid to narration, a kind of shorthand for a characterization. This is the time in America when the director of New York's Bronx Zoo, a white man, saw nothing wrong with the exhibition of a Congolese pygmy with monkeys in a cage (Keller).

The second scene in *Laughing Gas* (Edison, 1907) is in the office of the dentist and his assistant, where the woman is given the gas that relieves her toothache. She then starts her boisterous journey. GRAFICS collection.

The question arises as to whether *Laughing Gas* falls under the racist label. In an interview in the DVD *Edison: The Invention of the Movies,* Michele Wallace argues that it is not necessarily racist. The woman is the leading character of the narrative and, as Wallace notes, she is a big beautiful black woman whose vitality shines from the screen. The contagion of her laughter brings wild disorder not only in the black community but in the white world where she moves freely, even in the white family where she is employed as servant. Jacqueline Stewart (105) relates this figure to the stereotype of the "Mammy" and points out that the black female servant in white families had a freedom to move in white society that was not available to others.

There is a degree of ambiguity in the relation of this character to the larger picture of race relations in the United States. The depiction of black people in the period before the institutionalization of the cinema is not easy to characterize, because it varies widely. (An analysis in depth of the films portraying black people in this period, including this film, may be found in Stewart's essay.)

We might consider that the woman is out of control and, under the influence of laughing gas, cannot help herself. That lack of discipline could suggest the childishness and emotionalism of the "inferior race," characteristics also ascribed to the new immigrants from eastern and southern Europe. Nevertheless, the total assurance of the lovely heroine of *Laughing Gas*, the self-confidence and the enjoyment with which she throws herself into the situations and upsets everyone else, white or black, puts aside considerations of racism in this film, whatever the attitudes of the film's producers might have been.

There are eleven scenes, one of which is missing in surviving materials. The film begins and ends with large close-ups. In the introductory close-up, the young woman expresses the pain of a toothache, a swollen jaw and a white scarf tied around her head, and in the final close-up she is laughing at or with us, the spectators. These shots are in the tradition of the one-shot "facial expression" films offered as an attraction in the earliest days of cinema, and still used here for a similar purpose. The opening close-up goes a small step further than that, however, by providing the motivation for the film that follows. The second scene is in the office of the dentist and his assistant, both of them white: here she comes to attain relief, is given the gas, and starts her boisterous journey. Next, there is a group seated along the bench in a streetcar. When a woman enters, the men lift up their newspapers and read to avoid having to offer her a seat. These characters all appear to be white. The big black woman then enters and more or less falls down into a seat right in the middle of them, forcing them to move over and then to dissolve in laughter. According to Charles Musser, who restored the film for DVD, the fourth scene, in which the heroine breaks up the performance of a German street band with her laughter, is missing, and the next is an exterior scene in which the heroine meets a milkman and upsets his merchandise, bringing two policemen to the scene. Of course, all end up laughing. The heroine and the policemen appear in the police station in the following scene, where she again breaks up the proceedings. Next, there is another street scene: two bricklayers are in a fight and her laughter breaks it up. In the dining room of a white family, she brings in the dinner and upsets the soup on her employer's head, after which everybody ends up on the floor in the laughing melee. Then there is a scene in the moonlight (a George Méliès–like moon with a face that laughs) in which she meets a black man with whom there is a mutual attraction. But the romance cannot get anywhere while they are overcome with laughter. Finally, there is a scene in a church where the black preacher earnestly delivers his sermon to an enthusiastic audience, until the heroine enters, takes a seat, and breaks up the proceedings during a solemn prayer. In the true spirit of slapstick comedy, she brings down the forces of authority, the police, and the church. There is no scene in which she is humiliated, disrespected, or defeated. *Laughing Gas* demonstrates that racial films in early cinema were not always unambiguously racist.

The Problem of the Story Film: *College Chums*

Comedies about college life seem to appeal to almost all audiences, although higher education was probably out of reach for most of the nickelodeon audience. Collegiate comedies, already an established stage tradition, neglected the educational purpose of such institutions in favor of tales of sports, fun, and romance.

College Chums, from the Edison studio, had a lot to offer its audiences: a conversation by telephone, then sometimes referred to as "the lovers' telegraph" for reasons of its privacy; the misunderstandings of lovers; cross-dressing; and the mores, manners, and camaraderie of college life itself. A college man's fiancée sees him in the company of another woman and accuses him of perfidy. He makes up the false excuse that the woman is his sister. He does not have a sister. When the fiancée, accompanied by her parents, comes to visit him in his college rooms, his roommate is enlisted to dress up as a woman and pretend to be the "sister," leading to further misunderstandings and entanglements. The topic of cross-dressing was consid-

A conversation by telephone, often referred to at the time as "the lovers' telegraph" for reasons of its privacy (*College Chums*, Edison, 1907). GRAFICS collection.

ered acceptable material for comedy then as now; it could lead to misunderstandings and open many prurient possibilities. In *College Chums*, the father of the girl is drawn to the cross-dressing young man masquerading as the "sister" and carries on a suggestive flirtation until caught up by his wife.

College Chums has a complicated story to tell in one reel and in some ways lacks sufficient means to tell it. The main part of the story is told in a very lengthy shot of the characters in the college rooms filmed in long shot, as if we were looking at a stage set. Actually, it was made in several shots meant to appear as one, with continuous action from one shot to the next, because the director thought it preferable to complete all the action within one shot, even though more than one shot was necessary to achieve it. By avoiding calling attention to the cuts, and thus to the filmmaking process, he hoped to avoid distracting the spectator from the narrative. This avoidance of the shock of the cut to another shot might be related to a much later style known as classic cinema, but here it is more a reflex of the older style now about to give way to quite a different one. One can scarcely observe the facial expressions of the actors in *College Chums*, and only the broadest of gestures are used. Without advance knowledge of the plot or an aid of some sort, the audience may have found it difficult to follow. It is certainly difficult for a modern audience seeing it for the first time. However, *College Chums* got around these problems at the time with a well-rehearsed set of actors reading lines behind the screen in the theaters. The troupe, known as Actologue, traveled with *College Chums* from one theater to the next. The use of such acting teams was probably more prevalent this year than in any other, as filmmakers struggled with the problems of the story film. In August, Lyman Howe made a special feature of actors behind the screen at Ford's Opera House in Baltimore when producing "Moving Pictures That Talk" (Musser, *Before* 398). Another such troupe appeared under the name of Humanovo, employed by the exhibitor Adolph Zukor. Of course the troupe of traveling players added greatly to the cost of exhibiting *College Chums*. The small storefront shows could not make a profit from their nickel admissions if they had to pay such costs. By the time *College Chums* completed its run at the high-class theaters and music halls it was undoubtedly shown in the nickelodeons, but it would have been shown without the players. The exhibitor might have narrated it himself, or employed a single talker.

Telephones were still a novelty for many, used mostly for businesses, institutions, services, and shops, and as a private luxury for the well-to-do. The telephone lines did not yet reach great distance. It would not be until 1915 that New York could talk to San Francisco. For filmmakers, thinking of ways to film telephone calls was intertwined with a new understanding of links between distant spaces. Crosscutting of adjacent scenes was beginning to appear, as we have seen in *The Mill Girl*, but to relate distant spaces was another problem. The method devised for showing a telephone conversation in *College Chums* is a literal one: circles on each side of the screen enclose the speakers and a space showing rooftops fills the center, demonstrating the distance between the participants in the conversation. Similar compositions may be found for portraying phone calls in postcards of the time. It enables the filmmaker to complete the action of the scene in one shot and makes it clear that two distant images are linked in time. This mode of showing a phone call was popular for a few years before the widespread acceptance of editing together two shots of the two ends of a telephone conversation. Early this year, Pathé sent over from France *Médor au téléphone* (Spot at the Phone) (1906), a comedy with a conversation between a dog and his master that was intercut between the two speakers several times.

To further demonstrate that the telephone is a long-distance talking device, the conversation in *College Chums* takes place by means of animated letters tumbling across the screen between the speakers. In a clever touch, the letters express the emotions in the conversation: when the lovers quarrel, the letters meet and crash in mid-screen. The animated conversation, devised by Edwin S. Porter, took a lot of painstaking work, moving letters about between each frame. The hypothetical "one shot" here is actually composed of many shots planned to appear as one. The telephone sequence is a set-piece, an attraction, a magic trick. It also carries an important portion of the narrative, unlike some of the spectacle scenes in earlier films. This elaborate scene shows how some filmmakers found a literal solution to the problems of actions taking place simultaneously in distant spaces. It shows the resistance of a filmmaker like Porter to the concept of alternating edits between distant spaces, which soon become the common way to portray telephone conversations and, more generally, to represent the various threads of a narrative.

As the nickelodeons spread across the nation, fueled by large waves of immigrants and a rapidly growing audience in the midst of a depression, the motion picture industry wondered if this was a fad or if it had a real future, progressives worried about the effect of the new cheap amusement on society, and filmmakers struggled to find new ways to construct films to convey the more complex narratives that now appeared to be in demand. In this transition period, we can see a few hesitant steps, such as the various relationships of separate shots in space and time, toward a new way of seeing the moving image and the visual world in the new modern age of fast transportation and instant communication.

1908

Movies and Other Media

MATTHEW SOLOMON

Asked what achievements history would remember from this year, a dozen leaders in different fields had difficulty reaching a consensus, although several agreed that recent advances in aviation, including the Wright brothers' successful passenger flights and Count Ferdinand von Zeppelin's sustained dirigible flights in Germany would prove significant. Others pointed to the Root-Takahira Agreement, which averted possible war with Japan by settling U.S. and Japanese colonial interests in East Asia ("Striking Events"). In retrospect, one could add the introduction of the Model T automobile by the Ford Motor Company and the discovery of oil in the Middle East by the British to this short list of decisive events for the year. In the arts, the group of eight artists who would form the core of the Ashcan School joined together in an independent show with paintings that depicted much grittier visions of modern life.

In *The Melting Pot*, a hit play that opened in the nation's capital during the fall, the United States is a crucible in which a diverse group of immigrants are amalgamated into a new nation. As playwright Israel Zangwill's metaphor suggested, forging a unified national identity was proving to be a fiery process, for the country was fissured by heated racial, ethnic, and class differences. On 14 August, an angry mob in Springfield, Illinois, lynched two African American men during a violent race riot; several thousand more African Americans fled the city after their homes and businesses were burned. Racial enmity and anti-immigrant feelings were intensified by record levels of unemployment and fierce competition for jobs. Leading up to the November presidential election, the electorate was divided over a number of issues, including U.S. imperialism in the Philippines and limiting the power of big business or organized labor. The candidates of both major parties struggled to articulate viable solutions to the dire economic situation the country faced in the wake of the Panic of 1907.

In *The Financial Scare*, a film released by the Selig Polyscope Company in January, a man reads of a bank failure in the newspaper while at work and rushes home to tell his family and servants to withdraw their savings immediately. A chase ensues as the members of the household hurry to the bank, each hoping to arrive before the money is gone. Though they all succeed in withdrawing their money from the bank and hiding it throughout the home, all is lost to a passing thief who sees where the money is hidden, robs the house, and gets away. *The Financial Scare* was a fictional reminder of the financial panic that had gripped the country a few months earlier when a sharp drop in the stock market and an overextension of credit resulted in the failure of several banks and a run on deposits—a crisis exacerbated by the sensationalism of the yellow press and stemmed only by the intervention of the Treasury Department and large loans from several major financiers. While the film's unhappy ending might have served as a cautionary tale for those who rashly pursued alternatives to the banking system, its comedy tended to elide the rather unpleasant fact that bank failures were but one aspect of a severe recession that threatened the livelihood of workers and the nation's industries.

In the film industry, the recession made things difficult for film exhibitors and spectators alike. As one theater owner emphasized in a letter to the trade journal *Views and Film Index*:

> The truth is that both the United States and Canada are passing through a period of exceptionally hard times. The people of the States have indisputable proof of this in the suspensions of banks and the closing of shops, factories, and mills. On the east side of New York City alone there are between 130,000 and 150,000 unemployed people. . . . When people declare that they have not sufficient means to secure food, clothing, and other necessaries of life, how can the store show expect to fill their seats, even if they have one of the most popular forms of entertainment of the age and charge only five cents admission? (Sawtkin 4–5)

Although many people had less disposable income to spend, moving pictures were gaining an increasing share of the amusement market. New theaters opened in many locations. Many were nickelodeons or "store shows" set up in vacant storefronts with a minimal initial investment. Additionally, a number of existing theatrical venues were converted into movie theaters. An auspicious indicator of cinema's burgeoning status was the conversion of several of Keith and Proctor's vaudeville theaters into "Bijou Dream" movie houses. Movies continued to be seen in vaudeville theaters, amusement parks, skating rinks, churches, and even on steamships arriving in the United States via the Hamburg-American line ("New Field" 171).

The Edison Manufacturing Company and the American Mutoscope and Biograph Company, the two firms that controlled the most important motion picture patents, made competing moves to consolidate and re-organize the film industry, jockeying for position throughout the year. The lines were drawn early on, when the Edison Company, emboldened by recent victories in its campaign of patent litigation, issued licenses to the Kalem Company, the Vitagraph Company of America, Pathé-Frères, Georges Méliès, Sigmund Lubin, the Essanay Film Manufacturing Company, and Selig in exchange for royalties paid on every foot of film released. The films of the Association of Edison Licensees, as the combine was known, were staggered throughout the week and distributed by an affiliated network of licensed film exchanges at a standard rental price per foot. This network of film exchanges was initially called the United Film Service Protective Association, but in February it was renamed, more simply, the Film Service Association. Edison's chief domestic competitor, Biograph, bolstered by legal decisions in its favor and the purchase of several key patents, did not join the combine, opting instead to license several film importers, including the George Kleine Optical Company, to make use of its patents. A growing number of nickel theaters, many of which changed programs daily, created a massive demand for moving pictures. The members of the Edison and Biograph groups each upped their output to keep pace—so much so that some feared the industry was threatened by a crisis of overproduction. A few years earlier, Pittsburgh's Harry Davis had been one of the first entrepreneurs to invest in popular-priced movie theaters, but in July, he was hardly alone in claiming that movies were far more than a passing fad: "I know that the 'nickel craze' is not a craze, but an actual demand, and that so long as the manufacturers back up the efforts of the showmen with good subjects, moving pictures will continue to ride on a high wave of prosperity" (qtd. in "Life of the Nickelodeon" 12).

Double Vision, Double Purpose

What were "good subjects" for films? This was a question that preoccupied nearly everyone connected with the film business. Many within the industry were determined to "uplift" cinema and took definite steps to purge the medium of unsavory associations by pushing for reforms in film exhibition and supporting the production of "quality" films. Despite these well-publicized gentrification efforts, many of the films produced during the year were clearly addressed not so much to the emerging middle-class audience for cinema as to the vigorous existing base of spectators among the working class. Tom Gunning describes this fundamental ambivalence as "the double vision of the film industry in 1908": "Still derived from

fairgrounds and cheap urban amusements, the industry was rooted in a tradition of ungenteel showmanship. But from heads of production companies
to the exhibitors, the film business also desired the blessing of the middle
class—and the social respectability and financial security this would imply"
(88). This "double vision" was a defining feature of the year's cinema,
which oscillated between lowbrow slapstick comedies like Biograph's *The
Curtain Pole* and more highbrow subjects such as the adaptations of Ferenc
Molnár's celebrated play *The Devil* that were made by both the Edison and
Biograph Companies.

While there was no shortage of original scenarios, many moving pictures were derived from existing works as film producers looked to a variety
of other media for subjects and stories. Gene Gauntier, who wrote numerous scenarios for Kalem and Biograph, recalls the extent to which writers
and producers took advantage of unprotected material in other media:

> The woods were full of ideas. The surface had scarcely been scratched. A
> poem, a picture, a short story, a scene from a current play, a headline in the
> newspaper: All was grist that came to my mill. There was no copyright law to
> protect authors and I could and did infringe upon everything. We also traded
> on the names of successes though the plot might be totally different.   (183)

The theater was an especially rich source for filmmakers, many of
whom—like Gauntier, D. W. Griffith, and countless other actors and directors—had begun their careers on the stage and continued to work in the
theater while making films. And filmmakers borrowed not only from other
media but also from each other, quickly imitating successful films with their
own freely plagiarized versions.

In 1907, Kalem had been sued for producing an unauthorized film version of Lew Wallace's novel *Ben-Hur*. In May 1908, a U.S. Circuit Court
judge ruled that Kalem's *Ben Hur* (1907) had infringed on the author and
publisher's copyright as well as the theatrical rights to the story. The decision, the *New York Times* noted, "will have a most important effect on the
moving picture business all over the country, films of many popular plays
being in circulation and others in course of preparation" ("Must Pay"). The
case was subsequently appealed to the Supreme Court, which in 1911 ruled
against Kalem, forcing film producers to purchase the rights to copyrighted
works in other media.

The best publicized "intermedial" adaptations were films that borrowed
the titles—and, it was hoped, some of the cachet—of classic works of theater and literature. The plays of Shakespeare, which also happened to be in
the public domain, were abridged in adaptations of *Macbeth, Romeo and*

Juliet, *Richard III*, *Antony and Cleopatra*, and *Julius Caesar* by Vitagraph. Kalem and Society Italian Cinès also released versions of *As You Like It* and *Othello*, respectively. Like nearly all other contemporaneous films, each of these was less than one thousand feet in length, and thus considerably reduced from the theatrical or literary originals. Abbreviated film versions of much longer theatrical plays were sometimes incomprehensible to audiences who did not possess prior knowledge of the story; understanding was often aided by the use of lecturers or intertitles. "Quality" films were not aimed exclusively at the middle class, since the appeal of Shakespeare, for example, in fact cut across the class spectrum (Uricchio and Pearson 65-110). Nor were "quality" films exempt from the kinds of criticisms more often leveled at other kinds of subjects. In Chicago, for example, the police censor judged the scenes of dueling and stabbing in *Macbeth* inappropriate and ordered them removed ("'Macbeth' Pruned" 511).

Pathé-Frères also played an important role in the move toward "quality" films. Late in the year, Pathé began to release films like *L'Arlésienne*, which was produced in France in partnership with SCAGL (Société cinématographique des auteurs et gens de lettres)—a new production company involving prominent actors, dramatists, and authors—under the aegis of Films d'Art. Like Vitagraph's "quality" films, Richard Abel notes, "Pathé's *films d'art* had a double purpose: to 'educate' the masses but also to attract and hold the 'better classes'" (127). Pathé-Frères maintained a strong presence in the American market, as in many other markets around the world, and when Charles Pathé visited the United States, he stressed the need to uplift American cinema: "I must confess that while the United States is the country where the use of the cinematograph has spread to the greatest extent in the shortest amount of time, it is at the same time the country where the exhibitions lack most in refinement. I think, in their own interest, the exhibitors should be more particular regarding the quality of their films" (qtd. in "Chas. Pathé" 4). Despite Pathé's stated emphasis, many of his company's films were sensational melodramas, base comedies, and clever trick films that critics found to be decidedly lacking in refinement.

Regulating the Movies

The regulation of cinema focused not only on film content that was deemed problematic but also on the space of exhibition, which was fraught with dangers both real and imagined. On 13 January, a catastrophic fire during a movie showing in a Boyertown, Pennsylvania, opera house killed 170 people. Although the tragic blaze was eventually traced to an overturned kerosene lamp, initial reports attributed it to the film projector in use during the show. Fires were an ever-present danger that attended the projection of highly flammable nitrate films—a danger that worsened when equipment was not properly operated or projectionists smoked in the booth while turning the projector's crank over and over for hours on end. Fire inspectors and, to an even greater extent, the police exercised local authority to license, monitor, and, in cases where it was deemed necessary, shut down movie theaters.

Cultural concerns about the movies often highlighted the disproportionate numbers of women, children, and immigrants who were believed to make up nickelodeon audiences:

> Of all those who constituted the nickelodeon's mass audience (and variations, of course, existed from one region or city to another), several groups especially attracted attention. One was the disproportionate number of recent immigrants from eastern and southern Europe, concentrated in urban centers throughout the Northeast and the upper Midwest. . . . The other group was hardly mutually exclusive, consisting of women and children who, according to most accounts (however self-serving), made up the greater portion of nickelodeon audiences across the country.   (Abel 118)

Cinema's verisimilitude was judged acutely threatening to such impressionable spectators, who were especially likely—it was said—to be influenced by moving images of violence, crime, and immorality. In Chicago, two crime films, Kalem's *Night Riders*, which centered on the violent exploits of a group of mounted outlaws, and Essanay's *The James Boys in Missouri*, which showed the James brothers robbing, killing, and burning down buildings, were singled out for suppression. Exhibitor Jake Block protested to the courts that the violence seen in these films was an undeniable part of American history (Grieveson 74).

Never entirely comfortable with external censorship, the motion picture trade press, which now included three weekly journals devoted exclusively to developments in the film industry—*Moving Picture World*, *Moving Picture News*, and *Views and Film Index* (which in September became the *Film Index*)—maintained that such films brought unwelcome negative attention to the movies. One critic cited *The James Boys in Missouri* as a prime example of the "degradation of the motion picture entertainment": "One can have but little admiration for the pains and time spent in making such films in the first place . . . but one can wish heartily that the effort had produced something elevating, or at least harmless, instead of the seeming realism of bloodshed, crime, and brutality" ("Degradation" 308-09). In general, the trade press advocated industry self-regulation, urging film producers to avoid controversial subjects.

The regulation of cinema was in part a response to vocal attacks on motion pictures by religious groups. Municipal prohibitions against Sunday shows had a particularly deleterious effect on nickelodeon attendance, making it difficult or impossible for working people to come to the theater on their one day off. Exhibitors tried to circumvent these bans by screening travelogues or biblical films on Sundays—Pathé's *Passion Play* (1907) continued to be a popular subject, for example—or, as in several parts of the country, by taking the authorities to court, claiming that movies should not be subject to local "blue" laws. New York City, which was home to several major film production companies (Edison, Biograph, Vitagraph) as well as to several hundred nickelodeons, was an important battleground in struggles over regulation. The pitched battle between film exhibitors and New York City officials culminated on Christmas Eve, the day after a public hearing had given members of the clergy a platform for their grievances. Mayor George McClellan summarily revoked the licenses of all the city's moving picture shows, citing a widespread lack of adequate fire exits and religious opposition to Sunday exhibitions as primary reasons for his decision. In order to reopen, exhibitors were obligated to pass safety inspections and agree in writing not to operate on Sundays ("Picture Shows").

Film Nationalism

If movies and the cheap amusement problem were a key issue for local politicians in New York's Tammany Hall and elsewhere, the mass media also played a role in national politics and the race for the White House. Honoring a promise not to seek a third term in office, President Theodore Roosevelt chose William Howard Taft, his Secretary of War, as his successor. Even before Taft was chosen as the Republican presidential nominee, Kalem's film *Presidential Possibilities* was in wide circulation. Taft's opponent, the Democrat William Jennings Bryan, could subsequently be seen onscreen in films produced by Lubin and Vitagraph. In Chicago, supporters arranged "to can Mr. Bryan's personality as well as his voice, and the moving picture apparatus was on hand to rival the phonograph" ("How Bryan Poses"), leading one prophetic commentator to joke that campaigning could effectively be accomplished in the absence of the candidate by means of cinematograph films, phonograph cylinders, and a rubber hand with which to shake the hands of voters ("Film Campaigning"). In the end, Taft won by a fairly wide margin in the Electoral College, although Bryan

The Kalem Company filming Secretary of War William Howard Taft reviewing the troops at Fort Meyer, Virginia (*Views and Film Index* 11 April 1908: 5; original photograph by Frederic Bulkely Hyde [*Presidential Possibilities*, Kalem, 1908]).

carried the South and Socialist Party candidate Eugene V. Debs garnered 3 percent of the popular vote.

Presidential Possibilities largely consists of shots of Taft reviewing the troops and ends with the American flag being saluted. The lecture commentary meant to accompany the end of the film reads, "Long may it wave over our glorious country," cloaking partisan political differences beneath the rhetoric of patriotism and military pride (*Moving Picture World* 351). Nationalism was also clearly at play in Pathé's popular films of the London Olympic Games. This was especially true of *The Marathon Race*, which showed the controversial finish of the Olympic marathon, in which the Italian Dorando Pietri collapsed just before the end of the race and had to be helped across the finish line. Pietri was disqualified and the second finisher, John Hayes, was awarded the gold medal. The trade press synopsis (which may also have been used as an accompanying lecture) reads,

> Hayes and Dorando are leading, while the rest of the contestants follow the game little American, who appears to be as fresh as at the start, while the others are dropping out exhausted. . . . Dorando . . . goes down in a heap, but is quickly assisted to his feet and fairly carried by the attendants over the tape. Then along comes Hayes, and finished without the aid of any one, and seems to have plenty of vitality to spare for a longer distance. The distribution of the prizes is the next picture. . . . When Hayes very modestly steps up to receive

his he is fairly carried off his feet by his admiring friends, who place him on a table while four sturdy fellows bear him aloft before the thousands, proudly waving the Stars and Stripes.   (*Views and Film Index* 11)

In this text, Hayes's finish is presented as a worthy (but unassuming) victory of American endurance and persistence over a European rival, a victory supported and celebrated by his fellow Americans. After returning to the United States, Hayes appeared in a similarly nationalistic live theatrical act in which films of the marathon race were screened ("Cinematograph's Aid"). Furthermore, as a *Moving Picture World* editorial noted on 3 October,

> Many branches of the Young Men's Christian Association are making use of the moving pictures taken of the Olympian games in London, England, as an encouragement of athletics among members of the organization. . . . The power of patriotism suggests itself in connection with the movement. The United States figured gloriously among the victors in the games, and this, with the incentive involved, makes the pictures a success.   (251)

As the trade press indicated, nonfiction films of American victories in the Olympic Games were an instructive example of a good subject that could also serve as a useful object lesson in constructing virile American manhood.

Nationalist rhetoric also permeated discussions of appropriate subjects for story films, which were the industry's main product. If the wrong stories threatened to corrupt young people, women, and immigrants, the right kind of stories might have the opposite effect. Foreign film producers—Pathé in particular, as Abel has detailed—were increasingly scapegoated in cultural struggles to define cinema as "American." George Kleine, who distributed films imported from several European countries, complained that the Edison combine was explicitly attempting to exploit American nationalism to stoke the fires of this cinematic xenophobia for its own benefit: "A concerted attempt is being made to give the impression that Edison film licensees represent America. . . . By direct statement, by innuendo, by constant repetition, the idea is fostered that this is a patriotic movement fathered by Edison, to retain the plums of the trade for American manufacturers, which the wicked foreigners are trying to filch" (qtd. in Rabinovitz 173).

Criticism accentuated not just the foreign origins of imported films, but also the purportedly inaccurate ways that foreign films portrayed American life. In response, American producers proffered their films as authentic American products that represented the nation's shared values. Some, like Vitagraph's *A Cowboy Elopement* and Edison's *Pocahontas*, took place in the definitively American setting of the American West. Others, like

Kalem's *Evangeline, The Scarlet Letter, The Legend of Sleepy Hollow*, and *Way Down East*, were unauthorized versions of American classics that offered vernacular alternatives to more pretentious adaptations of European theater and literature.

■ "Talking" Pictures

Lecturers were an important part of the year's vogue for talking pictures, which encompassed both performed and mechanical modes of sound accompaniment. Lectures were delivered beside the screen for one or more films in a program, and could include lines of dialogue and explanatory or contextual information that aided the spectator's comprehension and enjoyment. Lectures were frequently paired with nonfiction films and religious or literary subjects. Critics like W. Stephen Bush of *Moving Picture World* (who was a professional lecturer himself) contended that lectures were an essential step in uplifting cinema from the debased realm of cheap amusement into the stratum of legitimate entertainment. Production companies facilitated lectures by distributing printed synopses with films; these synopses were sometimes reprinted in the trade press. Although the content of lectures was not necessarily edifying, the quasi-educational thrust of the lecture format also allowed film exhibitors to claim that they should not be subject to laws prohibiting Sunday shows (Altman 140–44).

Synchronized sound systems such as the Theaterphone, the Picturephone, the Cameraphone, and the Gaumont Chronophone were aggressively marketed to exhibitors. Each allowed audiences to hear words simultaneously as they were spoken on the screen. Many talking and singing pictures were films of stage performances that were screened as substitutes for live vaudeville. Any theater equipped with sound-film technology thus had access to quality vaudeville acts that could be used to supplement moving picture shows. While synchronized sound systems seem to have worked acceptably well, relatively few theater owners could bear the high rental or purchase prices of these systems, especially considering that talking pictures made up only one part of their programs. Other options for synchronized sound were available. An exhibitor could arrange for actors to speak lines of dialogue behind the screen in synchronization with a selected film, as one theater did with *Francesca di Rimini* ("Films That Please"). An exhibitor could also engage one of a number of companies of actors—Actologue, Humanovo, Ta-Mo-Pic (Talking Moving Pictures)—that traveled from theater to theater performing dialogue behind the screen in synchronization with specific films. Perhaps the most common form of nonmusical accompaniment was the use of sound effects to imitate noises made by trains, galloping horses, gunshots, and storms (Altman 152–78).

In all cases, going to the movies was a multimedia experience that typically included the playing of a piano, organ, or phonograph (though music, as Rick Altman has demonstrated, was not always played during the screening of the films themselves). Most nickelodeons incorporated illustrated song slides into film shows, which were projected from the projection booth and usually accompanied by a singer and a pianist. Illustrated songs were not just a musical interlude that covered reel changes (since most booths housed only a single projector) but in fact constituted one of the primary features of the picture show.

■ *'Ostler Joe*: Transgression and Containment

One film that lent itself especially well to verbal accompaniment was Biograph's *'Ostler Joe*, which was based on the popular poem of the same name by George R. Sims. Although the film's basic story of marriage, infidelity, and family tragedy is readily comprehensible without reference to the poem, it gains depth through a reading of Sims's ballad alongside it. Such readings seem likely because the poem was included in the *Biograph Bulletin* for the film and had long been part of the recitation repertoire (Mayer 42–43). Like the poem, the film tells the story of the humble stableman—hostler, or 'ostler—Joe (Edward Dillon), who weds Annie, a woman from the village. The couple has a child Joe adores, but Annie leaves them both for another man (played by D. W. Griffith) with whom she has begun an affair. The child dies. Many years later, Annie is destitute and falls ill. Joe has forgiven her and comes to her on her deathbed. Like her young son, she dies in Joe's arms. *'Ostler Joe* consists of seven shots, each of which is a fairly long take. Although film and poem are not exactly synchronous, five of these shots center on turning points in the story that roughly match lines or stanzas of the poem: the wedding of Joe and Annie; Annie running away with her lover after leaving a note for Joe; Joe returning home to discover Annie gone; the death of the child; and the death of Annie.

The other two shots of the film, however, do not really correspond to specific events in the poem. Instead, these provide telling glimpses of Annie's infidelity and her decadent life apart from Joe, moments that reveal her character, though neither is really a turning point in the story. Whereas Sims's poem focuses on Annie's seduction, the film jumps from the wedding, shown in the first shot, directly to the affair. In the film's second shot,

Annie is already a "fallen woman," as she welcomes another man into the home shortly after her husband leaves for work earlier in the shot. In place of the poem's brief chronicle of Annie's rise to fame in London as an actress, the penultimate shot of the film shows Annie enjoying the high life with her lover, dancing on a table while drinking and dining out with a gathering of the idle rich.

Both these shots—and the latter shot in particular—can be understood less as singular events than as examples of "iterative" narrative, as scenes that stand in for a series of similar events occurring repeatedly over a much longer period of time (Gaudreault "Singular Narrative"). Indeed, these two shots seem inserted less to depict specific story occurrences than to condense larger segments of the story. While the other shots in the film mark events that cannot really have been repeated, these two shots correspond to a rather different temporal order. They also have a rather different character. The rest of the film is constructed as a cautionary tale, with scenes progressing from the joining of conjugal bonds to their severance and the dire consequences that follow, but these shots show us the transgressions that the rest of the film goes to such lengths to contain. It is in these two shots in particular that one can most clearly see the "double vision" of the film, conforming at once to the uplift movement's emphasis on moralistic stories but in the process showcasing immoral behavior.

The film has a clear moral that shows not only Annie, but also her family, being severely punished for her marital transgressions. The deaths of the child and his mother follow in quick succession from her abandonment of the family. Joe's intense suffering, which is twice underscored by the dramatic gesture of him raising both arms to the sky, as he gazes upward, figures as the direct result of his wife's departure. Father and son both beseech a higher power, dropping to their knees to pray after Annie leaves (though it is not clear whether they are praying for her return or for the forgiveness of her sins). The child never gets up, for the next shot finds him lying in his deathbed. Nor does Joe ever recover. The contrast between the happy-go-lucky groom (pun intended), ecstatic on his wedding day and joyfully at play with his little boy, who rides around the room on his father's back, and the despondent husband after his wife's departure is inscribed on Joe's comportment. Once Annie is gone, he is seen with head buried in his arms as the doctor tries in vain to cure his sick child and kneeling sorrowfully by his wife's deathbed. The moral of the film was not lost on critics, one praising it as "a fine pictorial rendering of this well-known poem, which teaches a good lesson in its contrast between the simple life and the temptations of a great city" ("'Ostler Joe" 515).

As its title suggests, the film, like the poem, is very much Joe's story, concerned largely with his responses to the series of unhappy tragedies that befall him. Yet the film also offers a privileged view of Annie's experiences, scenes that provoke not only moral condemnation but also, perhaps, empathy. The transformations that married life have wrought on Annie are made clear in the transition between the first two shots of the film. At the wedding, she is nearly as eager and excited as her husband, whom she embraces with great alacrity after the wedding toast. But, in the beginning of the next shot, some years later, she is drained of enthusiasm. As Annie clears the dishes after the family has finished its breakfast, she moves about the room like an automaton, mechanically putting away the breakfast things, folding the tablecloth, and preparing the table for its next use, while her husband relishes a spontaneous game with the child. By contrast, Joe's work in the stables, however repetitive and mechanistic, remains entirely offscreen.

Only when Annie peeks through the window, anticipating the arrival of her lover, does she become livelier. Animated, she moves quickly to dispatch her husband to work before the lover arrives. When the lover walks through the door, they embrace passionately as her child stands in the corner of the room. Their sensual grasp of one another stands in stark contrast to the perfunctory kiss she has just given to Joe a moment earlier—and, for that matter, to the brief hugs they had exchanged in the previous shot after the marriage ceremony. This physical passion peaks in the next shot, when Annie is quite literally torn between her lover and her child. Violently pulling herself from her lover's arms several times, she manages to rush back to the child before being dragged forcefully from the room, eventually abandoning herself to her lover's firm grasp and to her own adulterous passions.

The lesson of the film is clear at the end, when Annie dies in misery—penniless, childless, yet not alone. But the ending cannot entirely efface the illicit pleasures Annie has indulged by giving in to temptation, pleasures the viewer has witnessed by watching the film.

Seeing Things: *After Many Years*

Biograph's *After Many Years* was advertised as a film "on the lines of Enoch Arden, although more intensely heart-stirring than the original play" (Niver, *Biograph* 399), suggesting that the film has closer links to one of several stage versions of the story than to Alfred Lord Tennyson's poem "Enoch Arden." Kalem's *Enoch Arden* film, released six months earlier, seems to have been much more faithful to Tennyson ("Latest Films"). *After Many Years* was directed by D. W. Griffith just a few months after he took over primary directing duties at Biograph. The film begins with the parting of sailor John Davis (Charles Inslee), who is going off to sea, from his wife (Florence Lawrence) and young daughter. John is shipwrecked, but survives on a deserted island. Years go by, and their daughter grows from an infant into a young girl. The wife faithfully awaits the return of John, refusing the entreaties of another suitor, Tom Foster (Harry Solter), who believes her husband dead. When at last John is rescued and restored home, he sees Tom with his wife and child. Mistakenly believing that he has been usurped, the crestfallen John vows revenge. He pursues them with a knife, but, stopping short, momentarily considers taking his own life. Before any harm can be done, however, he embraces his child and is seen by his wife. The misunderstanding is quickly resolved, and the nuclear family is reunited.

Little more than 150 feet longer than *'Ostler Joe, After Many Years* consists of more than twice as many shots, fifteen in all. Although the story departs considerably from the well-known original and is told in a less linear fashion, one trade press commentator praised it as "an interesting and easily understood plot . . . that holds the attention of the audience" ("Comments" 379). Much of the film's absorbing story is told by means of parallel editing, a cornerstone of the emerging "narrator system" Griffith was redefining as director. By alternating shots of John shipwrecked on an island with shots of John's wife at home, Gunning contends, "an omniscient narrator . . . unites on the screen what is separate in the space of the story" (113). The effectiveness of the film derives not only from its virtuoso use of parallel editing, but also from the way it stages much of the action in deep space along the axis of the spectator's vision, with characters approaching from background to foreground again and again to punctuate the dramatic moments that often conclude individual shots.

The backbone of *After Many Years* is a parallel-editing sequence that makes up the middle of the film, alternating shots of John waiting beside a hut on the beach (clad in animal skins) and of his wife standing inside their home and on the porch. The first two shots of this four-shot sequence, shots 8 and 9 of the film, are closer shots that afford the spectator a better view of the faces of the two main characters, whose emotions are conveyed— here and at other points in the film—through facial expressions and gesture. These shots in particular elicit a sense of unfulfilled longing, a sense that is further reinforced by the characters looking at pictures of each other, signaling their reciprocal devotion. In shot 8, John looks at a locket that hangs around his neck. In shots 3 and 10, his wife looks up at a picture that hangs on the wall. The characters' placement within the frame also serves to link them together, as Eileen Bowser points out: "Their positions within their respective shots reflect the emotional relationship, each gazing at the empty space that the other would occupy if they were in the same scene" (64). In terms of the story, John and his wife are separated by a great distance. Through parallel editing, the film figuratively collapses this distance, virtually bringing the couple together while rendering their mutual desire visible.

The emotional crescendo of the film comes in the succession of shot 8, which shows John standing on the beach, kissing the locket, and shot 9, which shows his wife standing on the porch and with outstretched arms. The action of John kissing the locket is interrupted by an uncharacteristically immediate cut to his wife. As Gunning explains, together these two shots are symptomatic of the way morality is embedded within the operations of Griffith's "narrator system":

> The editing creates a nearly supernatural link between the characters. . . . John's kiss is directed toward his absent wife and seems to be greeted by the wife's attempt to enfold her distant husband. Through editing, Griffith creates a space of the imagination in which these gestures meet in a phantom embrace. The desert island kiss resounds upon the welcoming wife outside the English cottage, as devotion overcomes geography. The sense of simultaneous prayers united by a transcendent witness is fully realized, in a space knitted together by mutual desire. The narrator system affirms these gestures of devotion, creating an omniscience that allows this paradoxical embrace. These two shots hint at the ultimate fulfillment of the couple's faithfulness, but their devotion is rewarded only in the final shot of the film, when they are reunited, along with their daughter. The film ends as the other man, Tom, walks out of the frame in disappointment, leaving the family kneeling together in a happy tableau. (113)

The reunion of the family does not follow directly from alternating shots of their extraordinary mutual devotion. What follows, in fact, is a chase and near-confrontation that threatens to violently destroy the family. These sensational scenes intervene before the plot is resolved. In order for the family to be reunited, John's erroneous vision must first be corrected. When John observes Tom with his wife and daughter beside the very hedge where he and she had once shared tender moments, he misconstrues their physical proximity as intimacy. John is heartbroken and nearly collapses. He follows them out of the frame and pursues them into the next two shots, lurking angrily just out of their view. He raises a knife as if to stab one or both of the apparent lovers, but as his wife and Tom go into the house, he abruptly decides to leave them to their happiness together—as Enoch Arden does both in Tennyson's poem and in Kalem's earlier film. But, as John embraces his child one last time, his wife emerges from the house and the three embrace, bringing about a swift and sudden denouement.

Through these respective sequences of longing and pursuit, *After Many Years* implicitly contrasts the supernatural vision of cinema, which makes desire itself visible, with the flawed—and here potentially fatal—vision of the individual. Next to cinema's privileged view, which transcends space, time, and fixed point of view, mere human sight is exposed as tragically flawed and prone to error.

The Thieving Hand: Trick Film/Comedy

While dramatic films like *'Ostler Joe* and *After Many Years* made up the majority of story films, comedies with much looser narrative structures—and much lower cultural reputations—were also numerous. Vitagraph's *The Thieving Hand* makes use of several trick film techniques to repeat variations on the gag of a disembodied kleptomaniac hand. Though the film may have been based on an original scenario, its style strongly resembles that of French trick comedy films produced by Gaumont, Pathé, and Méliès. A one-armed street peddler sells a pencil to a rich man. As the man walks away, the peddler notices that the man has dropped a ring and returns it to him. In gratitude, the rich man takes the peddler to a shop that sells limbs and purchases him the prosthetic hand and forearm displayed in the window. When the prosthetic is attached and cranked into action, it rapidly pilfers articles from everyone in arm's reach. The "thieving hand" subsequently steals from several passersby, who return to retrieve their possessions and scold the peddler. Exasperated, the peddler pawns the prosthetic. The pawnbroker places it in the window with other valuables, but the prosthetic takes this opportunity to slip rings onto all of its fingers and slide out of the pawnshop on its own power. It reattaches itself to the peddler. Discovering the missing items, the pawnbroker runs to get a policeman, who apprehends the peddler and brings him before a judge. The judge pronounces the peddler guilty, and even as he is led away, the hand continues to pilfer articles. The peddler is placed in a cell with several other prisoners, one of whom is missing an arm. The prosthetic is detached from the peddler and rejoined to the other prisoner (described in advertisements as its original owner), whereupon it begins to steal from everyone else in the cell.

Trick films with a primarily presentational format, many of which were French, continued to constitute a viable category that was used to fill out many film programs. Yet straightforward trick films that lacked a plot were becoming outmoded. Pathé's *Elastic Transformation*, for example, was described as "one of those atrociously colored spectacular and trick films" and dismissed as being hopelessly dated: "Moving picture production has gone beyond this transparent trick work, which belongs five years back in the development of the art" (qtd. in Dahlquist 23). But a related category of films that utilized cinematic tricks (often in outdoor settings) to achieve comedic results seems to have been far more popular with audiences. This move toward embedding film tricks within cinematic stories coincided not only with the predominance of the story film, but also with the publication of articles revealing the methods filmmakers used to mystify audiences. Greater public awareness of the artifice of film production was fostered by articles in the popular press—not to mention the "behind the scenes" knowledge available in such films as Vitagraph's *Making Moving Pictures: A Day in the Vitagraph Studio.*

Other trick film/comedies that similarly blurred the distinction between the two genres are Pathé's *The Runaway Horse* and Biograph's *The Invisible Fluid*. In *The Runaway Horse*, a horse goes on a high-speed rampage after eating an entire bag of oats, upsetting everything and everyone in its path even as it gallops backward. The film was cited as the "greatest laugh producer of recent issue" (*Moving Picture World* 112). In *The Invisible Fluid*, a messenger boy wreaks havoc by mischievously spraying a fluid that renders things invisible, causing much consternation and a wild chase. *Moving Picture World* noted: "At present the most acceptable of the films are the comics, and the best of these are what are called 'chasers.' This is a scene in which a runaway horse or thief is pursued by a crowd" ("Cult" 176).

Not exactly a "chaser" in this sense of the term, *The Thieving Hand* is a signal example of how cinematic tricks were becoming part of the essential repertoire of an emerging school of film comedy rather than ends unto themselves. As such, the film is a liminal example that combines characteristics of what Gunning describes, respectively, as a "cinema of attractions" and a "cinema of narrative integration" (6). The film's primary "attractions" are its clever trick shots, in which a patently lifeless prop is comically endowed with a relentlessly noncompliant life of its own. These "attractions" are only partly "narrativized" by the episodic story of the peddler, which avoids character development in favor of two-dimensional characterizations that can be easily played off the antics of the rampant prosthetic: the poor but honest peddler, the wealthy benefactor, the dili-

The prosthetic hand is placed in the pawnbroker's window with other valuables, but it takes this opportunity to slip rings onto all of its fingers (*The Thieving Hand*, Vitagraph, 1908).

gent salesperson, the Jewish pawnbroker (represented here by an especially crude stereotype), the lazy police officer, the unforgiving judge, the unrepentant criminal. Each of these characters, in turn, is upstaged by the irrepressible hand of the film's title, both when it is attached to a body and when it is not.

The most striking of the film's many trick shots make up the sequence immediately after the hand has been placed in the pawnshop window, as it purloins a number of rings, slides from the window over the counter, out the shop door, and into the street to rejoin its reluctant host, the peddler. In this sequence, the "thieving hand" becomes an independent—and uniquely cinematic—character. These trick shots contain no people and, moreover, are not seen by anyone in the film. (The pawnbroker is momentarily absent from the main part of the pawnshop; the peddler is seated on the curb, asleep, and is only awakened by the reattachment of the prosthetic; and the "thieving hand," of course, does not itself have eyes.) These shots are pure "attractions" that exist apart from the film's rudimentary story, purely for the pleasure of the spectator. After the hand gathers up a fistful of rings that are magically transferred to its fingers, it pauses for a moment to show off its ill-acquired baubles to the film's audience positioned on the other side of the pawnshop window.

In the next shot, the hand pauses once again momentarily as it slides over the pawnshop counter, where it is perched beside a conspicuous array of modern recording and communication technologies, including a phonograph, a gramophone, a telephone, and a box-like handled contraption that looks a lot like a movie camera (all of which have been relegated to the pawnshop). While each of these sound- and image-producing machines requires a hand to turn its crank, the "thieving hand" has, ironically, long ceased to require cranking. (Indeed, we see it cranked only once, by the salesperson who initially sells it.) After teetering on the edge of the counter, the disembodied hand leaves the other, inert, machines behind and slides away on its own inexorable inertia, having escaped yet another display window. As allegory, the film envisions the machine-body not just running freakishly amok, but stubbornly bent on disrupting commercial circuits of buying and selling.

Dime Novel Cinema: *The Boy Detective*

Biograph's *The Boy Detective* was advertised as the "first of a series of film stories, which will be presented periodically, recounting the experiences of Swipesy, the newsboy, whose astute sagacity wins for him, fame as a juvenile Sherlock Holmes" (Niver, *Biograph* 341). Although announced as the beginning of a series of films about a recurring character, no more of Swipesy's adventures appear to have been filmed. Like Eclair's *Nick Carter: The Doctor's Rescue* and Kalem's *Old Sleuth, the Detective*, both of which borrowed the names of long-running dime novel detective characters, *The Boy Detective* references dime novel detective fiction more than the Sherlock Holmes detective stories of Arthur Conan Doyle. The protagonist of Vitagraph's similarly titled *The Stolen Plans; or, The Boy Detective*, released a few months later, is an inventor's son who is described in an advertisement as "a student of 'Nick Carter's' novels" (*Views and Film Index* 14). The boy is pictured in an initial scene "reading a dime novel" and recovers the plans for one of his father's inventions by applying what he has learned from dime novel detective stories, disguising himself as a woman and later as an "Italian organ grinder" to fool the thieves ("Stolen Plans" 10-11).

Swipesy of *The Boy Detective* has much in common with the title character of the dime novel *New York Nell, The Boy-Girl Detective*, another paper seller who works as a detective (and like the woman actor who plays the role, masquerades as a boy). Along with the western, the detective story was one of the most popular genres of dime novels, many of which actually cost a nickel and were especially popular with working-class readers. Swipesy's rough shirt and cap clearly mark the character as a marginal underclass figure, as do his peddling of papers, smoking, and dice-playing with other children on the street. Like many dime novels, the film is set in a gritty urban milieu populated by characters that are seldom who they seem to be (Denning).

Despite its distinct parallels with *New York Nell*, *The Boy Detective* is not really an adaptation, in the strict sense of the term, of any single specific work of cheap fiction. Rather, it is what I would term a generic adaptation because it is based less on the particular story, setting, or set of characters in an existing work than on the common characteristics of an entire genre in another medium. *The Boy Detective* is a composite of the tropes of cheap detective fiction. The film is a variation on the structure of the chase and, like both *Nick Carter: The Doctor's Rescue* and *Old Sleuth, the Detective*, it mobilizes the chase through a story of a kidnapping and involves the detective's use of disguise. Swipesy overhears two men planning to abduct Mary, a woman they have been following. Swipesy shadows the men as they follow Mary to her home, then stop at a saloon. He manages to read a note meant to lure Mary to a spot where she can be waylaid, then races to her home to get there before the message does. With the help of Mary and her maid, Swipesy is disguised as a woman and takes her place in the carriage sent by the kidnappers. Swipesy leaps out wielding what appears to be a gun and holds the kidnappers at bay until the police arrive. The men are apprehended, at which point Swipesy reveals that what appears to be a gun is actually a gimmick cigarette case.

Like many dime novels, the narrative of *The Boy Detective* depends heavily on sheer physical action and chance occurrences. As Charlie Keil notes, "The film remains indebted to a model of narrative exposition derived chiefly from the chase format" (176). The film is itself an extended chase sequence that begins in the first shot and ends in the penultimate shot, moving rapidly through a number of different spaces. The chase is interrupted briefly by the men's stop at the saloon and Swipesy's subsequent visit to Mary's home. Many of the film's significant moments occur by chance, rather than thanks to the "astute sagacity" of the main character. It is chance that Swipesy happens to overhear the plot of the would-be kidnappers when the two men duck into a recess in the building next to where Swipesy is playing dice. It is also chance that in that same dice game he wins the cigarette case that proves so instrumental in foiling the attempted kidnapping.

Interrupting Swipesy's pursuit of the kidnappers, which was filmed entirely outdoors, is a carefully organized long take of the interior of Mary's home, shot in a studio set. This long shot is organized by the entrances and exits of three different characters: the maid, Swipesy, and the messenger boy. The staging is remarkably symmetrical: the three characters enter the frame a total of ten times and exit the frame a total of ten times, with five entrances and exits frame left and five entrances and exits frame right. This constant action creates a constant interplay of onscreen and offscreen space. Significant action occurs offscreen; at one point the frame is empty of characters for several seconds while Swipesy dons a female disguise with the help of Mary and her maid. Swipesy then promenades twice across the

Swipesy in *The Boy Detective* removes a cigarette from the case, lights it, laughs with— or at—the audience, and pats the gimmick confidently (Niver, *Biograph* 341; Biograph, 1908).

frame and back in drag, laughing, much to the amusement of the two women.

The narrative of *The Boy Detective* is structured by a series of deceptions that center on Swipesy's use of disguise and the manipulation of the cigarette case. In the first shot of the film, Swipesy is deceived by the cigarette case, drawing back as the messenger boy aims it at him like a gun after losing the dice game. Swipesy laughs when the gimmick is revealed and takes the cigarette case as part of the winnings. The gimmick reappears in the penultimate shot of the film, when Swipesy aims it at the two men. When the police arrive, Swipesy snaps the cigarette case open, laughs, and hands a cigarette to one of the police officers, who also begin laughing. The final shot that follows is an emblematic coda that parodies the celebrated shot in *The Great Train Robbery* (1903) in which the outlaw Barnes fires a revolver directly at the viewer. In *The Boy Detective*, Swipesy points a fake gun at the viewer and then to the left and right before revealing that it is a cigarette case by opening it to display the words "TAKE ONE" on the inside. He then removes a cigarette from the case, lights it, laughs with—or at—the audience, and pats the gimmick confidently. In *The Great Train Robbery*, smoke authenticates the discharge of the outlaw's pistol, confirming its "realism" (as the Edison catalogue described this final shot). In *The Boy Detective*, however, smoke issues not from Swipesy's fake gun but instead from the cigarette that is laughingly removed from it after it is revealed as a gimmick. To share in this laugh while watching this shot is to take pleasure in being fooled and to enjoy being in on the joke.

While revealing the instrument of deception in direct address to the audience, the final shot also reveals an extra-filmic level of deception: the actor playing Swipesy is a woman. This fact is rendered all the more ironic by the title of the film as well as the female disguise employed by "the boy detective." The boy disguised as a woman is thus actually a woman in drag as a boy, in drag as a woman.

Swipesy's look at the spectator crystallizes the double vision of the film industry and beautifully apotheosizes many of the concerns of cinema this year, addressing himself/herself with a laugh to women and men, to children and adults, and to the working class as well as to the "better" class of movie viewers. The story that precedes it is drawn from dime novels and is populated with archetypes of cheap fiction. Some would have found it familiar or entertaining, a story film that conformed to a different ideal of the rousing well-told tale, marked by sudden reversals of fate. Others might have found it coarse or displeasing, filled with seedy characters and unlikely situations. In the end, whatever threat the ambiguously gendered title character represents is neutralized. The street urchin is not a menace and in fact has gone to considerable lengths to protect a woman of the upper classes from harm, asking nothing in return. Armed only with cigarettes (which are happily shared), Swipesy dispels one's concerns with a good-natured laugh. The viewer of *The Boy Detective*, and by extension the viewer of any film, has nothing at all to fear.

Two Sides of Transformation

This year marks an early phase of the transformation (or transitional period) of American film history. Its films are fundamentally Janus-faced, looking backward to the elemental linearity of the chase, to the tableau style of scenes filmed in long shots and long takes, and to the exhibitionism of the "cinema of attractions," as well as forward to the simultaneity of parallel editing, to fragmented and elliptical treatments of time and space, and to the absorption in story characteristic of the "cinema of narrative integration." All these stylistic approaches coexisted to a greater or lesser degree through the inherent juxtapositions of nickelodeon film programs, which brought together films of various makers. This extreme stylistic diversity was matched only by the overall instability of cinema's place in the cultural hierarchy. The year's films spanned the range from highbrow to lowbrow, often uniting elements from opposite ends of the spectrum in a single film. Cinema's deep-seated cultural ambivalence is especially evident in its free-ranging "intermediality." Throughout the year, filmmakers made uplifting adaptations of high cultural theatrical and literary works, but they also insistently turned (in ways that have often been overlooked) to sensational melodrama, slapstick, and cheap fiction, among a range of less-esteemed genres. Understanding the unstable place of cinema in this broader "intermedial" context reminds us that the movement toward "quality" films and the consolidation of an ostensibly unified middle-class audience for the movies were neither unilateral nor uncontested.

I wish to thank Jennifer Bean, Eileen Bowser, Jennifer Chapman, Helen Day-Mayer, Alexander Geraghty, Tom Gunning, Charlie Keil, Ron Magliozzi, David Mayer, Michele Obler, Charles Silver, and Paul Spehr for helpful suggestions and assistance.

1909

Movies and Progress

JENNIFER M. BEAN

Talk of progress was everywhere in the air. I mean this quite literally if we recall that one sunny July afternoon Orville Wright flew a two-seater airplane with a passenger for just over sixty minutes at an average speed of forty miles per hour. The landing was safe, a record was set, and what followed marked the onset of military aviation: the Wright brothers sold the aircraft to the Army's Aeronautical Division, the U.S. Signal Corps. Then again, what the airplane did for the army, the railway did for another government agency, the U.S. Postal Service. On 22 May the front page of the *New York Times* revealed that "the Chicago, Burlington & Quincy and Northern Pacific Railroads have combined to inaugurate a service from Chicago to Seattle that will annihilate distance," promising that "the transmission of mails from NY to Seattle in four days is a certainty." Such speedy delivery to the Northwest certainly enhanced East Coast correspondence with the Pacific-Alaska-Yukon Exposition (P-A-Y), which opened on 1 June to an eager public with the express purpose of "boom[ing] Seattle as the shortest road to the fields of trade extension in the Orient" (*New York Times* SM4).

To move higher, faster, further: this is what it means to speak of progress more generally. The powerful mobility implied by the term "progress" thus conveys something of its privileged status as the ubiquitous catchword of industrial America, a nation proud of its capacity for seemingly infinite expansion, development, and growth. It also conveys something of the spirit that led one writer for the *New York Times* to make a bold historical claim in an "inventory" of the "history of the nation's progress": "In the Hundred and Twenty Years Since Washington's Inauguration the Country's Progress Has Been Continuous." Gliding deftly over tense "resting points" of recent memory—like the Money Panic of 1907—the writer calculates "astounding records" of "material progress" in the country's production of iron and steel, the vast spread of railway and shipping routes, the proliferation of telephones and telegraph stations, the advances in electricity and manufacturing techniques, and the steady increase in per capita wealth and bank clearances, life insurance policies, newspaper circulation, and the college student population. Emboldened by such evidence, the writer envisions an ever-greater America, a country marching to the tune of ongoing progress following the inauguration of President William Taft, which was slated for the coming week. The buoyant tone of the prophecy, however, depends little on the perceived capacities of Taft's leadership. It depends instead on the writer's assessment of a particular trend in American corporate structures during the most recent period of growth (1885–1909), specifically the "enormous development of public companies and the centralization of industrial control," a trend emblematized in the field of manufacturing by the "bigness" of the "Steel Trust" ("Nation's Story").

The newly formed film "Trust" may seem modest by comparison. But the centralization of industrial control for film production, distribution, and exhibition in America offered hitherto unimaginable stability for those companies entering the year as licensed members of the Motion Picture Patent Company (MPPC). It also ensured their dominance of the market. At base, the MPPC functioned as a patent-pooling organization, with sixteen of the most crucial patents—for such things as cameras and projectors—previously held by Edison, Biograph, the Armat Company, and Vitagraph combined and transferred to a holding company, the Empire Trust. Members included the most powerful and well-established production companies—Edison, Vitagraph, Selig Polyscope, Lubin, and Biograph as well as two French firms, Pathé Frères and Georges Méliès's Star Film—while stretching to incorporate two relative newcomers: Kalem and Essanay. A tricky bit of negotiation with George Kleine, of Kleine Optical in Chicago, the largest domestic distributor of foreign films, solidified the Patent Company's monopolistic control by foreclosing the American market to the majority of European firms and setting quotas on the importation of foreign footage. A prime objective, the MPPC revealed to exhibitors in early February, was to "eliminate the cheap and inferior foreign films which have been forced upon the market" (qtd. in Rosenbloom 46).

The Patent Company, in turn, quite effectively forced their films upon the market. The control of key patents, as well as an exclusive contract with Eastman Kodak for the supply of raw film stock, formed the basis for a series of interlocking agreements that allowed the MPPC to organize and regulate all areas of the motion picture industry. The system was nearly airtight: only licensed equipment manufacturers and producers could use patented machines and film stock; only licensed distributors could buy MPPC films; and only licensed exhibitors could lease them. Rental prices were fixed, and producers adhered to a one-reel maximum film length. In short, laissez-faire capitalism and internecine competition had turned to the organized pursuit of profit and hence to the possibility of exponential progress. "For the year 1909," Eileen Bowser neatly sums up, "the basis of an organized industry existed, and now the producers could confidently go forward to invest in expansion, with new and enlarged studios and laboratories, with increased production staffs, and with new assembly-line production methods. Now there could be a standardized product, easily marketed and consumed" (35).

Before agreeing that industrial progress as such is "easily" achieved, it is imperative to recognize that organized efforts to redress—to reform—the negative or uneven effects of corporate expansion underlie the historical significance of the term "Progressive," the ubiquitous catchword of the Progressive Era. Largely associated with the middle class, Progressive agendas sought to better the less fortunate by emancipating them from conditions that stood in the way: parochialism, habit, poverty, disease, illiteracy, and economic insecurity. Overt racism also stood in their way, and the inauguration of the National Association for the Advancement of Colored People (NAACP) in February overtly drew from Progressive rhetoric and ideals. It would be a mistake, however, to claim that all, or even the majority, of Progressives supported the struggle for racial equality. Nor was there agreement on how such "advancement"—or progress—for "colored people" might be achieved. While the NAACP advocated the more militant posture associated with W.E.B. Du Bois's all-black Niagara Movement, others adopted the policy of accommodation associated with black author and intellectual Booker T. Washington. For many Progressives, the point was simply moot.

Class-based tensions similarly pervaded attempts at labor reform. The "Uprising of the 20,000," for instance, began in late summer when thousands of predominantly immigrant, mostly teenage, working girls went on strike in New York's garment industry to protest the brutal and unsanitary conditions of the sweatshop factories. Progressive groups like the Women's Trade Union League (WTUL) and the International Ladies' Garment Workers Union (ILGWU) played an active role in the struggle, urging middle-class women not only to help raise funds for trade unionism but to help on the picket line, and hence to protect the immigrant poor from brutality by confronting police with the presence of refined or genteel middle-class women. Retailing this strategy for readers of the *Independent*, reporter William Mailly relayed the arrest of Mary Dreier, the league's president, whose elite social status was revealed at the station, at which point the arresting policeman exclaimed with a bit of dismay: "'Why didn't you tell me who you were. I wouldn't have touched you then?'" (Mailly 1417). Considering such radical differences in the social perception of class status, it is hardly surprising that the young strikers, mostly Jewish and Italian, pejoratively referred to their white, middle-class supporters as "the mink brigade." Nor is it surprising that police brutality, arrests for vagrancy, and even deportation to the workhouse on Blackwell's Island escalated throughout the fall. In early December the WTUL organized a march on City Hall to protest police violence against the strikers. Ten thousand marchers confronted New York mayor George McClellan, many carrying banners that read, "Peaceful picketing is the right of every woman" (Schofield 170).

Of particular interest in the current context is the fact that many of the same middle-class, reform-minded women loudly agreed with Mayor McClellan's policies for altering and uplifting the conditions of another industry: motion pictures. Like factory sweatshops, nickelodeons had been perceived as squalid and unsanitary, as prone to fire hazards, as sites of moral and spiritual degradation, and emphatically as locations where immigrant workers congregated en masse. In July, one writer for *Moving Picture World* recalled the advent of the nickelodeon around 1905 as the seedbed of a decidedly lurid realm: "For three or four years prior to December last the moving picture business occupied in public esteem a position so offensive, so contemptible, and in many respects so degrading, that respectable people hesitated to have their names associated with it" (81). The past tense employed in this description is illustrative since the moving picture business was perceived as rapidly improving through the year, beginning with "December last" when Mayor McClellan shut down approximately 550 nickelodeons on Christmas Eve, revoking all common show licenses in the city and ordering that future licenses prohibit the exhibition of motion pictures on Sundays.

Mechanisms designed to reform motion pictures appeared with amazing alacrity. Exhibitors in New York—the country's biggest marketplace for moving pictures—immediately formed the Association of Moving Picture Exhibitors of New York. The alliance enabled them to gain injunctions against the mayor's decision and reopen for business in the early part of the year, even as they sought to enhance modes of self-regulation that might obviate further state repressive mechanisms. They approached the People's Institute, a sympathetic civic reform organization, and generated the New York Board of Censorship, largely populated by middle-class female volunteers eager to aid the industry's reformation. The New York Board of Censorship met for the first time in March to review and inspect all films to be shown in the city. Two months later the organization became the National

Board of Censorship. Although not every film this year would be reviewed by the censors, the Board's formation noisily announced an organized system for controlling and countermanding what appeared on the screen.

We have reached a point where the moral regulations advocated by the Board, along with the financial stability imposed by the Trust, suggest a relatively coherent approach to motion picture progress this year. One need look no further than director D. W. Griffith's *A Drunkard's Reformation*—a film that draws from well-known theatrical sources, elaborates character psychology, and preaches family morality—to see how American cinema progressed by addressing the concerns of a middle-class public. The radical distinctions between this temperance drama and the structure of a socioeconomic editorial such as Griffith's *A Corner in Wheat*, however, raise the question of what, precisely, "progress" looks like when we examine its orchestration on the screen. Elsewhere the vestiges of a physically bawdy slapstick tradition, reanimated in the Essanay Company's release of *Mr. Flip*, or the flourishing of a brutally violent fight film tradition, exemplified by the *Johnson-Burns Fight*, intimate that the proliferation of formal principles and aesthetic pleasures may be the singularly definitive mark of progress this year—a volatile mode of advance as diverse and conflicted as America itself.

▩▩▩■ Trusts and Temperance: *A Drunkard's Reformation*

A witty tongue-in-cheek editorial published by *Life* magazine in November, "Life's Literary Trust," provides a playful yet telling transition. Parodying the corporate logic that led to the formation of monopolies, or "Trusts," the editors announced that the magazine had "secured control" over the majority of popular print publications and was proceeding anon with an economic plan that would heighten efficiency by streamlining each publication to a narrow field of specialization. *The Century*, for instance, would be headed by Mark Twain and would be devoted to the subject of "men's furnishings," while *The Outlook* (a notoriously serious journal of politics and art) would "continue" as a "humorous paper . . . under the able editorship of Eugene V. Debs." Detailed attention in particular was granted to the *Ladies' Home Journal*. "Under the efficient editorship of Mr. Jack Johnson," the editors intoned, the journal "will hereafter be the leading pugilistic organ of the world. It will also have departments devoted to gambling, tippling and kindred topics."

Whether or not *Life* had the film industry's newly formed "Trust" in mind as it made these jokes, especially the joke about the *Ladies' Home Journal*, is open to speculation. But it is hard not to read into this playful entry an anti-image of the reformist rhetoric spouted by the MPPC and fully endorsed by the many middle-class "ladies" whose concerns regarding motion pictures inspired their efforts to transform the nickelodeon into a "leading . . . organ" of respectable domestic values. More pointedly, reformers promoted the nickelodeon as an alternative to the saloon, as a place where men could cheaply amuse themselves in the company of their wives and children rather than waste precious coins blustering about with their male colleagues at the bar. It thus may come as little surprise that when the New York Board of Censors met for the first time on 26 March to review and inspect all films to be shown in the city, commentators "singled out" *A Drunkard's Reformation*, a temperance drama produced by the Biograph company and directed by D. W. Griffith, "as indicative of the newfound morality of cinema, heralding the film industry's 'transition from wickedness to grace'" (Grieveson 80).

The relatively simple plot of the film heralds a young man's transition from alcoholic abuse to domestic harmony. The tale begins when John Wharton (Arthur Johnson), husband of a trusting wife (Linda Arvidson) and father of an eight-year-old daughter (Adele De Garde), gets drunk at a saloon and returns home in a rancorous mood that terrifies his wife and daughter. The child, however, pleads with him to take her to the theater to see a stage performance of Émile Zola's *L'Assommoir*, and the example encourages the man to quit drinking. A peaceful scene of domestic bliss ends the film with the suggestion that the promise has been kept; the drunkard has been reformed.

One way of categorizing this film is to situate it within the many anti-drink dramas materializing on screens throughout the year. Biograph alone churned out a diverse array, including *The Expiation*, *A Change of Heart*, *What Drink Did*, and *A Broken Locket*, while Essanay offered *Ten Nights in a Barroom*, Selig Polyscope released *The Drunkard's Fate*, Kalem came in with *The New Minister; or, The Drunkard's Daughter*, and Vitagraph produced *The Honor of the Slums*. The temperance entry by Pathé-Frères, *Drink*, takes its title from the stage play on which it was based, Charles Read's adaptation of Zola's *L'Assommoir* (The Drunkard), the very play that the father and daughter attend in *A Drunkard's Reformation*.

These intertextual references, in turn, categorically situate Griffith's temperance tale within the broader *film d'art* movement, which flaunted adaptations of works by eminent writers and artists and by extension the respectability and cultural refinement of the motion picture industry. Introduced by the Pathé-Frères company, the *film d'art* movement directly inspired American imitators, in particular the Vitagraph and Edison Companies, while Biograph trumpeted a relation to reputable classics early in the year with productions like *Edgar Allen Poe*, *Resurrection* ("Free Adaptation of Leo Tolstoy's Powerful Novel"), and *A Fool's Revenge* ("A Free Adaptation of Rigoletto"). Insofar as the *film d'art* influence gravitated toward a theatrical model of presentation replete with increasingly elaborate sets, costuming, and makeup, however, it diverges sharply from Griffith's experimentations with a specifically filmic discourse: implied point of view; proto shot/reverse shot editing; parallel editing; frame composition; acting style; lighting techniques. These stylistic and structural innovations crystallize in *A Drunkard's Reformation*, enabling a relatively complex narrative system capable of enhancing the psychological drama of the reformed drunkard and of visually expressing the story's moral imperatives.

The effects of this system shimmer into view with the opening frames, which establish through editing an opposition between domestic space and its depraved other—the saloon. Shots 1 and 2 reveal the mother and daughter waiting and fretting at home, while the third shot reveals the father carousing at a saloon with his buddies. The fourth shot unites the family in the domestic space, but as the father enters and stumbles about, slamming his fist on the table, it is clear that the home has been infected by drinking. A fifth shot hints at a slight temporal ellipsis: the man is calmer, drinking coffee at the table, when the little girl pleads with him to take her to the theater. A noticeably longer take, this fifth shot proves a turning point in the drama, as man and child garb themselves for the event and leave the house. The static frame holds as the mother sits heavily on the now-empty dining room chair, cradling her head in her hands. This portrait of despair— as she bends knees to the floor and assumes a posture of fervent prayer— concludes the opening frame of the story and stages the transition to a second public, non-domestic space: that of the theater.

It is safe to say that the mother's prayer is answered at the theater, just as the promise of a narrative system capable of articulating character psychology finds its fullest elaboration in Griffith's career to date. Through an extended twenty-shot sequence, based on a continuous shot/reverse shot editing pattern, the theater scene reveals the husband-father's transformation from boredom to dawning recognition, uneasy agitation, and ultimate reformation as he watches the temperance play unfold on the stage. The remarkably consistent position of the frames complements the focus on Wharton's perspective and his experience as a spectator. With the exception of the initial shot (a sort of proto-establishing shot) that frames the action from the back of the theater as Wharton and his child enter and take their

seats, the design invariably frames the two sitting together in the front
lower-left corner of the frame, surrounded by audience members. Alternately, the stage performance is shot from a medium-long view, approxi-
mating the perspective of the father and child with the frame placed slightly
below the proscenium arch.

The editing pattern also enhances Wharton's perspective. A symmetrical, rhythmic balance of the shot/reverse shot cutting defines the first half
of the scene. The shots alternate between the audience and the stage action,
where the character Coupeau (Herbert Yost) pledges a temperance vow,
embraces his wife, Gervaise (Florence Lawrence), and spurns the attention
of another woman (Marion Leonard). Significantly, each cut back to the
audience, where Wharton alternately appears distracted, slightly amused,
and occasionally bored, occurs at a moment when the stage scene is changing. In shot 9, however, the reverse shot to Wharton *interrupts* the unity of
the stage scene, and for an obvious reason: Coupeau's young daughter
dashes onto the stage and sits on the lap of her father, who has pledged to
reform his drinking habits. Tom Gunning's intricate analysis of the film
attends to Wharton's gesture at this exact moment: he edges his daughter
closer to him in the theater seat and points to the stage twice, effectively
"drawing a comparison between the stage drama and his own life" (166).
The comparison intensifies as the play reveals Coupeau's downfall: his
friends coax him back into the saloon, he drunkenly struggles with his wife,
he suffers the effects of withdrawal, and he then exultantly drinks a bottle
of brandy left near his invalid's chair by the woman he spurned. Ultimately,
he terrorizes his family in their home and collapses to his death. As these
events progress through the remaining eleven shots of the sequence, the
pattern of cutting to Wharton in the "middle" of a stage action continues,
with each "reaction shot" progressively revealing his increasingly agitated
identification with the drama: he pulls his daughter ever closer, takes her
arm and then holds her hand; he frowns, bends low in his seat, grimaces,
and nods his head slowly. Ultimately, he perches on the edge of his seat,
tapping his chest and bowing his head as he embraces his daughter.

Given the film's careful visual design, it is possible to say that Wharton's
proximity to his daughter in the final shot of the theater scene (she is practically in his lap) visually rhymes the earlier action on the stage, the
moment preceding Coupeau's downward spiral, the moment when he
pledges never to drink again: the moment when *his* daughter perches happily on his lap. The visual parallel, so typical of Griffith, enhances the mean-
ingful resolution of the film's drama—an inverted mirror of the stage play's
development—as Wharton and his daughter return home and the reformed

father-husband vows never to drink again. A tableau of nigh perfect domestic harmony ends the film. Mother and father clasp hands and bend over their daughter, who is reading, the family lit by the glow of the hearth. The fact that the composition of this final tableau also suggests a visual parallel, a rhyme of sorts, must not be overlooked. The closely gathered family is located slightly to the left of the frame, with the daughter's seated position centering the view to the lower bottom corner in a position visually reminiscent of the consistent, repeated framing of daughter and father in the theater. It is thus that the non-domestic space of the theater is linked to the domestic space of the home. The reformation of the home—via the act of theatergoing—is complete.

A *Drunkard's Reformation* emerges as a reflexive commentary on the educational and redemptive effects of theatergoing. Put simply, the viewer ultimately reformed and educated by the film (and by the play it re-creates) is the one sitting in the nickelodeon. More precisely still, as Lee Grieveson aptly observes, "it is a *male spectator* who is represented as being reformed by edifying drama. . . . Male spectatorship in *A Drunkard's Reformation*, we may say, is actually about opening up to the instruction of [respectable, refined] women and children—and this mirrors the position of the industry more widely at this contested moment in cinema history" (111).

Slapstick and the Working Man: *Mr. Flip*

This "moment in cinema history" was indeed "contested." While the momentum to reform and regulate the industry progressed apace, and while the New York Board of Censors became the National Board of Censors by May, with manufacturers willingly supplying their films for review, not all audience members expressed a willingness to be reformed. Anti-drink films in certain areas, for instance, equaled anti-profit. Eileen Bowser recounts the story of one exhibitor in St. Louis who "was nearly ruined by rumors that he was a prohibitionist: his customers went from three hundred a night to forty, until he made a sworn oath to the contrary and displayed it behind glass outside his show" (188). Others protested the *film d'art* movement more generally. "There is too much high class drama, which cannot be understood by the average working man," complained one exhibitor near the end of the year: "a very large proportion seems to thoroughly enjoy the old Essanay slap-stick variety" (*Moving Picture World* 837).

The "old Essanay slap-stick variety" typically deforms (rather than reforms) people and things. The company's forty-year-old clown, Ben

Mr. Flip annoys the working women he encounters with his tickling, patting, leering, and mashing (*Mr. Flip*, Essanay, 1909).

Turpin, relayed as much on 3 April when he summarized his two-year career in motion pictures for readers of *Moving Picture World*: "I think I have broken about twenty barrels of dishes, upset stoves, and also broken up many sets of beautiful furniture, had my eyes blackened, both ankles strained and many bruises, and I am still on the go. This is a great business" (405). To be sure, the psychologically delineated characters so crucial to the narrative economy of *A Drunkard's Reformation* clash with slapstick's relentless focus on aggressive physicality, on a performance style that parades its denouement in the form of an actor's bruised body, with "eyes blackened" and "ankles strained." Then again, the drive to restore the sacral space of domesticity, so unerringly developed in Griffith's film, butts up against a slapstick tradition that flaunts the ruination of domestic things—of "dishes," "stoves," and "beautiful furniture." Admittedly, slapstick comedy often took its antics to the streets in the marvelously maniacal form of an extended chase. But Turpin's emphasis on the ruination of interior space may have been prompted by his most recent bruising, attained during the production of Essanay's split-reel comedy *Mr. Flip*, released just one week following *Moving Picture World*'s exposé in early April.

One should never judge a book by its cover, as the saying goes, and the same holds true when considering the title of *Mr. Flip*. The viewer who anticipates an acrobatic tour de force, a display of physical leaps or "flips" designed to defy the laws of gravity, will emerge disappointed. The title might more aptly be read as a referent to character behavior—and this is the closest we will come to speaking of "character"—in the sense of the clown's "flippant" disregard for acceptable standards of behavior and his defiance of the laws governing social interaction, especially with women. He just can't keep his hands to himself. Decidedly naughty and irritatingly flirtatious, the scrawny, cross-eyed clown annoys the working women he encounters with his tickling, patting, leering, and mashing. Thus the film begins; and thus it ends. This is another way of saying that Mr. Flip's behavior changes not at all through the course of the film's six scenes—and seven shots. Repetition, rather than progression, structures its temporality.

Repetitious, too, is the film's spatial design: a series of interior settings that may or may not be interrelated, that may or may not be proximate one to the other. Lacking clear screen direction of any sort, spatial contiguity adheres primarily by virtue of each scene's common signifying features, each of which represents a public place where women work: a store, a manicurist's station, a telephone operator's office, a shaving parlor, a saloon, and a café. The reiterative camera set-up, which approximates a medium-long ("nine-foot rule") distance, and an unwavering straight angle offer little diversity of perspective. Indeed, even the props are replicated; the counter and stools utilized in the "store" scene, for instance, reappear in the space of the "saloon." Whereas the repetition of spatial features in *A Drunkard's Reformation* enables a visual rhyme that enhances the narrative's meaning-making economy, the repetition in *Mr. Flip* is just that: repetition, the kind that lacks both rhyme and reason, just like Mr. Flip himself.

But if Mr. Flip's compulsion to repeat himself again and yet again reflects the dull redundancy of the film's form, then the women provide a source of difference, of ingenuity and cleverness, of quick reflexes and rather creative cruelty. When Mr. Flip flirts with the busy telephone operator, for instance, she encourages him to pick up a nearby receiver, at which point she wildly cranks the telephone transfer device, laughing as Mr. Flip devolves into a series of trembling, electrified pirouettes. When he glides into the shaving parlor and accosts a female attendant, she and her friend tilt back his chair, lather his chin, and layer steaming washcloths on his face. The final scene takes place in a café where, as Mr. Flip reaches across the counter toward the serving girl, she reaches down for a pie and casually, albeit forcefully, heaves it in his face.

The more significant point is that *Mr. Flip* can ultimately be read as a fable, however farcical, of working women's struggles to reform untoward masculine behavior. A comparison again proves useful: the psychological reformation of Griffith's drunkard here becomes the physiological reformation of the flirt, and the physicality of the women's reformist agenda is far from subtle. The flamboyant difference of the "average" working woman's reformation of the "average" working man effects a wild variable in the filmic discourse as well, which appears in the film's second scene. The scene opens with a medium long shot of a manicurist's parlor, but radically alters the viewer's perspective by offering a detail cut-in: a close-shot insert reveals a long needle that one of the women places under Mr. Flip's seat.

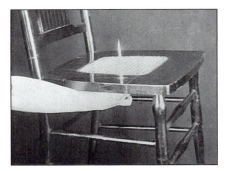

A close-shot insert reveals a long needle that one of the women places under Mr. Flip's seat (*Mr. Flip*, Essanay, 1909).

As he lowers himself unknowingly onto the razor-sharp point he becomes—quite literally—the butt of the joke.

One rarely speaks of butts in polite company. Thus slapstick's bawdy physicality suffered in the wake of the Trust's commitment to respectability, and Essanay would produce for the moment other, more domestic-oriented comedies, such as *Two Sides of the Story*, in which an older man and woman marry, each unaware that the "other" already parents a squadron of "small troubles," which is to say: children. Among the best known domestic comedies of the year must be counted the "Mr. and Mrs. Jones" series that Griffith directed at Biograph, all of which avoided calling attention to the lower regions of physical anatomy. The head, however, was a different matter altogether; it proved a perfectly respectable comic target. To be more precise, the sartorial splendor with which refined women covered their heads proved the target of Griffith's semi-reel comedy, *Those Awful Hats*. Designed as a live-action version of the ubiquitous "Ladies Will Kindly Remove Their Hats" lantern slides shown at the beginning of film programs, the film stages its action in a movie theater where a variety of women sporting ornately decorated hats enter one by one. The most remarkable of millinery designs plume upward and outward atop the stick-thin figure of actress Flora Finch, who sashays into the theater, seating herself with a feathery sway of the head, thus effectively blocking the view of the patron seated behind her. More remarkable still, an enormous crane-like mechanism descends from the ceiling and scoops up Finch and her offending hat, effectively clearing the patron's sight line while offering viewers of *Those Awful Hats* a near perfect (nigh invisible) stop-camera cut in which a dummy is substituted for the actress.

The ironic reversal of historical terms is good for a laugh or two. By substituting more sophisticated comic play for slapstick's grotesqueries, Griffith spoofs the very "ladies" whose increasing presence in nickelodeons ensured the respectability of the environment, and whose vocal endorsement of films like *A Drunkard's Reformation* ensured the viability of motion-picture morality. Of course *Those Awful Hats* nestles among an array of cultural jokes in which the proprieties associated with middle-class women offered grist for the humor mill, including the parody at play in "Life's Literary Trust." As we have seen, to envision the *Ladies' Home Journal* as the "leading pugilistic organ," with special departments in "tippling" and "gambling," playfully nods at those home-oriented ladies whose opposition to the public realms that catered to "primitive" masculine behavior was well known. Less playful, however, is one critical detail of "Life's Literary Trust" that we have thus far overlooked. When the writer claimed that control of the ladies' journal would be placed in the "efficient hands" of "Mr. Jack Johnson," the joke veered dangerously toward white Americans' concerns regarding race. The powerful "hands"—or better, fists—of Mr. Johnson belonged to a champion African American boxer.

▰▰▰▰▰▰▰ Black and White: The *Johnson-Burns Fight*

Jack Johnson's unique status as the first black man to hold the world heavyweight title foddered debates well before the *Johnson-Burns Fight* premiered in the United States in Chicago on 21 March and subsequently in New York on 12 April. The fight recorded by the Gaumont Company's camera had taken place in Sydney, Australia, on 26 December 1908, where Johnson trumped white boxer Tommy Burns in a swift fourteen rounds. Not surprisingly, Johnson rapidly attained the status of a revolutionary icon for African American masculinity, a powerful symbol of black "progress" and a perceived threat to white supremacy. "No event in forty years has given more genuine satisfaction to the colored people of this country than has the signal victory of Jack Johnson," offered one editorial in January, implicitly equating Johnson's victory with the signing of the Emancipation Proclamation during the Civil War (qtd. in Streible 173).

Of course in the years since the abolition of slavery, legal rulings effectively sketched a color line between white and black America by upholding the principle of segregation and ushering in a new era of Jim Crow policies. A signed document was released on 12 February—the centennial of Abraham Lincoln's birth—officially inaugurating the National Association for the Advancement of Colored People (NAACP). Echoing the focus of W.E.B. Du Bois's militant all-black Niagara Movement, and avoiding the accommodation policies of black intellectual and author Booker T. Washington, the NAACP's stated goal was clear. The "advancement," or progress, of "colored people" was radically, viciously imbalanced; the association sought to secure for all people the rights guaranteed in the Thirteenth, Fourteenth, and Fifteenth Amendments to the U.S. Constitution, which promised an end to slavery, the equal protection of the law, and universal adult male suffrage, respectively.

Although the NAACP would eventually play a critically voluble role in a country defined by ever-escalating racism, the initial formation of the association barely registered in public discourse. In striking contrast, the spectacle of potent black masculinity afforded by Johnson's victory in the ring generated dire anxiety for white Americans regarding a race generally conceived as mentally and physically inferior. "A Negro is the champion pugilist," warned the *Detroit Free Press* in February: "[The] dark-colored peoples of the earth are threatening to ply the mischief generally with the civilization of the white man. . . . Is the Caucasian played out? Are the races we have been calling inferior about to demand to us that we must draw the color line in everything if we are to avoid being whipped individually and collectively?" (qtd. in Streible 173).

Dan Streible, who has done more than any other historian to recover the fraught reception of the Johnson fight films, claims it is quite possible that prints of the *Johnson-Burns Fight* circulated on the emerging all-black theater circuit. The most obvious venue would have been impresario Robert T. Motts's black-owned and -operated theater, the Chicago Pekin. Although materials regarding these potential screenings remain scarce, the image of Johnson and the description of the film that circulated in the black press laud the champion as an image of black pride, a veritable gladiator of racial "uplift." Additional pomp and circumstance by "the New Yorkers of his race" greeted Johnson's arrival in late March, shortly before the film premiered at the Broadway Theater: "Forty-second Street about the Grand Central Station, Broadway and the Tenderloin wore a dusky hue through all the morning," wrote the *New York Times*, adding that the boxer's arrival at the station generated the "noisiest kind of a demonstration by his negro admirers, a brass band in a big sightseeing automobile leading the clamor . . . and a line of other motor cars, all filled with negroes, formed in a parade when Johnson passed through the crowd" ("Jack Johnson Arrives").

Although some limited, segregated seating may have been available to Johnson's "negro admirers" at the film's New York premiere the evening of 12 April, newspaper reviews hint at the predominantly white composition of the audience. Consider, for instance, the description offered by one reporter for the *New York Times*, who lauded the "remarkably clear and distinct" qualities of the film, praising its capacious inclusion of "practically every move made prior to and during the fight," before adding: "To the

majority of those who witnessed the exhibition, the pictures were a dis-
appointment on account of the miserable showing made throughout by
Burns." The implicitly racist audience—the "majority" disappointed by the
white boxer's poor performance—mirrors in turn the implicitly white perspective dominating the construction of the film, specifically the footage
shot "prior to" the event. According to the writer, it "was apparent from
these [scenes] that Burns before the contest was a big favorite." It was
painfully clear that once the fight began "there was not a single minute
from the tap of the first gong up to the time when the Police Inspector
stopped the contest in the fourteenth round that Johnson was not clearly
the master of Burns" ("Johnson-Burns Fight Here").

For a black man to "master" a white one deeply troubled white Americans, whose distaste trebled because of Johnson's cocky attitude, his resistance to performing humility of any sort. According to Jack London's
oft-cited editorial, Johnson's egoistic pride extended beyond his control
over the white boxer to include his determination to control the image he
projected for the screen. Describing the action in the ring, London intoned:
"He [Johnson] cuffed and smiled and cuffed, and in the clinches whirled his
opponent around so as to be able to assume beatific and angelic facial
expressions for the cinematograph machines" (qtd. in Strieble, 173). Johnson's self-assurance, interpreted as a smile of mockery, generated a racial
call to arms, a plea for the retired white heavyweight champion, Jim Jeffries, to reenter the ring and exact justice in the name of Caucasians everywhere. Thus London concluded his editorial: "Jim Jeffries must now
emerge from his alfalfa farm and remove that smile from Johnson's face.
Jeff, it's up to you. The white man must be rescued" (qtd. in Grieveson
124).

The near histrionic demand to "rescue" the "white man" spurred a
series of fights, and fight films. Johnson defended his title against Stanley
Ketchel on 16 October, an event the Kalem Company recorded and released
as the *Johnson-Ketchel Fight*. The bout with Ketchel lasted twelve rounds
before Johnson rendered his white opponent unconscious with a single
blow, thus undercutting white hopes while also cutting the film's length a
reel or so shorter than the fourteen-round *Johnson-Burns Fight*.

I am speculating on screen duration since prints of the Johnson fight
films have not survived the century extant, thus presenting us with an
absent archive (so endemic to the era) and forcing a detailed consideration
of related evidence, such as the reviews and editorials we have been dis-
cussing. A glance back at the *Times*'s review of the *Johnson-Burns Fight* premiere in New York, for instance, clarifies that along with the fourteen

rounds of the match and the incorporated scenes of the boxers' training and preparation, a "considerable delay" preceded the projection. The event began, rather, when W. A. Brady, former manager of (white) boxing champions Jim Corbett and James J. Jeffries, introduced Hugh D. McIntosh, the referee and promoter of the Johnson-Burns fight, who then functioned as lecturer for the film. What he might have said, by way of "editorializing" the film and "educating" the audience, is anyone's guess. It takes less guessing to surmise that the *Johnson-Burns Fight* shattered the standard one-reel film length elsewhere mandated by the MPPC, thus presenting a filmic form and a theatrical event that deranged dominant modes of regulation, much like Johnson himself.

Economics and Editorials: *A Corner in Wheat*

As we have seen, any assessment of the "lost" Johnson fight films depends on a historical methodology willing to sift through what remains, through reviews and editorials and a wide array of cultural perspectives and published arguments, all of which refract in differing lenses the querulous celebrity status of Johnson's appearance on the screen. But what does it mean to speak of a fiction film as, itself, an editorial, an argument, or a cultural commentary? Historically put, it means to speak of D. W. Griffith's directorial tour de force, *A Corner in Wheat*, one of the most remarkable films of the year, if not of the era.

The qualitatively different nature of this film was hardly lost on contemporary reviewers. "This picture is not a picture drama," wrote "The Spectator" for readers of the *New York Dramatic Mirror*, "although it is presented with dramatic force." Offering a clearer definition, he continued:

> It is an argument, an editorial, an essay on a subject of deep interest to all. The theme is the rising cost of living, the inability of the masses to meet the increase and the part played by the speculator in bringing about this unfortunate condition. No orator, no editorial writer, no essayist could so strongly and effectively present the thoughts that are conveyed in this picture.

If the process of conveying "thoughts" in a picture works differently than do words on a page, then the same might be said of every narrative film produced to date. But the radical difference of *A Corner in Wheat* lies in its refusal to develop a plot, to tell a story, to offer a singular protagonist. In other words, rather than proffer a narrative system geared toward the linear, teleological model of development capable of expressing, say, the psychological transformation of the father in *A Drunkard's Reformation*, in which the interrelation of the characters across different spaces and times builds to a climactic resolution, this representational system operates according to paradigmatic contrast. In so doing, it innovates a system capable of formally expressing the abstraction of an economic system in which a "speculator," much like a stock broker, could buy and sell farm commodities in terms of "futures" (crops not yet harvested; animals not yet slaughtered) and who could profit from the goods without ever seeing or handling a sheath of wheat or a slab of meat.

The film's subject, of "deep interest to us all," specifically addresses the speculation in grain, or what was referred to in the press that spring and summer as, pointedly, "The 'Corner' in Wheat." To inflate the price of flour, to render the most basic of foods unaffordable for the poor, generated a public outcry that few rebutted. "How much longer will the American people suffer such crimes to continue?" remonstrated one writer for the *Christian Observer* in April, noting that one active speculator, Mr. James Patten, was being everywhere denounced, and that "congressional action is everywhere demanded which will forbid speculation in the necessaries of life." Federal law in this instance, however, was envisioned as a means of ensuring a much higher law, that of the eighth commandment ("Thou shall not steal"), although the writer does not quote from Exodus or Deuteronomy but rather from Proverbs 11:26: "He that withholdeth corn, the people shall curse him" ("'Corner' in Wheat"). The oscillation between human and eternal laws played a role in the promotion of the film as well. By the time of its release in early December, the *Biograph Bulletin* would claim that "laws are being framed with a view of suppressing such nefarious transactions," while also claiming that "one of the sins that cries to heaven for vengeance is denying food to the hungry" (qtd. in Niver, *Early* 66).

The shift to the heavens, to the "hand of God," seems to have suggested itself to the *Bulletin* writer as the only means of explaining a filmic event—the death of the "Wheat King," the speculator—which occurs without any explicit cause-effect relation to those who have suffered. We return to the particularities of the death scene momentarily, but let us first note that the magical (or heavenly, if you prefer) alchemy of the film lies precisely in its deflection of cause-effect logic in favor of a systematic method of stark contrast.

The film propels its viewer into this system with the opening three shots. The first two show wheat farmers wearily heading out to their fields and then sowing the grain, while the third (following an intertitle: "The Wheat King. Engineering the Great Corner") cuts to the interior office of a grain speculator instructing his assistants to buy up wheat in "the pit" (a

Customers shuffle past the counter of a bakery (*A Corner in Wheat*, Biograph, 1909).

term used for the floor of the Chicago Commodities Exchange). The type of "labor" contrasted in these initial three shots could not be more obvious, with those working the earth to produce and those working the floor to buy separated by the exterior and interior settings as well as by their respective class status. Whether or not the "Wheat King" is speculating on the very crops that the farmers are sowing, however, remains unclear, nor will the two scenes, the two narrative strands, ever overlap. The Wheat King will never visit the farm; the farmers (who appear only in two other shots, among them the closing shot which echoes the opening image) will not communicate or overlap with the speculator. The connection between these figures is predicated solely on the abstract nature of their economic relation.

The film elaborates its economic "argument" as it develops its initial contrast (farmers, speculator) to include a third (consumers). The Wheat King travels from his office to the pit, then to a lavish party, the latter introduced by an intertitle: "The Gold of the Wheat." Another intertitle, "The Chaff of the Wheat," introduces the following shot, which cuts to the interior of a bakery where a prominently placed sign declares, "Owing to the advance in the price of flour, the usual 5 cent loaf will be 10 cents." Customers shuffle past the counter, their bent postures and homespun garb sharply contrasting with the lifted glasses of wine and flashy evening dress of the Wheat King's party. As the final customers, an older woman accompanied by a young girl, reach the counter and realize they cannot afford the new price, they leave the bakery and the film cuts back to the party, where guests eat and drink. That the Wheat King is now contrasted with the poor urban customers is clear, although once again temporal and spatial relations remain abstract, thus perfectly capturing (and critiquing) the abstract economic relations enabled by uncontrolled capitalism, by greedy speculators who profit at the expense of both producers and consumers whom they neither see nor consider.

Perhaps no image better illustrates the film's propensity for abstraction than the cut that returns to the bakery, where the action is frozen. I mean this quite literally, as long as we recognize that the image is not a freeze-frame, although it readily could be mistaken as such. What Griffith offers, rather, is a tableau vivant, in which all the actors remain still in a fixed position for the duration of the shot. Importantly, the bakery customers have cleared out, and these individuals stand in a breadline, seeking charity, seeking bread for which they cannot pay. The tension captured in the image—bodies poised expectantly mid-action, yet simultaneously bowed in despair—carries a force that moves in a way a moving image could not. Halted, hungry, lifeless, limp: the poor have been stripped of the power of animation per se, and the viewer's gaze arrested. Hence, while the starkness of the image heightens the visual contrast between the bakery and the active gaiety of the Wheat King's party, the very strangeness of the tableau vivant also heightens the film's status as a mode of contemplation, of economic and cultural reflection.

Some might say that another variation on the stilling of life—in this case, the death of the Wheat King—alters the film's paradigmatic operations by suggesting a "resolution" of sorts to the story of the speculator. And yet the method of the telling retains the film's emphasis on contrast, while adding what Tom Gunning aptly calls a "metaphorical" dimension to the argument. After taking his guests on a tour of the grain elevators where the wheat is stored, the Wheat King receives a telegram informing him of his global monopoly and, just as he exults in triumph, he falls into an elevator and is buried by the grain. But the scene of his live burial is interrupted, suspended slightly, as the film cuts back to the bakery, to an indeterminable moment in time, where a riotous crowd rushes the baker and is subsequently held at gunpoint by the police. As the protesters are held suspended in action, the film returns to the grain elevator where the Wheat King's hand flutters briefly before disappearing entirely into the massive heap. By "comparing the violent death of the Wheat King to the violence he has unleashed in society," as Gunning puts it (248), the cut operates on a "metaphorical axis," one in which the vengeance wrought by the "hand of God," which the *Biograph Bulletin* attributes to this scene, functions more deterministically in the manner of social commentary, economic argument, or editorial.

Significantly, the film ends with an image of neither violence nor vengeance. It returns instead to the sowing of the field, to the farmer whose weariness echoes the opening image, thus producing a visual rhyme that suggests a cyclical pattern rather than a pattern of closure, resolution, or containment. Shot by cameraman Billy Bitzer, the image of the farmyard that frames the film is justly famous, not only for its allusion to Jean François Millet's painting *The Sowers* but also for the manner in which early morning or late evening sun is utilized for back and edge lighting. Outdoor shooting of this sort incurred a variety of complications, such as the fact that placing one's actors against the source of the light could obscure their faces (as evident in earlier Biograph films shot on exterior locations), a problem that Bitzer corrected in *A Corner in Wheat* by a simple innovation: he utilized reflectors.

One wonders in turn what innovative techniques might have been employed when Griffith shot the remarkable outdoor scenery that defines the latter half of *A Politician's Love Story*. Here the rather weak comic plot of a romantic *pas-de-deux* is entirely (and fortuitously) overwhelmed by the visually rich ambiance of snow-covered parks and ice-laden trees, each of which may have functioned as an infinite series of miniature reflectors. The luscious outdoor setting of the film is particularly valuable, however, as a historical reminder that extended on-location shooting could be especially treacherous, if not downright impossible, during the long, gray winter months.

Coda: Peripatetic Progress

It may be a truism to note that the pursuit of sunny weather and exotic atmospheric settings spurred the peripatetic movements of many companies, while such settings in turn catalyzed the proliferation of certain genres, among them the "Wild West" films flaunting "cowboy performers" like G. M. Anderson (soon to be known as "Broncho Billy"), co-founder of the Essanay Company. In September, Anderson's search for authentic western settings and winter-season shooting spurred him to leave Chicago in the company of Essanay cameraman Jesse Robbins and a handful of players. In Golden, Colorado, he reportedly recruited genuine cowboys with roping and riding skills as extras to enhance the action of his films, and shot a series of westerns before heading further south to El Paso, Texas, in November, and then onward to Mexico. Although Essanay would not settle a permanent base in Niles, California, this year, the New York Motion Picture Company (NYMPC) sent a group of players to Los Angeles in November who never returned, thus establishing what may be the first permanent studio base in the area we now call Hollywood.

The migration of the American film industry to the South and West had begun. But as the ironies of historical progress would have it, an escape from the harsh winter climes of the East only partially motivated the NYMPC's departure to the far reaches of the West Coast. An attempt to escape the detectives and spies of the Patent Company was another. As one of several newly formed "independent" film companies, the NYMPC operated outside the Trust's centralized system of control, and hence violated the patent laws by utilizing cameras and equipment without the proper license. Although it would be a mistake to believe that the move to California deterred the Patent Company spies altogether, the geographical distance between the MPPC headquarters in New York and the lawsuits taking place in court systems on the West Coast certainly complicated the Trust's capacity to seek immediate legal recourse.

It would be a mistake as well to consider California as the preeminent winter-season climate at this time, or even to assess the companies affiliated with the Trust as equally powerful and productive. Whereas the Biograph, Vitagraph, and Edison studios utilized relatively ample indoor stages for interior shooting, the Kalem Company owned no studio proper at all. With only offices based in New York, and with principal director Sidney Olcott shooting on location in Coytesville, New Jersey (and occasionally in the Catskills and Connecticut), it is hardly surprising that Kalem's band of adventurous players headed due south, to Jacksonville, Florida, as the year began. Practicing frugality, the "Kalemites," as they were often called, labored to integrate the local citizenry into their productions, often depending on picturesque southern homes for visual backdrops and borrowing props from local families.

The budding relationship between the town and the "movie-people," however, was momentarily threatened early in the year by the production of *A Florida Feud*, which dealt with the poorest of the local population and portrayed a version of Jacksonville displeasing to the township. Sensitive to the community's mood, Gene Gauntier, the company's principal scenarist, responded immediately by altering "the thrust and tone of her scenarios," often by explicitly adopting a southern perspective (Harner 189).

That Gauntier also adopted a female perspective is nowhere more visibly pronounced than in her wildly popular Civil War action series *The Adventures of the Girl Spy*. As its title suggests, the central character of this sensational thriller was young. She was also capable of a clever ingenuity, mixed with gritty physical daring, which easily foiled groups of high-ranking male officials, defied entire armies, and even out-spied the occasional counter-spy. Although film prints of the series' multiple episodes from this year have not survived the century, the memorable success of Gauntier's girl spy provocatively recalls the basic point with which we began. Any normative assessment of "progress" remains questionable, depending on who or what one is addressing, and why.

SOURCES FOR FILMS

Many films from this decade are difficult to find. Some titles are only available in film archives. Some may be acquired for personal use, but only from small companies that distribute "collector's copies" on VHS or DVD-R. Typically mastered from video copies of battered and "dupey" 8 mm or 16 mm prints, these copies are often well below normal commercial standards. Quite a few silent films have been released by commercial distributors, but individual titles, particularly short films, can be difficult to locate when they appear on multi-title DVDs that vendors or libraries might catalogue using only the overall title.

This guide will aid readers in locating sources for the films that are examined in detail in this volume. DVDs, like books, may go out of print over time, but the information below will nevertheless assist in the placement of interlibrary loan requests should a title become otherwise unavailable. A good source of information about the availability and quality of silent films on DVD and VHS is www.silentera.com.

All the companies and organizations listed below have web sites that can be located easily by typing their full names into any Internet search engine. For companies whose titles appear multiple times within the following list, we have abbreviated the full names as follows:

> Grapevine = Grapevine Video
> Kin = Kino International
> LOC = Library of Congress

For titles discussed in this volume that do not appear in the list below, the reader may assume that the film has survived (unless the discussion indicates otherwise) but is available only in a film archive. Specific information about the location and preservation status of virtually all surviving films from this era may be found in the FIAF International Film Archive Database, an online database available from Ovid (www.ovid.com) via library subscription.

FILMS AND SOURCES

Annabelle Butterfly Dance (1894) is on DVD on *Edison: The Invention of the Movies* (Kino).
Annabelle Serpentine Dance (1895) is on DVD on *Edison: The Invention of the Movies* (Kino).
Band Drill (1894) is on DVD on *Edison: The Invention of the Movies* (Kino).

Black Diamond Express (1896) is on DVD on *Edison: The Invention of the Movies* (Kino).

Blacksmithing Scene (1893) is on DVD on *Edison: The Invention of the Movies* (Kino).

College Chums (1907) is on DVD on *Edison: The Invention of the Movies* (Kino).

Corbett and Courtney Before the Kinetograph (1894) is on DVD on *Edison: The Invention of the Movies* (Kino).

A Corner in Wheat (1909) is on DVD on *D. W. Griffith, Years of Discovery: 1909–1913* and on *Griffith Masterworks: Twenty-Three Complete Films, 1909–1913* (Kino).

Dream of a Rarebit Fiend (1906) is on DVD on *Edison: The Invention of the Movies* (Kino).

A Drunkard's Reformation (1909) is on DVD on *D. W. Griffith: Director* (Grapevine).

Electrocuting of an Elephant (1903) is on DVD on *Edison: The Invention of the Movies* (Kino).

Enchanted Drawing (1900) is on VHS on *Origins of American Animation, 1900–1921* (LOC).

Films of the San Francisco Earthquake (1906) is on DVD on *Edison: The Invention of the Movies* (Kino).

Fire Rescue (1894) is on DVD on *Edison: The Invention of the Movies* (Kino).

The Gay Shoe Clerk (1903) is on DVD and VHS on *Edison: The Invention of the Movies* (Kino) and *The Movies Begin* (Kino).

The Great Train Robbery (1903) is on DVD and VHS on *Edison: The Invention of the Movies* (Kino) and *The Movies Begin* (Kino).

How a French Nobleman Got a Wife through the New York Herald "Personal" Columns (1904) is on DVD on *Edison: The Invention of the Movies* (Kino).

Humorous Phases of Funny Faces (1906) is on VHS on *Origins of American Animation, 1900–1921* (LOC).

Jack and the Beanstalk (1902) is on DVD on *Edison: The Invention of the Movies* (Kino).

The John C. Rice–May Irwin Kiss (1896) is on DVD and VHS on *Edison: The Invention of the Movies* (Kino) and *The Movies Begin* (Kino).

Laughing Gas (1907) is on DVD on *Edison: The Invention of the Movies* (Kino).

Life of an American Fireman (1903) is on DVD and VHS on *Edison: The Invention of the Movies* (Kino) and *The Movies Begin* (Kino).

McKinley at Home (1896) is on DVD and VHS on *The Movies Begin* (Kino).

McKinley Parade (1896) is on DVD on *Edison: The Invention of the Movies* (Kino).

Mr. Flip (1909) is on DVD and VHS on *Slapstick Encyclopedia* (Kino).

Pan-American Exposition by Night (1901) is on DVD on *Edison: The Invention of the Movies* (Kino).

Sandow (1891) is on DVD and VHS on *Edison: The Invention of the Movies* (Kino) and *The Movies Begin* (Kino).

Serpentine Dance (1895) is on DVD and VHS on *The Movies Begin* (Kino).

Sioux Ghost Dance (1894) is on DVD on *Edison: The Invention of the Movies* (Kino).

The "Teddy" Bears (1907) is on DVD on *Edison: The Invention of the Movies* (Kino).

What Happened on Twenty-third Street, New York City (1901) is on DVD on *Edison: The Invention of the Movies* (Kino).

WORKS CITED
AND CONSULTED

Abel, Richard. *The Red Rooster Scare: Making Cinema American, 1900–1910*. Berkeley: U of California P, 1999.

Altman, Rick. *Silent Film Sound*. New York: Columbia UP, 2004.

American Film Institute Catalog: Film Beginnings, 1893–1910. Compiled by Elias Savada. http://www.afi.com.

"The Armenian Massacres." *New York Times* 30 Aug. 1901.

"The Astoria Concerts: E. Burton Holmes's Lecture." *New York Times* 25 Feb. 1898: 6.

Bancel, Nicolas, Pascal Blanchard, and Sandrine Lemaire. "Les zoos humains: le passage d'un 'racisme scientifique' vers un 'racisme populaire et colonial' en Occident." *Zoos humains*. Ed. Nicolas Bancel et al. Paris: La Découverte, 2002. 69.

Benjamin, Walter. *The Arcades Project*. Cambridge, Mass.: Harvard UP, 2002.

———. "Paris, capitale du XIXe siècle." *Œuvres III*. Paris: Gallimard, 2000. 52–53.

Bettelheim, Bruno. *The Uses of Enchantment / The Meaning and Importance of Fairy Tales*. New York: Alfred A. Knopf, 1976.

"The Biograph Better." *Washington Post* 2 Feb. 1897: 7.

Biograph production records. Film Study Center, Museum of Modern Art, New York.

"Biographing Jumbo." *Hartford Times* 8 Apr. 1897: 1.

Bogdanovich, Peter, and Orson Welles. *This Is Orson Welles*. Ed. Jonathan Rosenbaum. New York: Da Capo, 1998.

Boston Herald 17 May 1896: 32.

Bowser, Eileen. *The Transformation of Cinema, 1907–1915*. Berkeley: U of California P, 1990.

Brooklyn Daily Eagle 14 May 1901: 1.

Burch, Noël. *Life to Those Shadows*. Berkeley: U of California P, 1991.

———. "A Primitive Mode of Representation?" *Early Cinema: Space Frame and Narrative*. London: BFI, 1990. 224.

Catalogue. F. Z. Maguire & Co. March 1898. 31.

"Chas. Pathé Makes a Statement." *Views and Film Index* 16 May 1908: 4.

Cherchi Usai, Paolo, and Cynthia Rowell, eds. *The Griffith Project*. Vol. 1, *Films Produced in 1907–1908*. London: BFI; Pordenone: Le Giornate del cinema muto, 1999.

"Cinematograph's Aid." *Views and Film Index* 12 Sept. 1908: 5.

Coissac, G.-Michel. *Histoire du Cinématographe. De ses origines à nos jours*. Paris: Cinéopse/Gauthier-Villars, 1925.

"Comments on Film Subjects." *Moving Picture World* 14 Nov. 1908: 378–80.

"Conférence de M. Louis Lumière à la Société d'Encouragement pour l'Industrie Nationale." *Bulletin du Photo-Club de Paris* no. 51 (Apr. 1895): 125–26.

"The 'Corner' in Wheat." *Christian Observer* 28 Apr. 1909: 7.

Crafton, Donald. *Before Mickey: The Animated Film, 1898–1928*. Cambridge, Mass.: MIT Press, 1984.

"Crowd Cheered the Picture—Biograph Representation of Maine Caused Tremendous Enthusiasm." *Washington Post* 27 Feb. 1898: 4.

"Cult of the Motion Picture." *Moving Picture World* 5 Sept. 1908: 176–77.

Dahlquist, Marina. *The Invisible Seen in French Cinema before 1917.* Stockholm: Aura förlag, 2001.

"The Degradation of the Motion Picture." *Moving Picture World* 17 Oct. 1908: 308–09.

Denning, Michael. *Mechanic Accents: Dime Novels and Working-Class Culture in America.* London: Verso, 1987.

Dickson, William Kennedy Laurie. *The Biograph in Battle.* London: Fisher Unwin, 1901. Rpt. Trowbridge, Wiltshire: Flicks Books, 1995.

"Does Its Work Well." *Boston Herald* 1 June 1897: 7.

"Dreamland and the Beautiful Is Pearl of Coney Island." *The Billboard* 9 June 1906: 6.

Edison: The Invention of the Movies. DVD. Kino International and the Film/Media Department of the Museum of Modern Art together with the Library of Congress. 2005.

Edison Manufacturing Company advertisement. *New York Clipper* 28 Apr. 1906.

"Editorial." *Moving Picture World* 3 Oct. 1908: 251.

"Film Campaigning." *Film Index* 26 Sept. 1908: 9.

"Films That Please." *Moving Picture World* 21 Mar. 1908: 233.

"Fine Day for Biograph." *Hartford Times* 12 Apr. 1897: 1.

Gaudreault, André. "Detours in Film Narrative: The Development of Cross-Cutting." *Early Cinema. Space, Frame, Narrative.* Ed. Thomas Elsaesser, with Adam Barker. London: BFI, 1990 [1979]. 133–150.

———. "Fragmentation and Assemblage in the Lumière Animated Pictures." *Film History* 13.1 (2001).

———. *From Plato to Lumière: Narration and Monstration in Literature and Cinema.* Toronto: U of Toronto P, 2009.

———. "From 'Primitive Cinema' to 'Kine-Attractography.'" Trans. Timothy Barnard. *The Cinema of Attractions Reloaded.* Ed. Wanda Strauven. Amsterdam: U of Amsterdam P, 2006.

———. "Singular Narrative, Iterative Narrative: *Au Bagne* (Pathé 1905)." *Persistence of Vision* 9 (1991): 66–74.

Gaudreault, André, and Philippe Gauthier. "Crosscutting, a Programmed Language." *The Griffith Project.* Vol. 12, *Essays on D. W. Griffith.* Ed. Paolo Cherchi Usai and Cynthia Rowell. London: BFI; Pordenone: Le Giornate del cinema muto, 2008.

Gaudreault, André, and Tom Gunning. "Le cinéma des premiers temps: un défi à l'histoire du cinéma?" *L'Histoire du cinéma, nouvelles approches.* Ed. Jacques Aumont, André Gaudreault, and Michel Marie. Paris: Publications de la Sorbonne, 1989. 49–63.

———. "Early Cinema as a Challenge to Film History." Trans. Wanda Strauven and Joyce Goggin. *The Cinema of Attractions Reloaded.* Ed. Wanda Strauven. Amsterdam: U of Amsterdam P, 2006.

Gaudreault, André, with the assistance of Jean-Marc Lamotte. "Fragmentation and Segmentation in the Lumière Animated Views." Trans. Timothy Barnard. *The Moving Image* (Spring 2003): 110–31.

Gauntier, Gene. "Blazing the Trail." *Woman's Home Companion* (October 1928): 7–8, 181–84, 186.

Grieveson, Lee. *Policing Cinema: Movies and Censorship in Early Twentieth Century America.* Berkeley: U of California P, 2004.

Gunning, Tom. "The Cinema of Attractions: Early Film, Its Spectator and the Avant-garde." *Early Film.* Ed. Thomas Elsaesser and Adam Barker. London: BFI, 1989. 56–62.

————. *D. W. Griffith and the Origins of American Narrative Film: The Early Years at Biograph.* Urbana: U of Illinois P, 1991.

Hansen, Miriam. *Babel and Babylon. Spectatorship in American Silent Film.* Cambridge, Mass: Harvard UP, 1991.

Harner, Gary W. "The Kalem Company, Travel and on-Location Filming: The Forging of an Identity." *Film History* 10.2 (1998): 188–209.

Herbert, Stephen. "Major Woodville Latham, Grey Latham and Otway Latham." *Who's Who of Victorian Cinema.* http://www.victorian-cinema.net/latham.htm.

Herbert, Stephen, and Luke McKernan. *Who's Who of Victorian Cinema.* http://www.victorian-cinema.net.

"How Bryan Poses." *Film Index* 26 Sept. 1908: 8.

"Jack Johnson Arrives." *New York Times* 30 Mar. 1909: 10.

"Johnson-Burns Fight Here." *New York Times* 13 April 1909: 11.

Keil, Charlie. *Early American Cinema in Transition: Story, Style, and Filmmaking, 1907–1913.* Madison: U of Wisconsin P, 2001.

"Keith's New Theater." *Boston Herald* 24 May 1896: 10.

Keller, Mitch. "The Scandal at the Zoo." *New York Times* 6 Aug. 2006.

Kessler, Frank. "Cinématographie et arts de l'illusion." *The Tenth Muse: Cinema and the Other Arts.* Ed. Leonardo Quaresima and Laura Vichi. Udine: Forum, 2001. 535–42.

"Latest Films of All Makers." *Views and Film Index* 2 May 1908: 10–12.

Levy, David. "Re-Constituted Newsreels, Re-Enactments and the American Narrative Film." *Cinema 1900–1906: An Analytical Study.* Ed. Roger Holman. London: National Film Archive, 1982. 243–60.

"Life of the Nickelodeon." *Views and Film Index* 18 July 1908: 12.

"Life's Literary Trust." *Life* 23 Sept. 1909: 408.

Loughney, Patrick. "A Descriptive Analysis of the Library of Congress Paper Print Collection and Related Copyright Materials." Ph.D. diss., George Washington U, Washington, D.C., 1988.

"'Macbeth' Pruned in Chicago." *Moving Picture World* 13 June 1908: 511.

Mail and Express 3 Nov. 1896: 4.

Mailly, William. "The Working Girls' Strike." *The Independent* 23 Dec. 1909: 1416–20.

Mannoni, Laurent. "Etienne-Jules Marey." *Who's Who of Victorian Cinema.* http://www.victorian-cinema.net.

"The Marathon Race." *Views and Film Index* 5 Sept. 1908: 11.

Mayer, David. "'Ostler Joe." *The Griffith Project.* Vol. 1, *Films Produced in 1907–1908.* Ed. Paolo Cherchi Usai and Cynthia Rowell. London: BFI; Pordenone: Le Giornate del cinema muto, 2008.

Morris, Peter. *Embattled Shadows: A History of Canadian Cinema 1895–1939.* Montreal: McGill-Queen's UP, 1978.

Motion Pictures 1894–1912. Washington, D.C.: U.S. Copyright Office, the Library of Congress, 1953.

Moving Picture World 15 Feb. 1908: 112.

Moving Picture World 18 Apr. 1908: 351.

Moving Picture World 17 Oct. 1908: 208–09.

Moving Picture World 3 Apr. 1909: 405.

Moving Picture World 17 July 1909: 81.

Moving Picture World 4 Dec. 1909: 837.

Musser, Charles. *Before the Nickelodeon: Edwin S. Porter and the Edison Manufacturing Company.* Berkeley: U of California P, 1991.

———. *Edison Motion Pictures, 1890–1900.* Gemona: Le Giornate del Cinema Muto; Washington, D.C.: Smithsonian Institution P, 1997.

———. *The Emergence of Cinema: The American Screen to 1907.* New York: Charles Scribner's Sons, 1990.

Musser, Charles, and Carol Nelson. *High Class Moving Picture: Lyman Howe and the Forgotten Era of Traveling Exhibition, 1880–1920.* Princeton: Princeton UP, 1991.

"Must Pay Royalties on Moving Pictures." *New York Times* 6 May 1908: 5.

"The Nation's Story in Five Great Periods." *New York Times* 28 Feb. 1909: SM7.

"A New Field for Pictures." *Moving Picture World* 5 Sept. 1908: 171.

"The Newspaper's Latest Competitor." *Washington Post* 2 July 1899: 14.

New York Clipper 10 Mar. 1900: 27.

New York Daily News 24 Apr. 1896. Clipping. Raff & Gammon Collection, Harvard Business School, Baker Library, Boston.

New York Herald 13 Mar. 1898: 9.

New York Times 22 May 1909: 1.

New York Times 13 June 1909: SM4.

Niver, Kemp, ed. *Biograph Bulletins 1896–1908.* Los Angeles: Artisan Press, 1971.

———, ed. *Early Motion Pictures: The Paper Print Collection in the Library of Congress.* Washington, D.C.: Library of Congress, 1985. 66.

"'Ostler Joe." *Moving Picture World* 13 June 1908: 515.

"The Passion Play." *Hartford Courant* 2 Dec. 1899: 9.

"The Passion Play." *Washington Post* 27 Nov. 1898: 23.

"Passion Play in Pictures." *New York Times* 15 Mar. 1898: 7.

Perkins, Dexter. *The Monroe Doctrine, 1867–1907.* Baltimore: Johns Hopkins UP, 1937. 136.

Phonoscope June 1897: 11.

"Picture Shows All Put Out of Business." *New York Times* 25 Dec. 1908: 1.

"Pictures of the Pope." *Washington Post* 26 Nov. 1898: 2.

"Pope in Moving Pictures." *Washington Post* 1 Dec. 1898: 10.

Rabinovitz, Lauren. *For the Love of Pleasure: Women, Movies, and Culture in Turn-of-the-Century Chicago.* New Brunswick: Rutgers UP, 1998.

Ramsaye, Terry. *A Million and One Nights.* New York: Simon & Shuster, 1926.

Reyes, Aurelio de los. *Los origenes del cine en Mexico (1896–1900).* Mexico City: Fondo de Cultura Economica/Cultura, 1983.

Rosen, Philip. *Change Mummified: Cinema, Historicity, Theory.* Minneapolis: U of Minnesota P, 2001.

Rosenbloom, Nancy J. "Progressive Reform, Censorship, and the Motion Picture Industry, 1909–1917." *Popular Culture and Political Change in Modern America.* Ed. Michael Barkun, Lizabeth Cohen, Larry Bennett, Ronald Edsforth. Albany: State U of New York P, 1991.

Rydell, Robert. "Africains en Amérique: les villages africains dans les expositions internationales américaines (1893–1901)." *Zoos humains.* Ed. Nicolas Bancel et al. Paris: La Découverte, 2002. 213.

Sawtkin, J. G. "The Merits of Films." *Views and Film Index* 15 Feb. 1908: 4–5.

Schofield, Ann. "The Uprising of the 20,000: The Making of a Labor Legend." *A Needle, a Bobbin, a Strike: Women Needleworkers in America.* Ed. Joan M. Jensen and Sue Davidson. Philadelphia: Temple UP, 1984. 167–82.

Simmel, Georg. "The Metropolis and Mental Life." *The Sociology of Georg Simmel.* New York: Free Press, 1950.

Sirois-Trahan, Jean-Pierre. "Mythes et limites du train-qui-fonce-sur-les-spectateurs." *Limina. Le Soglie del Film/Film's Thresholds.* Ed. Veronica Innocenti and Valentina Re. Udine: Forum, 2004. 203–21.

Smith, Albert E., with the assistance of Phil A. Koury. *Two Reels and a Crank.* Garden City, N.Y.: Doubleday, 1952.

The Spectator. *New York Dramatic Mirror* 25 December 1909: 15.

Spehr, Paul C. "La production cinématographique à la 'Biograph,' entre 1900 et 1906." *Les Cahiers de la Cinémathèque* 29 (Winter 1979): 152–59.

Stewart, Jacqueline. "What Happened in the Transition? Reading Race, Gender, and Labor between the Shots." *American Cinema's Transitional Era: Audiences, Institutions, Practices.* Ed. Charlie Keil and Shelley Stamp. Berkeley: U of California P, 2004. 103–30.

"Stirring Scenes at the War-graph." *Washington Post* 6 Oct. 1898: 10.

"The Stolen Plans; or, The Boy Detective." *Views and Film Index* 19 Sept. 1908: 10–11.

Streible, Dan. "Race and the Reception of Jack Johnson Fight Films." *The Birth of Whiteness: Race and the Emergence of U.S. Cinema.* Ed. Daniel Bernardi. New Brunswick: Rutgers UP, 1996.

"The Striking Events of the Year 1908." *New York Times* Dec. 27 1908: SM2.

"Striking Pictures of the Pope." *Boston Daily Globe* 18 Dec. 1898: 24.

Thompson, Kristin. *Exporting Entertainment: America in the World Film Market, 1907–1934.* London: BFI, 1985.

Uricchio, William, and Roberta E. Pearson. *Reframing Culture: The Case of the Vitagraph Quality Films.* Princeton: Princeton UP, 1993.

Vardac, Nicholas. *Stage to Screen: Theatrical Method from Garrick to Griffith.* New York: Benjamin Blom, 1968. 17, 34–35.

Views and Film Index 19 Sept. 1908: 14.

Wallace, Michelle. "Commentary." *Edison and the Invention of the Movies.* Kino Video, 2005.

Wheeler, Charles Edgar. "Taft the Pacificator." *Outlook* 2 Jan. 1909: 28–31.

Wheeler, Edward L. *New York Nell, the Boy-Girl Detective; or, Old Blakesly's Money.* Cleveland: Arthur Westbrook, 1899.

"Without Sanctuary: Photographs and Postcards of Lynching in America." © 2000–2005 Collection of James Allen and John Littlefield. 15 June 2007 http://withoutsanctuary.org.

"Wonderful is the Vitascope." *New York Herald* 24 Apr. 1896: 11. In Musser, *Edison:* 200–201.

CONTRIBUTORS

JENNIFER M. BEAN is director of Cinema Studies and associate professor of comparative literature at the University of Washington. She is co-editor of *A Feminist Reader in Early Cinema* (2003) as well as a special issue of *Camera Obscura* entitled "Early Women Stars." She is the author of *The Play in the Machine: Gender, Genre and the Cinema of Modernity* (forthcoming) and is currently at work on a study of silent-era slapstick and modern theories of laughter.

EILEEN BOWSER is curator emerita at the Museum of Modern Art Department of Film. Her primary publications include *The Transformation of Cinema: 1907–1915* (1994), *Slapstick Symposium* (editor and author, 1985), *The Movies* (co-author, 1972), *Biograph Bulletins 1908–1912* (editor and introductory essay, 1973), *Film Notes* (editor and primary author, 1969), and *D. W. Griffith* (co-author, 1965). She has received several honorable distinctions, including the Prix Jean Mitry (1989), and she is an honorary member of Domitor, FIAF, and the Society for Cinema Studies.

ANDRÉ GAUDREAULT is a full professor in the Département d'histoire de l'art et d'études cinématographiques at the Université de Montréal, where he leads the research group GRAFICS (Groupe de recherche sur l'avènement et la formation des institutions cinématographique et scénique). His books include *Du littéraire au filmique: Système du récit* (1999; an English translation is forthcoming in 2009 under the title *From Plato to Lumière: Narration and Monstration in Literature and Cinema*), *Le Récit cinématographique* (with F. Jost, 2005), and *Cinéma et attraction: Pour une nouvelle histoire du cinématographe* (2008). He is also director of the scholarly journal *CiNéMAS*.

TOM GUNNING is Edwin A. and Betty L. Bergman Distinguished Service Professor at the University of Chicago in the Department of Art History and the Committee on Cinema and Media. He is author of two books, *D. W. Griffith and the Origins of America Narrative Film* (1991) and *The Films of Fritz Lang: Allegories of Vision and Modernity* (2008), as well as over a hundred articles on early cinema, the avant-garde, film genres, and issues in film theory and history.

PATRICK LOUGHNEY is curator of the Motion Picture Department at the George Eastman House. Previously he was head of both the Moving Image Section and the Motion Picture and Television Reading Room of the Library of Congress. He is an archivist and historian who has worked in the field of motion picture preservation for thirty years.

CHARLES MUSSER is professor of American Studies, Film Studies, and Theater Studies at Yale University, where he co-chairs the Film Studies Program. His numerous books on silent cinema include *The Emergence of Cinema: The American Screen to 1907* (1990), *Edison Motion Pictures, 1890–1900: An Annotated Filmography* (1997), and *Moving Pictures: American Art and Early Cinema, 1880–1910* (co-authored with Nancy Mathews, 2005).

LAUREN RABINOVITZ is chair of the Department of American Studies, director of Interdisciplinary Programs, and professor of American Studies and Cinema at the University of Iowa. She has published widely on film and television, including much research on early American cinema. Her list of early cinema publications includes *For the Love of Pleasure: Women, Movies, and Culture in Turn-of-the-Century Chicago* (1998) and *Yesteryear's Wonderlands: Introducing Modernism to America*, a CD-ROM (2008).

JEAN-PIERRE SIROIS-TRAHAN is an assistant professor in the Département des littératures at Université Laval. He holds a joint Ph.D. from the Université de Montréal and Université Paris III–Sorbonne nouvelle. He co-edited an issue of the journal *CiNéMAS* (fall 2003) on the cinematic apparatus. He has also published several articles and co-edited two books on early cinema: *Au pays des ennemis du cinéma . . . Pour une nouvelle histoire des débuts du cinéma au Québec* (1996) and *La vie ou du moins ses apparences. Émergence du cinéma dans la presse de la Belle Époque* (2002).

MATTHEW SOLOMON is an assistant professor of Cinema Studies in the Department of Media Culture at the College of Staten Island, City University of New York. He is the author of *Disappearing Tricks: Silent Cinema, Houdini, and the New Magic of the Twentieth Century* (forthcoming) and the editor of *Méliès's Trip to the Moon: Fantastic Voyages of the Cinematic Imagination* (forthcoming). His work has also been published in *Theatre Journal, Nineteenth Century Theatre and Film, Cinema & Cie, Quarterly Review of Film and Video,* and a number of anthologies.

PAUL C. SPEHR is an archivist and a film historian. He is also the former assistant chief, Motion Picture, Broadcasting & Recorded Sound Division, Library of Congress, now retired. He is the author of *The Civil War in Motion Pictures* (1961), *The Movies Begin* (1977), *American Film Personnel and Company Credits, 1908–1920* (1996), and several other articles on early film history. He recently completed a book on the career of William Kennedy Laurie Dickson.

INDEX